PSYCHIC
POWERS

Soraya believes:

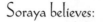

You are **magical**.
You are **mystical**.
You are **spiritual**.

Magick is a very effective tool for realising your own potential in all areas in your life. Soraya gives this ancient and often misunderstood practice a new place in today's world. **Spells and Psychic Powers** is written in simple, everyday language to help you to change your life as she did.

Soraya has become one of Scotland's favourite psychics, especially since she predicted a huge win for someone who, three months later won 2.8 million pounds in the National Lottery!

A Reiki Master, for several years she has been teaching Reiki to employees within the medical profession and to private students.

In addition, Soraya is featured regularly in local and national newspapers, on radio and TV and was astrologer and agony aunt for **The Sunday Post.** She is also an avid and renowned numerologist.

She is mother to three children, Ian, Claire and Tori, grandmother to three grandchildren, Ashi, Jack and Eva, and wife of artist Martin Conway.

Spells &
PSYCHIC
POWERS

By Soraya

**GEDDES &
GROSSET**

Dedication

Thanks and blessings to my husband
Martin and my youngest daughter Tori
whose patience, support and assistance
have been invaluable.

My life is mine that I can change
By the power of my will
Yours you do with as you wish,
Or change and be fulfilled.

This combined edition published 2006 by Geddes & Grosset
David Dale House, New Lanark, ML11 9DJ, Scotland

Book of Spells first printed 2001
Reprinted 2002, 2004, 2005

How to Enhance Your Psychic Powers first printed 2005

Text © Soraya 2001, 2005

Spells artwork © Martin Conway 2001

Fortune Cookie by Mark Mechan

Chakras by Tom Cross

Layout and cover design © Geddes & Grosset 2006

ISBN 10: 1 84205 594 1
ISBN 13: 978 1 84205 594 6

Printed and bound in Poland

POLSKABOOK

Positive thoughts and actions
can work miracles

Like most people today, I choose to believe that there is a higher power at work in all our lives.

In this combined volume of *Spells and Psychic Powers* I will demonstrate that our own inner strength is vastly increased by having a clearer focus and understanding of how to connect with the higher power within us.

I will also explain the value of creating the right environment and the importance of drawing strength from the higher power.

This book contains 48 different spells using everyday items, candles, oils and symbols to help you empower your life for the better. I will also teach you how to unlock your mind to allow your innate psychic powers to become free.

I was born in 1947, in Bethlehem, on Christmas day, to an Arabian mother and a Scottish father, and came to Scotland with my parents when I was just 3 months old. I was named after my Arabian grandmother and the name Soraya means 'the brightest star in the galaxy of seven stars'.

My life has been a series of coincidences and sometimes life-shattering events that have made me who I am today. Years of study, and my own life experiences, have shown me that individuals can create their own futures by using the power within themselves. I want to share this knowledge with you in this book.

Soraya

Spells

Part One:
Magick by the Light
of the Moon

Preparing Your Magickal Tools 69

Part Two:

Making the Magick

Happen

Contents

PSYCHIC
POWERS

CONTENTS

Spells

Part One:

Magick by the Light of the Moon

The Magick Has
Already Begun

DO YOU believe that there is a reason for everything? Do you believe that if you wish hard enough anything is possible? Do you believe that you can do more in your life? Have you noticed that sometimes what you want happens almost before you express the desire?

Where are you now? Standing in a shop or sitting in your favourite chair at home? Perhaps someone has given you this book – perhaps you have been drawn to it – either way the magick has already begun.

But what is magick?

Magick is the art of causing change in accordance with your will. In other words, magick is the art of making things happen, as you would wish them to. Magick is simply the manipulation of energy.

Some people are afraid of magick, and so they should be because magick is powerful stuff. Some say that magick is black or evil, white or good, but the truth is there is no black, evil, good or white magick – it's all the same. There are, however, good people and evil people. If your heart is filled with evil or wicked intentions then this book is not for you.

But then again, perhaps it is because this book may have come to you so that you can change your ways. The first rule of magick is:

And it harm none so be it.

Be careful what you wish for

The reason for this is simple: whatever you put out will come back to you threefold. In other words, if you send out good wishes or words then three times that amount will come back to you. If you send out bad wishes or words then the same will apply: three times that amount will come back to you.

To understand this, you have to understand a little more of how magick works. When we desire something the thing we normally do is to think of it. Then we might talk about it to someone close. Some people take things a little further and do something about achieving what they want. If it is an item that can be purchased, they might start saving for it. Making the magick happen is as simple as that, but with knowledge and practice it can go much further.

Be careful what you wish for

When I was a child, I was always wishing for something. My mother would tell me to be careful about what I wished for because I might get it and then be sorry. It was years before I began to really understand what she meant. Any time that I questioned her she would tell me that I would understand when I was older.

One day, I asked for new ice skates and my mum said that I could not have them. I pleaded with her and finally she explained that she could not afford them. I replied that I wished we were very rich and could afford everything. My mum was furious. She turned to me, pointing her finger, shaking it at me in anger and told me never to wish for such a thing. I was shocked at her reaction. I only wanted to be rich, what was wrong with that? Mum explained to me that I would feel very bad if my wish came true as a result of something bad happening to someone. I still could not understand so she almost whispered her fears.

'What would you feel like if someone you loved very much died and left you a lot of money?'

That made me stop and think. She was right. I would have been heartbroken if I had lost someone I loved.

You might wish for a new car and think there is nothing wrong with that. But what sequence of events might have to happen to enable you to get your dream? The money you need for the car might come from an unfortunate source like the insurance money for an accident or injury. You might wish a passionate lover to come into your life and when he or she arrives, the person might be passionate and exciting but might not touch your heart with love. I can speak from experience on that one.

One day I spilled some coffee on my lovely new cream-coloured, canvas espadrilles. I decided to wash them to get rid of the stain. Later, after they had dried in the sun, I inspected them only to discover that there was no difference. The stain was still there. As I looked at them, I realised that the stain was in the shape of the sun. Not realising what I was doing, I began to create a magick spell. I took a coloured pen and drew round the stain. Now that I had done this on one shoe, I had to balance it up on the other one too. I drew a crescent moon on the other shoe. I tried both shoes on and admired my handiwork. I began to think of the symbols that I had used.

Moon   Sun

The sun is masculine and the moon is feminine .!. mm! I did not have someone special in my life so I thought it would be fun to see if drawing a masculine symbol on my shoe brought someone into my life. I was beginning to get quite carried away with myself. My sign is Capricorn so I drew the appropriate glyph on the shoe

Be careful what you wish for

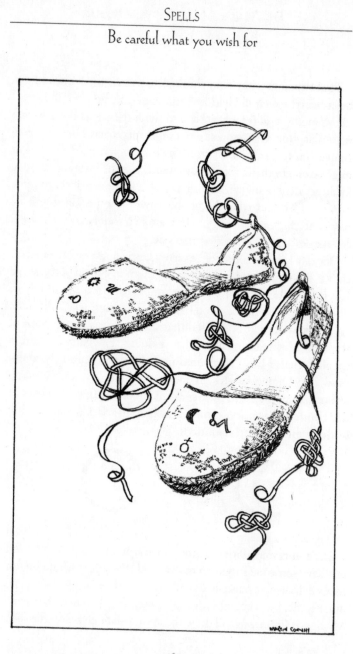

Be careful what you wish for

with the moon symbol. Now I really had to think. What would be an exciting sign to be in a relationship with? Well, I knew that the sign of Scorpio was quite a sexy sign so without further ado I drew the glyph for Scorpio on the shoe with the sun symbol on it. I needed some action in my life so on went the symbol for Mars and, to balance this, the other shoe was given the symbol for Venus.

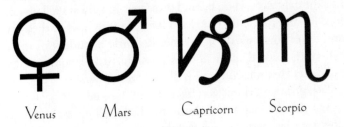

Venus Mars Capricorn Scorpio

I was very happy with the finished result and was proud to wear my previously ruined shoes. If only I had realised! Within the week, someone who was born under the sign of Scorpio befriended me. He was passionate, sexy and attractive and although this certainly brought some action into my life, he did not love me, nor I him. The tragedy was though, that when I tried to tell him how I felt, he did not want to listen. No matter what I said or did, I was not able to convince him that this relationship was not what I wanted. I cried many tears over this and eventually I had to hurt his feelings and damage his pride. I felt bad and I am sure that he did too and, to this day, he has never forgiven me.

I created magick without thinking about what I was doing and without considering the effects that my magick would have on another person's life. And that brings us back to the first rule of magick:

And it harm none.

You may wonder in what way this inadvertent spell came back to me. Simple really – the next person that I dated broke my heart.

Never speak ill of anyone

The power of magick begins with the words that you speak and the depth of feeling behind these words. I always tell people I know, and particularly my students, to watch what they say and never to speak ill of anyone. Recently a student of mine called and asked me if it was possible to hex someone by accident. Hex means to wish ill on another person.

'What do you think you have done?' I asked.

At first, she was a little hesitant about telling me, perhaps doubting her own magickal skills.

'I had a conversation with my boyfriend before the Christmas holidays and he told me of a secretary who was causing problems in the office. I told him that she deserved to be fired and he told me that she never would because she had been with the company for a very long time.'

My student then went on to tell me that when her boyfriend went back to work, he found out that the secretary had been fired. They were both amazed by this piece of news but for very different reasons.

My student had indeed hexed this person.

'Perhaps it's just a coincidence,' she said, trying to ease her troubled conscience.

Perhaps it was, but was she willing to take the chance?

'What can I do to fix things, I don't want to feel guilty or have this hanging over my head?'

I told her to light a small candle and dedicate it to the secretary, to wish her success in her chosen field and to wish that she would find a new job that she would like as soon as possible.

Some things were meant to be

The second rule of magick is, if you think that you have made a mess of something, do something to fix it immediately. If you utter negative words to or about someone, immediately say:

I take these words back and wish you well

Powerful stuff this magick!

Never interfere with a person's will

Never, ever, interfere with another person's will. You may think at this point that you only want to create magick for yourself but what if you were in a situation where your best friend had separated from his or her partner or lover. You might be tempted then to magick them together again. This is probably the worst thing that you could do! If they are destined to be together, then they will be and if they are destined to be apart then they should be left to get on with the painful experience of parting.

You know what they say: 'That which does not kill us makes us stronger and wiser.' Richard Bach in his book *Illusions* puts it in a rather more interesting way when he says: 'Here is a test to find out if your mission on earth is complete. If you are alive it is not.'

Some things are meant to be

Experiences that we are destined to have, for whatever reason, should not be changed. That does not mean that you cannot do something to help during experiences. You can create a spell for someone to have peace of mind during his or her difficult time. You can create a spell to help someone recover his or her self-esteem, which is so often damaged during the break-up of a relationship. You can also create a spell that will draw in love and friendship.

Do you have to be a witch to cast a spell?

I will repeat that: you can create a spell that will *draw in love and friendship*. Not to draw a *particular* person towards you because that would be interfering with their will. If you do attempt this and create a spell to draw a particular person toward you then you may end up having that relationship but it would be a very unhappy one.

Do you have to be a witch or a wizard to cast a spell?

I have been asked that question so many times. The answer is simple. No, you do not have to be, but only a witch or a wizard can teach you the fundamentals and the ethics of spell casting. You can learn this craft by studying with a mentor or by reading some of the many books that are available. This question is usually asked when someone has the desire to cast a spell or make magick happen in his or her life. If you are asking that question, I suppose the real answer is that you probably *are* a witch or a wizard.

The word *witch* comes from the words *wise* or *wisdom* and originally witches were called the *wise ones*. Witches are healers who study natural remedies and the influences of the cycles of moon and the planets. Witches seek to harm none, knowing the energy they send out comes back threefold.

I discovered that I was a witch or a pagan when someone gave my sixteen-year-old daughter a book on witches. Panicking, I took the book from her and told her that I would read it first and if it was suitable then I would give it back to her. Within the first two chapters, I discovered that I was reading about things that I had believed most of my life and, to be truthful, I felt as though this book had been written about me. I could liken different experiences that I had had as a child and as an adult to those in this book.

I knew that the things that the authors talked of in the

first few pages had been with me all my life. It was this same sense of knowing that had always made me feel different and had alienated me from others. This was the first time that I had heard the word Wicca and the first time that I had understood the word paganism.

What is paganism?

My understanding of paganism until that time had been people who do not believe in or worship God. In fact, The *Collins English Dictionary* describes a pagan as a person without any religion – a heathen.

Recently the subject of pagans came up in a group discussion and one woman stated that pagans worshipped Satan. This makes me feel quite sad.

I am a pagan. I do believe in God and I believe that I have a greater understanding of God than I ever had before. The word pagan was derived from the Latin word *pagus*, which means countryside. This then became *paganus*, which referred to someone who lived in the countryside. The word heathen originally meant heath dweller.

The three principles of the Pagan Federation, of which I am a member and former office bearer, are:

1 Love for and kinship with nature. Reverence for the life force and its ever-renewing cycles of life and death.
2 A positive morality in which each individual is responsible for the discovery and development of their true nature in harmony with the outer world and the community. This is often expressed as 'Do what you will as long as it harms none'.
3 Recognition of the Divine, which transcends gender, acknowledging both the male and female aspect of Deity.

What is paganism?

A pagan is someone who believes in a supreme Being who is above, below and all around us. A being that is in the life-giving air that we breath, in the fire that warms us, in the water that washes us clean and sustains us and in the earth that carries our weight.

A pagan is someone who recognises that this supreme being is made up of masculine and feminine elements, as we all are. A god and goddess combined (*see* the illustration of this on page 32). Father God who reigns above us and Mother Earth beneath our feet.

Think of that for a moment and realise why pagans all over the world are saddened by the destruction of our Mother Earth.

It is these same pagans who meet on regular intervals at badly littered, overgrown and neglected ancient sites and spend their own precious time cleaning up the mess that is left by others.

A pagan is someone who respects the choices that each individual makes in practising their beliefs. Paganism is not a religion, paganism is a faith.

Pagans believe in observing the laws and signs of nature, believe in life after death, believe in the God-given gifts of healing and believe in the power of word, deed and action – magick.

If you have reached a stage in your life where you believe that there must be more, if you feel as though you are searching, as I did then perhaps this path is for you.

Is Wicca a new religion?

Wicca or paganism is not a religion at all. Wicca is a Goddess-based belief system that can be dated back at least 25,000 years. However, its usage as a term used for those who practice paganism is relatively new. Pagan faiths have existed on most continents since history began and there are many disciplines. Some people are drawn to the Egyptian philosophy, others to Druidism. Some are drawn to the Anglo Saxon tradition and others follow a Native American path. Some people are known as kitchen witches, green witches or solos. Green witches focus on the earth and are likely to be involved in replenishing or restocking wasteland to introduce trees, shrubs, flora and fauna that may be dying because of pollution or mankind's general neglect or abuse. They may also be involved in the production of natural herbal remedies. Kitchen witches, whilst being supportive of green issues will also produce their own self-grown herbal remedies and potions but on a much smaller scale. A solo can be a green witch or a kitchen witch. The term means that they work alone rather than in a group. They may, from time to time, join other groups for celebrations.

As with all faiths there are offshoots and varieties and that is because everyone is different and their needs are different too. Wicca or paganism is something that you believe in and practise in a way that suits you.

Imagine a time long ago

The roots of paganism are buried deep in history. To understand this time, thousands of years ago, imagine a time when our ancestors lived in tribes or clans – no means of communication other than the spoken word, no means of transport other than one's own feet.

Life was harsh in those far off days and if you wanted to eat you had to find your food in your surroundings. Wild animals were hunted for meat and clothing and people would forage for edible plants. Before winter came, food and firewood had

Imagine a time long ago

to be gathered and stored to last through this difficult season and the nights would be cold and dark if supplies ran out.

The children, the youths, the maidens, the hunters or warriors, the mothers and the old wise women or medicine women would be safe in the cave, gathered round a camp fire listening to the stories that the elders would tell.

The elders would speak of the things that they had learned from their elders when they were young. Sometimes perhaps they would sing their stories and everyone would join in and this would make these lessons, for that's what they were, easier to understand.

The elders would speak of the stars in the night sky, of the sun and the moon and how each morning the sun would chase away the moon but as the sun slept, the moon would reappear. Their knowledge of the stars and the planets in the night sky gave them the wisdom that helped them to survive in those bygone days. As the younger ones grew to maturity they would in turn teach others.

The wise ones, having spent many years watching their clan grow and watching seasons change had a great understanding of time and the patterns of nature. These old men, once hunters or warriors themselves but too old to hunt now, had a valuable place in the society. To the warriors or hunters, they would tell stories of their grandfathers and of hunts of which they in turn had been told. Mostly these old men would be shamans.

Often someone who was disabled or disfigured in some way and could not hunt would be regarded as special and singled out to be the apprentice of a wise one. Perhaps they recognised that where one sense was weakened another sense was strengthened. At certain times the shaman would speak with the spirits and ask for guidance on matters concerning the clan.

Many different methods were used to do this but old traditions were always adhered to.

The old women had their place in the scheme of things too. As they grew up they would have been taught by the wise woman or medicine woman of their time of the properties of the herbs and plants that they gathered. They would have amassed great knowledge and understanding of all the plants, the times that they grew, the best places to find them, and their medicinal properties. They would know through practised skills which plants would heal or treat certain conditions. Traditionally these skills would be passed from mother to her first-born daughter. If they had no daughter, they would watch as the youngsters grew and they would choose the girl who showed most promise to carry on this wisdom.

Soon the nights would grow shorter. Those who survived the harsh winter would venture out to the fields or plains to begin hunting for fresh meat and gathering again those wild plants and herbs. This would be a time of celebration. During this first celebration people could now look forward to the arrival of spring.

After the spring equinox the people of the clan would be aware of the longer days, the grass, green beneath their feet, and the skies above them, blue. Flowers would begin to bloom and new life would be everywhere. Hunting, fishing and farming or gathering could begin in earnest. Fresh food would be the staple diet but the harshness of the winter that had passed would not be forgotten so food would be dried and stored for future use.

As the Wheel of the Year turned and summer approached children played happily, lovers kissed and laughter filled the air. Traditionally this would be a time for members of many clans to make plans to meet each other. Food would be in good supply so some would be set aside for sharing with neighbouring clans. Romance would be in the air and young men and women would be thinking of their sweethearts.

Soon the Summer Solstice would arrive and the clans would be gathering to celebrate summer, to trade and exchange goods and to visit family members who had married into other clans. The elders of the tribe would have been playing matchmaker and marriages between the clans would be planned and carried out.

Time does not stand still though, and soon it would be time to celebrate and give thanks for the gifts, which have already been bestowed by Mother Earth. Soon it will be time to harvest the plants and make ready again for the approach of winter.

At the Autumn Equinox, the clan is busy gathering plants that have been tended over the summer period. Vegetables, fruits berries and herbs have been prepared for storage for use in the long winter. Meat has been dried, skins cured for clothing and other uses. All too soon winter would be returning. A large bonfire would be lit to show weary travellers the way home before the winter snows would make the journey impossible. A sense of quiet overcomes everyone as they realise that some will survive this winter whilst others will journey to another time, another place.

As the Wheel of the Year makes its final turn, and the Winter Solstice arrives, the clan would celebrate that soon winter would be over and they could once again look forward to spring.

These are the cycles and the teachings that are followed by modern day pagans all over the world and with each turn of the wheel we pagans give thanks to our ancestors who handed down their secrets and rejoice for the season just past and the new one approaching.

Why Do People Think
Witches Are Bad?

Bad press

Not too long ago if anyone had suspected you of being a witch they would have reported you to the authorities. For just being suspected of witchcraft you would have been burnt at the stake for your crime or, you would have been sealed into a barrel and thrown over a cliff, or perhaps hung from high rafters. Once dead, you were then buried on unhallowed ground.

Macbeth

It is said that it was Shakespeare, in his play Macbeth, who stereotyped witches as evil, ugly old hags but he was not the only one. There were many before him who were responsible for this and other accusations against witches.

In the fourth act of Macbeth, the first scene is set on a stormy night with thunder crashing all around. In the middle of the cave stands a cauldron round which stand three witches.

First Witch: Thrice the brinded cat hath mew'd.
[The striped cat has mewed three times]
Second Witch: Thrice and once the hedge-pig whin'd.
[The hedgehog whined four times]
Third Witch: Harper cries: 'Tis time, 'tis time.

First Witch: Round about the cauldron go;
  In the poison'd entrails throw.
  Toad, that under cold stone
  Days and nights hast thirty-one
  Swelter'd venom sleeping got,
  Boil thou first i' the charmed pot.
  [Throw the poisoned entrails into the pot and stir them with the remains of the toad that has sweated under a rock for thirty days. Boil the mixture in the cauldron . . . stirring to prevent it from sticking. Yuck, disgusting!}

All: Double, double, toil and trouble;
  Fire burn and cauldron bubble.
  [Boil for a good period over a hot fire until it bubbles]

Second Witch: Fillet of a fenny snake,
  In the cauldron boil and bake;
  Eye of newt, and toe of frog,
  Wool of bat, and tongue of dog,
  Adder's fork, and blind-worm's sting,
  Lizard's leg, and howlet's wing,
  For a charm of powerful trouble,
  Like a hell-broth boil and bubble.
  [Take a fillet of snake caught on the fens, add the eye of a newt and the toe of a frog, the wool of a bat and the tongue of a dog. Don't forget the adder's tongue, the sting from a blindworm, the wing of an owl and a lizard's leg. (Who are they kidding?)]

All: Double, double, toil and trouble;
  Fire burn and cauldron bubble.

Third Witch: Scale of dragon, tooth of wolf,
  Witch's mummy, maw and gulf
  Of the ravin'd salt-sea shark,
  Root of hemlock digg'd i' the dark,

Salem

Liver of blaspheming Jew,
Gall of goat and slips of yew
Sliver'd in the moon's eclipse,
Nose of Turk and Tartar's lips,
Finger of birth-strangled babe
Ditch-deliver'd by a drab,
Make the gruel thick and slab:
Add thereto a tiger's chaudron,
For the ingredients of our cauldron.
[Add a dragon's skin. A wolf's tooth. The stomach and throat
of a hungry shark. Hemlock root that has been dug up in
the dark, the liver of a Jewish person (in Shakespeare's time
there was a lot of prejudice against Jewish people, even more
than now), a goat's gall bladder and the nose and lips of a
Turkish person. Not forgetting a finger from a stillborn child
delivered in a ditch by the roadside by a whore. Top this lot
off with tiger's entrails. (Yeah right!)]
All: Double, double, toil and trouble;
Fire burn and cauldron bubble.

Just ask yourself one question: 'Where would one acquire all
these ingredients?' No wonder witches had a bad name!

Salem

Many of you will have read *The Crucible*, by Arthur Miller,
possibly when you were at school. It's an allegorical play based
on the Salem witchcraft trials between 1692 and 1693, through
which Miller was satirising the events of the communist 'witch-
hunts' of Senator Joseph McCarthy in the 1950s. But if you
read the play on a purely historical level, it's an interesting
insight into the hysteria that arose in Salem at that time. Set in
a Puritan village in Massachusetts the play begins in the home
of Reverend Samuel Parris. Elizabeth, his daughter, had become

ill when her father discovered her, her cousin Abigail Williams, and several other local girls, dancing 'like heathens' in the woods.

Various suggestions have been put forward as the real reasons for the girls' behaviour: repressed sexuality, the repression of women, local politics and feuds, or the presence of a cereal disease, known as ergot, in the flour which could have given rise to a form of food poisoning causing hallucinations. A popular and plausible suggestion was that Elizabeth Parris and Abigail Williams had become interested in the occult from stories about voodoo that they had heard from Tituba Indian, a servant who had been brought from Barbados by the Reverend Parris.

Whatever the reason, the girls were happy to go along with the witchcraft theory and point the finger of suspicion at several local women. The hysteria escalated and many more were accused.

Landowner Giles Corey was tortured because he remained silent throughout his indictment, and he was gradually, horrifically crushed to death under a plank of wood weighted with large rocks. In all, nineteen people were executed because of the dubious testimonies of the girls.

Even more were sentenced to death but for various reasons did not actually go to the gallows. The girls felt they were in a position of extreme power and that they could accuse anyone and get away with it. But they were quite wrong. They chose to accuse the wife of the governor, William Phips. This was a step too far and finally Phips dissolved the court that had been trying the supposed witches.

The girls themselves were lucky to escape punishment and didn't show any desire to repent or ask for forgiveness (except for Ann Putnam who, fourteen years later, delivered her half-hearted confession in Salem Church saying she had been deluded by Satan and that the guilt lay with him). Steps of atonement were taken by clergy and state, an Official Day of Humiliation was held in 1697 and the colonial legislature of Massachusetts eventually financially compensated the families of the executed in 1711.

The Paisley witches

The persecution of witches was at its peak in the 14th century and continued for another 300 years, during which time thousands of country folk were tortured, maimed and murdered as witches and Devil worshippers throughout Europe. The following is just one example of hundreds that interested me because it is a story originating from Scotland, in fact, from my own town.

In Paisley in Renfrewshire, a horseshoe is embedded into a major crossroads to mark the spot where witches were hung.

It is recorded that in 1697, an eleven-year-old girl, named Christina Shaw, the daughter of John Shaw of Bargarran, accused her maidservant, with whom she had frequent quarrels, of bewitching her. Christina was reported to have had a spiteful temper. It has also been suggested that she could have been suffering from epilepsy or indeed that the whole thing could have been one big sham.

Her story was believed, unfortunately, and it led to the conviction of over twenty folk from neighbouring villages and parishes throughout Renfrewshire. Paisley Tollbooth, which was demolished in 1897, is where these poor innocents were tried, and seven of the accused were found guilty as charged, condemned to be 'strangled' on the gallows and burnt in a peat fire on the Paisley Green. One of the convicted, 'The Warlock', John Reid was imprisoned in the Renfrew prison where he committed suicide, cheating the executioners and spectators maybe, but adding fuel to their tales of possession and demonology. The talk in the town back in 1697 was that the Devil had come to claim his own. It was said to have been impossible for John Reid to hang himself as he did but that is another story.

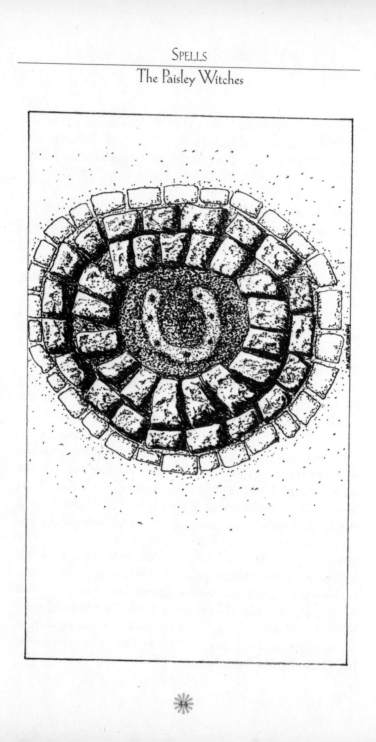

The Paisley Witches

The other six, convicted by the word of a mere girl, were indeed marched to the site of execution and paraded through the town to the delight of spectators who had journeyed from as far a-field as Edinburgh for this gruesome spectacle. A very basic set of gallows were set up, and one by one, the six folk were pushed off and hung by their necks and left struggling till they breathed no more. The mortal remains of the poor folk were thrown onto a peat fire and the dirty deed was blown away in the breeze. The spectacle was so shocking that even the lesser-educated people of the day actually questioned the reality of it all. The Minister of one of the local Parishes even called a mass fast to try and incite some forgiveness into this dreadful act.

This trial excited considerable disgust in Scotland. The Rev. Mr Bell, a contemporary writer, observed that, in this business:

'Persons of more goodness and esteem than most of their calumniators were defamed for witches.' He adds, that the persons chiefly to blame were 'certain ministers of too much forwardness and absurd credulity, and some topping professors in and about Glasgow.'

The whole thing was so serious that the horseshoe was solemnly placed on the site of the gallows. Was this to prevent evil spirits from seeking revenge on the town for this horrible deed, or was it to serve as a reminder to the people of Paisley of the tragic crime that their ancestors had committed?

Christina Shaw grew up to become quite a celebrity in Paisley. Following her travels around the world she brought various thread-making skills back to Paisley and created quite a sensation in the weaving industry. This industry became a major concern in Paisley, perhaps thanks to Christina Shaw of Bargarran, but at what cost.

As rumours grow and become myths and legends, so the witch trial became linked to the weaving industry. It was said if the horseshoe was ever removed that a curse would befall the weaving community. Another story goes on to say that a young local man on his way back from his favourite tavern after one or two beers too many thought it would be amusing to remove the horseshoe. Apparently over the next few weeks there were about six mysterious suicides among the local weaving community. The young man was so distressed he turned himself in to the constabulary of the time and confessed his 'prank'. The horseshoe was returned immediately to its resting-place and indeed it can be seen there to this very day over 300 years after the witch trials.

The other 16 or so folk who were originally accused, may have escaped the gallows but records show they were still imprisoned over a year later, living in very poor conditions, half starving no doubt. Many people are quite passionate that a memorial of some kind should be placed in Paisley to formally admonish the accused of 1697.

It was another forty years before the laws changed to prevent such ridiculous accusations being taken so far and it became illegal to accuse someone of bewitchment. The repeal of the Witchcraft Act was passed in 1951.

Good press

In Paisley today you can go into jewellery stores and find pentacles, the witches' sign, on rings, bracelets and necklaces. Other shops stock all types of books on Wicca, paganism, spiritual development healing and magick. Look at the success of the *Harry Potter* books by J. K. Rowling, books originally written for children but read and loved by adults too. *The Secret Garden* by Frances Hodgson Burnett was the first story I read as a child that made me see that if you believed in something enough you could really make it happen.

Back in the Sixties, two programmes helped to turn things around and make magick less of a threat and more like entertainment. The first of these was *Bewitched*, with the late Elizabeth Montgomery. The lead character Samantha twitched her nose to make things happen. No matter how hard I tried I could never manage to twitch my nose and my mouth wiggled instead. *I Dream of Genie* with Barbara Eden was my other favourite, about a soldier who found a genie in a bottle.

Switch on the television today and you can watch programmes that feature modern-day witches and magick. *Charmed*, *Sabrina the Teenage Witch*, *Buffy the Vampire Slayer*, *Angel* and many children's programmes too.

Films have been made about the Old Craft some of them are quite good whilst others are laughable. *The Craft*, for example is a tale of four college students who possess supernatural powers. Exaggerated of course, but it is one of the best because it does show what can happen when people start dabbling in magick and have no real understanding of the power of their actions. *The Fifth Element* with Bruce Willis is another, and I particularly enjoyed this one because it identified the fifth element as being love.

Misuse of magick

Afternoon radio and television programmes feature all kinds of psychics and one television channel devotes an entire programme to the Mysteries. It is so popular that it runs twice a week. No doubt people are fascinated enough to justify the volume of coverage that these subjects receive and they are all linked in one way or another to Wicca.

People appear on these programmes and declare that they are white witches. Well, what else would they say? Would they be likely to admit that they have taken the other path and practise black magic?

Misuse of magic

Recently a national daily newspaper produced an article featuring someone claiming to be a witch. The article included a spell for binding someone to you for life. Can you even begin to imagine how terrible that would be?! How often have you heard of a person who has fallen in love with someone and married or lived with that person and then later found them to be violent or abusive?

If you bind someone to you for life, it means life – not only this life but all your lives, for all eternity. Good or bad this is a permanent spell. It can be hard enough getting out of a difficult relationship in one lifetime without having to endure it for infinity.

People change and, with the passage of time, what they want often changes too. Sometimes we meet and fall in love with someone and later we find that the person that we fell in love with is not who we had thought them to be. Under normal circumstances, ideally, you discuss your feelings with this person and either find a way to sort out your differences or find a way to break up the relationship as painlessly as possible. But, if you have been stupid enough to cast a binding spell, or worse, someone else has done this to you, then your problems begin.

We've all heard stories in the press and on television of the misery that can be caused by stalkers. Their compulsive obsessions can create this kind of magick. Not because they have knowledge of magick but probably because they do not understand that the power of their intentions create magick. Good, bad or indifferent, magick is all around us.

Knowing how to use magick for the highest good becomes crucial.

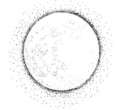

A Magickal Journey

THIS is not a journey to undertake lightly or just because you are curious. Wicca is a way of life that has been handed down over centuries by our ancestors. This way of life has been given to us to guide us on our path, to show us that everything that we do has a reaction, to teach us that we must honour and respect the world in which we live and the people with whom we share this world, regardless of their race, colour, creed, status, or opinions. This is a high demand. Can you live up to it?

If and when you decide that you are indeed a witch, or, more precisely, a pagan, it will be like the first day of a magical journey. There will be so many questions to ask and so many new things to try. That is when the real task begins because the chances are that you will not know where to begin and who to ask. That is normal. For me this is the Goddess's way of making sure that you are serious in your undertaking. Faint heart falls by the wayside. If it was easy anyone could do it, but it is not easy. The first recognition of how hard it can be is if friends think that you are some sort of weirdo and begin to drift away. Then you may have to endure derisory, ignorant comments from people who do not know what they are talking about, and worse, do not want to know.

You may feel for a time that you are going round in circles, bewildered and insecure, and that is the way that it should be. This is part of your apprenticeship. This is where you begin to understand yourself, your desires, your motives, your fears and your strengths. Overcoming all of this will lead you to your first teacher. In the craft, as we pagans call it, 'When the student is ready the teacher appears'. Teachers are also very aware that students have a lot to teach them too. We all learn and grow from our experiences.

Gradually, you will begin to recognise that you are being drawn towards like-minded people, and them to you, and new friends will be made. Do not, however, be lulled into the assumption that because these new friends are pagans like you that they must be nice. There are nice and not so nice people in the craft too. You will begin to find books that point you in the right direction. You will spend a lot of time on your own studying everything that you can lay your hands on about the mysteries. You will have a deeper understanding of the ever-renewing cycles of birth, life, death, and rebirth.

Do I have to join a coven?

Many people, myself included, prefer to work alone. I do have many students who call, write and e-mail me when they need guidance on their next step or if there is something that they do not understand. My reason for working alone is simple: I like to be in control of my own destiny and what happens in my circle. I also do not have the spare time required to go and meet with other like-minded people. Occasionally though I pine for the sharing that working with others brings.

A coven is simply a group of like-minded people who gather together to practise, learn and celebrate. Traditionally a coven was made up of thirteen people. Immediately you are probably thinking 'spooky', that thirteen is a bad number, but Jesus had twelve apostles so when they gathered to talk and learn or celebrate, they would be thirteen. As a numerologist, which means I have an understanding of the hidden meaning of numbers, the number thirteen for me becomes four, (i.e., 1 + 3) and four is the number of stability and security.

When taking the Wiccan path it is important that you do what is right for you and if you want to work alone then so be it. If however you prefer to work with others then take your time. You must have great respect, admiration and trust for your High Priest or High Priestess. This person, or these people, will be your mentors or guides and they should never abuse you or your trust in them. They too will take their time in getting to know something about you to make sure that they are not letting someone who has unscrupulous motives for choosing a pagan path into their group. That is the way that it should be, for if a coven is eager to accept you without question then they are not discriminating enough about who their members are. This has nothing to do with their sex, colour, or creed. The motives that lie behind the desire to follow a pagan path must be genuine. If the motives of the student and the motives of the coven are true and honourable then they will work well together.

What does a coven do?
Covens meet, to exchange ideas, to talk, to share and to perform rituals. Some rituals are for the purpose of healing those who are sick. This can be generalised to everyone who is suffering from some kind of illness or it can be focused on a more personal level and directed to friends or family known to that group. Some rituals are performed for the benefit of healing Mother Earth, the planet: to ease the wars, famines, oil spills, earthquakes or floods. Covens meet and perform rituals to ease the suffering of the earth, of man, of animals and of plants.

One particularly notable ritual was carried out early in the Second World War. A group of witches gathered on the shores of Britain and performed a ritual to banish the threat of a German invasion and to invoke the safe return of British and allied forces. The Dunkirk evacuation was spread over the period May to June 1940. The British Army were compelled to fall back due to the collapse of their allies the Belgians and French. Initially, only small numbers of men could be evacuated by Royal Naval vessels which were under constant air attack. Sixty-eight thousand troops were rescued on one day by a flotilla of small vessels, channel ferries and Navy war ships. Although the losses were staggering, many were saved. More than 338,000 were rescued. Did this ritual have anything to do with this? We will never know but the power of prayer is a wonderful thing and magick is simply a prayer of a different kind.

The *Collins English Dictionary* describes prayer as 'A personal communication or petition addressed to a deity in the form of supplication, adoration, praise, contrition or thanksgiving'. Almost every faith or religion has some form of prayer. Muslims use a prayer mat to kneel or prostrate themselves whilst praying to their god. Buddhists use a prayer wheel, which is filled with prayers. Each spin of the wheel is likened to these prayers being offered.

A pagan ritual is a form of prayer in the style chosen by the coven to the deity, God and Goddess of the coven.

Do I have to dance naked in the moonlight?

Well … you can if you want to … but that will be your decision. In Wicca, some people prefer to work 'sky clad', as we call it, but, to be honest with you, I can't see the necessity for this. When people work with magick and rituals they are working with energy. This energy is so powerful that it can change the course of events. If you believe that to be so then it must follow that this energy must be powerful enough to go through clothing.

The term 'naked and unadorned' is often used in rituals, however, I see this as a metaphor for being stripped of ego. Rituals are performed for the highest good, using pure energy and there is no room here for ego. My ego would have me being too worried about stretch marks and blemishes or prying eyes to concentrate on my tasks so I prefer to work clothed, but some like to work sky clad and that is their choice.

Others like to wear robes or gowns that have been made especially for their circle work (see *Why Cast a Circle?* page 79). It is nice to have something special to wear when you are working in your circle and making your own gown is all part and parcel of making your ritual special. This can be as elaborate or as simple as you like. I found some wonderful fabric in an Asian fabric shop. My name, Soraya, translated means 'the brightest star in the galaxy of seven stars' so you can imagine how thrilled I was to find some vibrant blue silk organza embroidered all over with gold beads in the shape of stars. I have two pieces of this and I use one as an altar cloth and the other as a cape. This is fine for working indoors but something more substantial is required for working outside, especially in cold weather. The Pagan Federation's quarterly magazine, *Pagan Dawn*, often carries advertisements for people who specialise in handmade gowns and robes if you are unable to make your own.

How often do covens meet?

Covens meet as often as they wish to. Some will meet weekly to talk, exchange ideas and plan their celebrations. Others may meet on a monthly basis on, or around, the time of the full moon. The full moon is a special time for pagans and some sort of ceremony will be carried out. They may simply light a candle on their work station or altar and spend a few minutes in quiet meditation or they will perform a ritual ceremony which is known as a Full Moon Esbat.

A working witch will cast a fresh circle every morning and be in or around it for the rest of the day, and magick in any shape or form can be practised at almost any time. There are special times though when circles will be cast even if magick is not being performed. Circles are cast at times of the full moon to honour the cycle of the moon, to honour the goddess or god associated with that time of year and festival, to draw down the power and energy of the moon.

There are eight special festivals during the year when pagans will gather together or work alone to celebrate these special days know as sabbats.

In the Wiccan calendar there are four great sabbats or festivals and four lesser sabbats or festivals. The eight sabbats are:

Imbolc
(Greater Sabbat) which is celebrated on February 2. Imbolc is known as a festival of light.

The Spring Equinox
(Lesser Sabbat) which is celebrated on March 21.

Beltane
(Greater Sabbat) which is celebrated on April 30.

The Summer Solstice
(Lesser Sabbat) which is celebrated on June 22.

Lammas
(Greater Sabbat) which is celebrated on July 31.

The Autumn Equinox
(Lesser Sabbat) which is celebrated on September 21.

Samhain
(Greater Sabbat) which is celebrated on October 31.

Yule
(Lesser Sabbat) which is celebrated on December 22.

Rituals in the
Pagan Tradition

IT IS not just weddings that are different in pagan tradition.
In fact all ceremonies are different whether they be
weddings, christenings or funerals. A few of these are outlined
below with some explanation regarding the symbolism involved.

How do witches marry ?

A handfasting is a pagan wedding and ceremonies vary
according to the traditions of different groups or couples. The
term handfasting comes from 'hand fastening', and in most
ceremonies it is usual to tie the hands of the bride and groom
together using cords or ribbons to symbolise their union.

In addition to the ritual of the ceremony, spells for love,
passion, fertility, prosperity and continued good health may
be included. In a handfasting, the bride and groom represent
the God and the Goddess, he is the hunter that provides and
she is the mother earth that nurtures and loves. Often when
pagans talk of getting married they refer to jumping the
broomstick and a handfasting would be incomplete if the bride
and groom did not jump over the broom. No matter how
solemn the ceremony, it would be difficult to suppress the
clapping and cheering at this part of the ceremony. The broom
represents binding together male and female aspects. The three
parts of the broom are the handle, which is a representation of

How do witches marry?

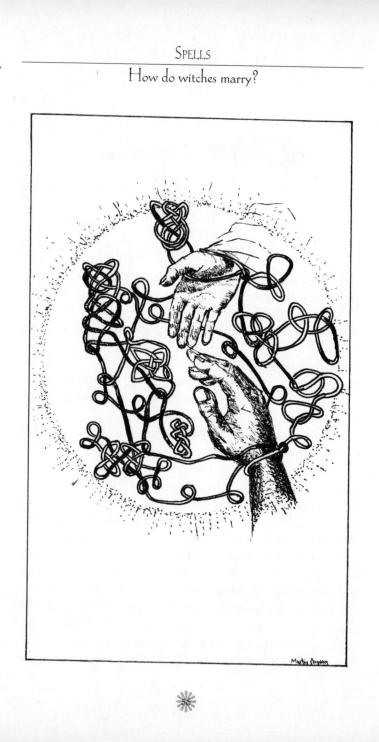

the male phallus, the bristles represent the female, and the twine is that which binds masculine and feminine together. The broom also sweeps away the old and allows the couple to have a fresh new beginning.

Couples may choose to marry for eternity and that means forever, in this life and in future lives. Other couples may choose to unite 'till death do us part' or they may choose to be united while their love burns strong and sure. They may also choose to be united for a year and a day. At the end of this time they may renew their vows and lengthen the period or separate.

Naming ceremonies

Naming ceremonies are the equivalent of Christenings but more thought is given to the Christening gift than for a conventional ceremony. To begin with, mother witch would have consulted an astrologer to find out her new baby's strengths and weaknesses, based on the child's time date and place of birth and this chart would be used to understand where the child may require extra encouragement. As the time for the naming ceremony approaches, those who will attend will already be thinking of the gifts that they will bestow. These come in the form of blessings. An artist would focus on blessing the child with the gift of creativity. Someone who had a good singing voice or was skilled with a musical instrument would bless the child with the gift of music. Each person would bestow on the child his or her greatest gift. A circle would be cast and each friend or coven member would, one by one, place their hand on the baby and as they did so they would visualise the child being proficient in that skill or talent.

Last rites

Even in death there is celebration and though we witches mourn the passing of a loved one in the flesh we believe in celebrating the passage into another time and dimension. It is traditional for mourners to wear white or pastel shades rather than black, and most pagans prefer to have a woodland burial or, if a cremation is preferred, the ashes may be scattered in a favourite woodland area. A tree is often planted instead of a headstone.

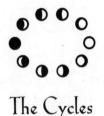

The Cycles

IN MAGICK, the cycles are important. Not just the cycles of birth, life, death and rebirth but an hour, a day, a week, a month, a quarter (thirteen weeks) then a year. Sometimes magick can be very quick and a spell can produce a result in an hour. Other spells take time and you may have to wait a month, or even a year. If we begin our magickal journey with a compass we start at the east, move to the south, the west and lastly the north.

East corresponds to the element of air. Air is the formation of an idea or a thought or a plan.

South corresponds to the element of fire. In the south, we bring energy to our plan.

West corresponds to the element of water. This is where we introduce purity, love and flowing movement to our magick.

North corresponds to the element of earth.

This is where our magick begins to grow and is blessed with abundance. The face of the compass is round reminding us again of the cycles of birth, life, death and rebirth. In Native American traditions, the dream catcher reminds us of this too, formed round the sacred hoop with ancient symbols.

When we are small children we are in the east quarter of our

Invoking rituals

lives and as we grow with knowledge and understanding we move to the south. In our middle age, we are in the west and we move in our old age to the north. Death and rebirth occurs and we begin again in the east.

Invoking rituals

All invoking rituals, where you want to bring something towards you or another person, are performed when the moon is rising. When the moon is rising, it is called a waxing moon. The waxing moon is the best time to invoke good health, recovery from illness or strife, peace of mind and contentment, protection, romance, and career opportunities.

Banishing rituals

Banishing rituals are performed when the moon is reducing or waning. In a banishing ritual you would send away or repel situations. You would banish illness, disease, anxiety, threats, jealousy, poverty, and loneliness.

The four stages of the moon

There are four stages or quarters to the moon's progress. In the first quarter, the new moon begins to appear first as a tiny sliver and grows in strength each evening. In the second quarter, we can see half of the moon and since we know that it is growing, it is waxing. During the third quarter the moon grows in strength and beauty and becomes full. The fourth quarter is when the moon begins to wane and reduce in size.

The chapter Phases of the Moon, at the end of this book includes the cycles of the moon and indicates when the moon is in a particular sign so that you know when it is best to cast a spell.

The moon and the signs of the zodiac

As you become more aware of the movement and influence of

The moon and the signs of the zodiac

the moon and the planets you will realise that when the moon is in particular planets or signs of the zodiac your magick can be more focused or empowered.

There are times though, when the moon is in between two signs of the zodiac when it is known as being 'void of course'. This is not a good time to perform any kind of magick that demands a certain outcome.

The moon travels round in a cycle, which lasts a little more than twenty-eight days. During this journey, the moon passes through the twelve signs of the zodiac. It remains in each sign for a period of two to three days. It does not appear in one sign and then jump immediately to the next sign. It is a gradual process. During the short period when the moon reaches the point when it is in neither one sign nor the other, unexpected things occur and plans tend to go awry. For that reason, it is best not to perform magickal rites during these times because it is more likely to go wrong.

If you incorporate some knowledge of the qualities of the planets and the signs of the zodiac in planning your working spells you will have greater results. Being aware of the qualities of each sign will help you to choose the best time for any given spell.

Aries ♈ 🐏

Dates: 21st March–20th April
Element: Fire
Quality: Cardinal
Symbol: The ram
Nature: Masculine
Day: Tuesday
Metal: Iron or steel
Gem: Bloodstone
Colour: Red
Occupation: Politics

The moon and the signs of the zodiac

Governs: The head
Key word: Energy
Positive influences: Courage and action
Negative influences: Greed and destruction
Ruler: Mars, God of War ♂

Taurus ♉ 🐂
Dates: 21st April–20th May
Element: Earth
Quality: Fixed
Symbol: The bull
Nature: Feminine
Day: Friday
Metal: Copper
Gem: Moss agate
Colour: Red and orange
Occupation: Economics
Governs: The ears, neck and throat
Key word: Love
Positive influences: Patience, affection and persistence
Negative influences: Stubbornness, aggression and jealousy
Ruler: Venus, Goddess of Love ♀

Gemini ♊ 👯
Date: 21st May–21st June
Element: Air
Quality: Mutable
Symbol: The twins
Nature: Masculine
Day: Wednesday
Metal: Quicksilver
Gem: Emerald
Colour: Orange

The moon and the signs of the zodiac

Occupation: Education
Governs: Hands, arms, chest and lungs
Key word: Expression
Positive influences: Affection, intelligence, and astuteness.
Negative influences: Pretentiousness, shallowness and restlessness.
Ruler: Mercury, God of Knowledge ☿

Cancer ♋ 🦞
Date: 22nd June–22nd July
Element: Water
Quality: Cardinal
Symbol: The crab
Nature: Feminine
Day: Friday
Metal: Silver
Gem: Moonstone
Colour: Orange and yellow
Occupation: The land
Governs: The chest and stomach
Key word: Enigmatic
Positive influences: Self-reliant, loyal and kind
Negative influences: Unforgiving, selfish and deep.
Ruler: The Moon, Goddess of Life ☽

Leo ♌ 🦁
Date 23rd July–22nd August
Element: Fire
Quality: Fixed
Symbol: The lion
Nature: Masculine
Day: Sunday
Metal: Gold

The moon and the signs of the zodiac

Gem: Ruby
Colour: Yellow
Occupation: The arts
Governs: The heart
Key word: Creativity
Positive influences: Considerate, dynamic, and charming
Negative influences: Egotistic, forceful, quick tempered.
Ruler: The Sun, God of Life ○

Virgo ♍ ♍
Date: 23rd August–22nd September
Element: Earth
Quality: Mutable
Symbol: The maiden
Nature: Feminine
Day: Wednesday
Metal: Quicksilver
Gem: Diamond
Colour: Yellow and green
Occupation: Public services
Governs: The digestive organs and the intestine
Key word: Expression
Positive influences: Balanced, organised and courteous
Negative influences: Negative, fretful and exacting
Ruler: Mercury, God of Knowledge ☿

Libra ♎ ♎
Date: 23rd September–22nd October
Element: Air
Quality: Cardinal
Symbol: The scales

The moon and the signs of the zodiac

Nature: Masculine
Day: Friday
Metal: Copper
Gem: Jasper
Colour: Green
Occupation: Law
Governs: The loins, kidneys and back
Key word: Affection
Positive influences: Charming, refined and affectionate
Negative influences: Cutting, harsh and arrogant
Ruler: Venus, Goddess of Love ♀

Scorpio ♏ ≈
Date: 23rd October–21st November
Element: Water
Quality: Fixed
Symbol: The scorpion
Nature: Feminine
Day: Tuesday
Metal: Plutonium
Gem: Topaz
Colour: Green and blue
Occupation: Finance
Governs: The reproductive areas
Key word: Transformation
Positive influences: Determined, magnetic and sincere
Negative influences: Challenging, secretive and headstrong.
Ruler: Pluto, God of the Underworld ♇

Sagittarius ♐ ≈
Date: 22nd November–21st December
Element: Fire
Quality: Mutable

The moon and the signs of the zodiac

Symbol: The archer
Nature: Masculine
Day: Thursday
Metal: Tin
Gem: Turquoise
Colour: Blue
Occupation: Travel
Governs: The thighs
Key word: Progress
Positive influences: Adventurous, thoughtful and independent
Negative influences: Impulsive, self-centred and domineering
Ruler: Jupiter, God of Fortune ♃

Capricorn ♑ 🐐

Date: 22nd December–19th January
Element: Earth
Quality: Cardinal
Symbol: The goat
Nature: Feminine
Day: Saturday
Metal: Lead
Gem: Lapis
Colour: Deep blue
Occupation: Civil service
Governs: The knees
Key word: Authority
Positive influences: Independent, refined and disciplined
Negative influences: Insecure, critical and proud
Ruler: Saturn, God of Time ♄

The moon and the signs of the zodiac

Aquarius
Date: 20th January–18th February
Element: Air
Quality: Fixed
Symbol: The water carrier
Nature: Masculine
Day: Wednesday
Metal: Uranium
Gem: Sapphire
Colour: Indigo
Occupation: Parliament
Governs: The calves and ankles
Key word: Confrontation
Positive influences: Affectionate, modest and intelligent
Negative influences: Judgmental, critical and extreme
Ruler: Uranus, the God of Air

Pisces
Date: 19th February–20th March
Element: Water
Quality: Mutable
Symbol: The fishes
Nature: Feminine
Day: Friday
Metal: Platinum
Gem: Pearl
Colour: Violet
Occupation: Health care
Governs: The feet
Key word: Inspiration
Positive influences: Intuitive, sensitive and kind
Negative influences: Argumentative, excessive and selfish
Ruler: Neptune, God of the Sea

Preparing Your
Magickal Tools

ALMOST everything that you will need to practise your own magick and to work in a circle you will find in your own home, or it will be easily obtainable or easy to make from equipment that you already have in the home.

A Book of Shadows

The first thing that you must have is a Book of Shadows. Think of this as a homework book. Everything that you learn about in the craft should be written in your Book of Shadows. For this, buy the best that you can afford. When I began, I started with a hardback notebook, but that means transferring all the information into your special book. Some of the things that you may want to write about are spells, when spells were carried out and at what point they achieved a successful outcome, rituals, remedies, supplies and suppliers. It will be your book and it is something very special that can be handed down for generations to come.

Magickal tools

A broom
A wand
An athame (magickal knife)
A bolline (working knife)
A pentacle, the five pointed star

The broom or besom

A cauldron
Four candles which are placed at the four quarters
A cup or chalice
A bell
A table or large tray
A mat on which to kneel or sit
A large white altar candle
A large black altar candle
A dinner candle
A small pouring jug filled with water
A small dish of salt
A small empty dish
A small pointed knife
A censer, some incense or smudge sticks
Matches or a lighter
A candle snuff
A towelling cloth, a face cloth is ideal.
Some crystals, if you have them, to place round your working surface

Now that you have assembled your tools, you will want to have some understanding of what they are for and why you would want to use them.

The broom or besom

A besom is a broom, traditionally made using ash for the handle and birch twigs for the brush. They are inexpensive to purchase and can be personalised by carving or painting the handle and adding symbols of your choice. I have several of these, the first one given to me by my children many years ago. Another of my favourites is one that I have decorated with turquoise suede and feathers typical of Native American styles. The besom is used primarily as a purifier, and many Wiccan rituals begin by sweeping the area where the sacred circle is to be cast in order to remove any negative energy. The besom can also be used as a protective implement by laying it under the bed, across a windowsill or across the threshold of your property.

Wand

A wand is used to draw magickal symbols on the ground or in the air, for directing energy, and for calling upon the Goddess. A wand can be made of crystal or a branch from a tree can be used. Each sign of the zodiac is associated with a particular tree so if you would like to have a wand that is compatible with your sign the following information will help you:

Astrological Sign	Tree
Aries	Alder
Taurus	Willow
Gemini	Hawthorn
Cancer	Oak
Leo	Holly
Virgo	Hazel
Libra	Vine
Scorpio	Ivy
Sagittarius	Elder
Capricorn	Birch
Aquarius	Rowan
Pisces	Ash

Athame (magickal knife)

The dagger is used for connecting the energy from the source of infinity above, the sky – the stars and the air – with the source of the energy below, Mother Earth. It is used to direct energy and to open and close doorways to your circle. In Wicca, we would use a traditional dagger, which is called an athame. You can also use a sword, a crystal wand or a small wooden branch taken from a favourite tree. Remember though that a tree, as with any plant, is a living element and some courtesy should be shown here. To remove a branch from a tree, stand quietly in front of the tree and explain the purpose for which the branch is intended. It is also nice to leave a small gift of some fruit or a coin as an offering. Some people use two athames, one for consecrating and sealing the circle and another for working on their altar. I use one for consecrating and closing my circle and I use a large crystal wand for my altar work.

Bolline (working knife)

The knife is usually white handled and is used in the gathering of herbs and plants, cutting wands, and to inscribe symbols into candles when you are using candle magick or for inscribing symbols on to your broom or wand.

Pentacle

A pentacle is an ancient symbol in the shape of a five-pointed star, which has one point at the top, one each to the left and right and two more at the bottom. The top point of the pentacle points to infinity above and, moving clockwise, the next point symbolises water, the next fire, and the next earth and lastly air. The space in the middle is the space that mankind symbolically occupies. A circle symbolising infinity and protection generally surrounds this five-pointed star. Most

Wiccans wear a pentacle as a piece of jewellery around their neck or on a ring. Some consider the symbol too sacred to be seen by the eyes of other people and always keep it covered. The choice is yours to do as you wish.

The pentacle is always used in circle work, drawn in the air and placed on the altar and this reminds us of the ever-renewing cycles of balance, life, death and rebirth in all aspects. The pentacle can be used for evoking spirits and calling upon the Goddess. Pentacles can be purchased in most New Age shops but can also be made.

If you have a computer, a simple way to draw one is to open a Microsoft Word document, click on 'insert', and on the drop down menu click on 'picture'. When you have done this a new box titled 'AutoShapes' will appear. Choose the stars and banners icon, click on this, click on the five-pointed star and your pointer on the screen will become a cross. Hold down the left mouse button, press the shift button (this will give you a perfectly proportioned shape) and drag the mouse until the star appears in the size that you want. Print this out and use it as a template to help you draw or paint your own pentacle. If you are artistic, you could even make one from plaster, papier-mache or wire. Your pentacle should be placed on the centre of your altar.

Cauldron

What self-respecting witch would be without a cauldron? However, it took me ages to find mine. I searched high and low, looking in second hand and antique shops and finally I resorted to magick. At the Pagan Federation Annual Conference in Edinburgh I found it. My cauldron's home is in my lounge and a candle burns in it most days. At special times of the year my cauldron is brought outside to my circle and I use it during my rituals. During a full moon it can be filled with water and used for scrying (seeing into the past or the future). Spells can also be created in the cauldron.

Candles

Four candles are placed, one at each of the four quarters, the east, the south, the west and the north, on the outside rim of the circle. You can use tea lights or altar candles for this. In addition to these candles you will need a good supply of a variety of candles in different shapes, sizes and colours. I buy mine in bulk and make some too. When I am working with candle magick I save the end pieces and recycle them, losing none of the power and energy that I have been working with.

Cup or chalice

The cup or chalice is used for symbolically joining the male and female aspects. The cup is feminine and the athame is masculine. At the end of a ritual you would drink your water, wine or fresh juice from the chalice. If you can afford to splash out you can buy one made of silver, brass or gold or you may already have something suitable.

Bell

Ringing a bell will purify and clear the air or the energy around you and, as a feminine object, the bell can be used to call the Goddess. Any bell can be used but the finer the peel the better. I found my bell in a second hand shop. It is made of Caithness glass and has a beautiful sound.

A tray

A large tray is required to carry your tools to your circle, whether you are working inside or out, and this can be used as your work surface if you do not have a table. In Wicca, your work surface would be called an altar. There is nothing sacred about an altar but the purpose for which it is used is sacred. For this reason, many Wiccans will keep their table or tray in their magickal cupboard away from prying eyes or, more aptly, negative vibrations. Each time it is brought out for use it would be carefully washed and blessed for its value and purpose.

A censer or incense stick and burner

Censers can be quite elaborate and expensive but if you pop into any hardware store or gift shop you should be able to find a small brass hanging-plant potholder complete with chains. Put some salt or sand in the bottom, add a charcoal disc which can be purchased from most New Age shops and, when it is white hot, herbs and grains of crystallised gums can be sprinkled on top. This makes it easy to carry around your circle when you are invoking the element of air. If you find it difficult to obtain the loose incense you can use an incense cone or stick instead. This represents the element of air and should be placed at the east section of your table. If you prefer you can substitute a smudge stick instead. Again these can be purchased from any good New Age shop or you can make your own smudge sticks by drying your favourite herbs and then binding them together in a bunch with some twine.

They can be difficult to use initially because after lighting them it is important to blow on them and fan them to create the smoke. It is also important that they are extinguished properly. I use a small pottery jar half filled with salt and when I am finished I place the glowing end of the smudge stick into the salt and press it down firmly. If you are working indoors remember to check it later to ensure that it has gone out.

Other objects
A **table** to use as your altar.

A **mat** comes in handy for kneeling or sitting on, especially if you are working outside. I use a prayer mat purchased from an Asian store. I remember when I went into the shop to buy it the salesman was not going to let me have it. He asked me if I knew what it was and what it was used for. I managed to convince him that it would be used for a good purpose.

One large **white altar candle** is placed on the left of the altar to symbolise the feminine element, the Goddess. You can use a green candle instead.

One large **black altar candle** is placed on the right of the altar to symbolise the masculine element, the God. You can use a red candle instead. These two candles represent balance and harmony just the same as is seen in the yin and yang symbol.

One **dinner candle,** representing the element of fire, should be placed at the south section of your table.

One small pouring **jug** filled with water, representing the element of water, should be placed at the west section of your table.

One small **dish of salt** representing the element of earth should be placed at the north section of your table.

One small **empty dish** should be placed within your reach in front of you to use for blending water and salt during your ceremony.

Do not forget
Your matches or lighter and candle snuff to put out your candles.

> Never, ever blow your candles out
> or you will undo all your work.

The towelling cloth is important for cleaning your hands

especially if you are using essential oils for anointing candles. If you like working with crystals or just like having them around you, you can scatter these around your altar.

Why Cast a Circle?

MOST rituals take place within a magick or sacred circle. Whilst working within the circle we are between this world and the astral world. It can be likened to meditating. There are guidelines for laying out a magic circle but they are not always necessary. Traditionally, a circle would be 9 feet (2.74 metres) in diameter and a sacred ceremonial chord, which measures 4 feet 6 inches in length (1.37 metres), would be used to measure this. However larger circles would be used for groups performing outdoor rituals and smaller circles may be used if you are working in a tiny space at home.

The most important thing that you can do though, is to prepare your ritual in advance so that you have everything that you need and know exactly what you are doing before you begin. It is not a good idea to break your concentration in the middle of a ceremony in order to go and get something that you have forgotten. This would be considered as an insult to the Goddess and it would also allow negative feelings or energy to enter your sacred space.

A circle is cast to keep the energy pure and focused. Part of this focus is a personal one. If I am working and do not wish to be disturbed, I close my office door so that my concentration is not broken. In my circle, I do the same. Once I am in my sacred space I do not wish to be interrupted or distracted by anyone and I will not stop what I am doing for a telephone call or a visitor at the door. The other reason that I cast a circle is that I do not want negative energy coming into my space. I consider negative energy to be that energy which is created by negative thoughts, deeds, words or actions. If you have just cleaned the carpet in your lounge because you are expecting important guests then you do not want your dog running over it with muddy paws, so you close the door. If this were to happen, by the time your guests had arrived you would be in an apologetic mood and it could spoil the occasion. It is as simple as that.

Where should my circle be?

When you begin to do your work, you will do so in a specific fashion. If you work in an office, the first thing that you would attend to would probably be the mail and telephone messages. You might then finish tasks that were unfinished before you went home the previous evening. Every day you do the same job and more often than not in the same fashion.

Circle magic has an orderly pattern too. This can be done in the home, the garden, or in your own favourite location.

Working outside is more difficult though. The weather is the first disadvantage. No one wants to work in the pouring rain and it is difficult to light candles when your matches are wet, or when the wind is blowing so fiercely that your candles are blown out. Another disadvantage when working outside is the presence of people out walking, perhaps with their dogs or children. I love dogs and children but I do not want to be distracted by them when I am working.

My favourite place to work is in my home but if the weather is fine, I have a special place in my little garden with some large stones placed round the edge of my circle.

Where should my circle be?

Preparation

I remember the day that my garden circle was created. The back garden was overgrown with couch grass, weeds and was full of debris. No work had ever been done on it. My partner Martin and I were surveying the overgrown mess and Martin asked what I would like done with it. I closed my eyes and pictured the scene: a special place where I could sit and meditate surrounded by wild flowers and herbs. I made a few suggestions of how I imagined it and thought no more about it. The next day I left early in the morning for a business meeting in Perth. The sun was shining and it was a beautiful day. Much later, when I came home, I was busy chatting to Martin about how my day had gone. I asked him what he had been doing all day and he told me that he had been sitting in the garden. The sun was still shining so we made some tea and took it outside to enjoy the last of the fine day and relax before dinner. I could not believe my eyes when I walked round the house.

Martin had cleared the overgrown jungle and had created a split-level garden. My Buddhas and Chinese lanterns were placed in among shrubs that he had transplanted and he had cleared and re-turfed a circle around which he had placed large boulders. At either side of the entrance to my new circle stood two large planters filled with lavender. I was so excited and touched by the effort that he had made to create my dream that I cried. Martin was happy too and eager to show me all that he had done. When we looked at the stones in my circle we were amazed to discover that each quarter of the circle had a stone which was perfectly placed for due east, south, west and north. Now that is what I call magick!

Preparation

If you are going to work outside the first step is to cast your circle. In traditional circle casting, a broom would be used to sweep round the circle sweeping it clean. A broom can be used

to measure the distance of the circle. If you would like to try this then lay the broom on its side with the bristles to the centre of the circle. Place one stone at the bristle end and another at the spot where the end of the handle rests. Moving to the opposite end of the circle and repeating this process would give the diameter. This process would be repeated twice more just like quartering a giant cake. This circle would now have four quarters. The first quarter is the east, the second quarter is south, the third quarter is west and the fourth quarter is north. You can now place stones in the spaces between your quarter stones and there you have it, your own circle.

At this point you must begin to prepare yourself and you do this as you would for any other important event in your life. You can start with a warm bath with essential oils to prepare your mood. My favourites for any kind of spiritual work are marjoram and frankincense.

A nice way to prepare is to lay out the clothes that you have decided to wear and any jewellery that has special meaning to you. Place four small tea light candles at each corner of your bath and light them, starting with the candle at the front left edge of your bath. Then light the furthest left, the furthest right and the front right candle last.

Turn the water on to fill your bath and as the water is running add a few drops of your favourite oil. Next take some sea salt and beginning at the left of your bath sprinkle the salt into the water in a figure-of-eight movement. When the temperature of the water is as you like it, place some of your favourite crystals into the water, turn out the bathroom lights and step into your bath.

While you are lying there go over in your mind those tasks that you are about to perform in your circle. Focus your attention on the energies of the salt, the water and the crystals and feel these energies cleansing and purifying your mind, body and spirit. Finish with a short meditation of your choice.

When you are ready, step out of the bath and then remove the plug and allow the water to drain away. As the water drains away it will remove any negative energy. Do not remove the plug before you are out of the bath or you will drain away all the good energy that you have invoked into your body.

Finally rinse your crystals in clean water. Both you and your circle have now been prepared and you can begin to place all your magickal tools on your altar and set your quarter candles in place.

Casting a circle

Starting at the east, then west, then south and then north, place one small, white candle in each quarter. The sun sets in the west and rises in the east but if you are still unsure of the direction then place the east candle to your left as you face your working surface which is in the centre of your sacred space or circle.

Once this has been done, stand at the edge of your circle and visualise white light pouring into it from infinity above. The best time is when the moon is full and moonlight blesses the circle. Focus your mind on the source of infinity above you, Father God, and the strength of the earth beneath your feet, Mother Earth. I prepare myself spiritually and mentally and think of my intentions. Visualise a temple of light and love growing over your circle. When you are ready, say these words.

> The circle is about to be cast and the temple erected.
> Let the light and the love and the energy which fills my sacred space be pure and work for the highest good and harm none.

Enter your circle and walk to the altar, and, taking your

Casting a circle

lighter or matches, light first the large white altar candle then the large black altar candle and lastly the dinner candle. Remove the dinner candle from its holder and move to the east of your circle. Light the east candle from the dinner candle and as you do so say these words:

> May the watchtower of the east be blessed with light and air to illuminate this temple and bring it life.

> May the watchtower of the south be blessed with light and fire to illuminate this temple and bring it warmth.

> May the watchtower of the west be blessed with light and water to illuminate this temple and wash it clean.

> May the watchtower of the north be blessed with light and earth to illuminate this temple and bring it strength.

Returning to your altar replace the candle in its holder and pick up the athame. Hold it high above your head with your arms at full stretch. Face the moon and ask again for the blessings from infinity above you. You may feel the energy beginning to course down through your arms. Lower your arms and walk to the east quarter of your circle. Point the athame to the ground and begin to walk round the edge of your circle visualising that you are drawing a golden white line of light with the point of your athame.

Starting at the east, move to the south, then the west, then the north, and back to the east. Move back to where you entered your circle and place the point of the blade into the ground where it will remain until you are ready to finish. If you are working inside your house, you can lay your athame across the entrance to your circle.

Returning to your altar, put your index finger into the container of salt and, as you do so, visualise light energy flowing down through your arm into your hand and into the salt and say these words:

> Let this salt of life purify my body and spirit that I may use it for the highest good.

Place three pinches of salt into the water and stir it clockwise three times.

Return to the east rim of your circle and begin to sprinkle the salt and water round the edge of your circle saying as you do so:

> I bless the east with salt and water to purify, cleanse and protect my circle.
> I bless the south with salt and water to purify, cleanse and protect my circle.
> I bless the west with salt and water to purify, cleanse and protect my circle.
> I bless the north with salt and water to purify, cleanse and protect my circle.

Move to the east to complete the circle and then return to your altar. Place your dish on the altar and pick up your incense and then say:

> I bless the east with this sacred scent to purify, cleanse and protect my circle.
> I bless the south with this sacred scent to purify, cleanse and protect my circle.
> I bless the west with this sacred scent to purify, cleanse and protect my circle.
> I bless the north with this sacred scent to purify, cleanse and protect my circle.

Move to the east to complete the circle and then return to the centre of your circle and place your incense on the altar.

Draw an invoking pentacle

Return to the east edge of your circle and using your athame, crystal, or your index finger, draw an invoking pentacle in the air at the east quarter as you say these words:

> May the watchtower of the east, element of air, guard and protect this sacred space and grant me the blessings I require to fulfil my desires so that they harm none.

Draw an invoking pentacle

Drawing down the moon

May the watchtower of the south, element of fire, guard and protect this sacred space and grant me the blessings I require to fulfil my desires so that they harm none.

May the watchtower of the west, element of water, guard and protect this sacred space and grant me the blessings I require to fulfil my desires so that they harm none.

May the watchtower of the north, element of earth, guard and protect this sacred space and grant me the blessings I require to fulfil my desires so that they harm none.

Move to the east to complete the circle and then return to your altar and draw an invoking pentacle above you.

Drawing down the moon

Ring the bell three times and replace it on your altar. Open your arms wide, raise your hands high above your head, focus all your attention on the moon above you, and visualise the Goddess sending down her light and love to you (see the illustration on the next page). Draw this energy into your heart, into your spirit and into your body. Give thanks for those blessings that you have already received, your health, your career, your family and your loved ones. Lower your arms and extend them out by your sides saying:

I call upon the Goddess to ask for assistance with my task. May she be ever=present in my work and in my life.

I am grateful for those gifts and blessings that I have already been given and I am open and ready to receive those that are waiting to come to me.

This is known as 'drawing down the moon'. What we are really doing here is drawing on the energy of the moon to bring our energy into contact with the energy of the Moon

Drawing down the moon

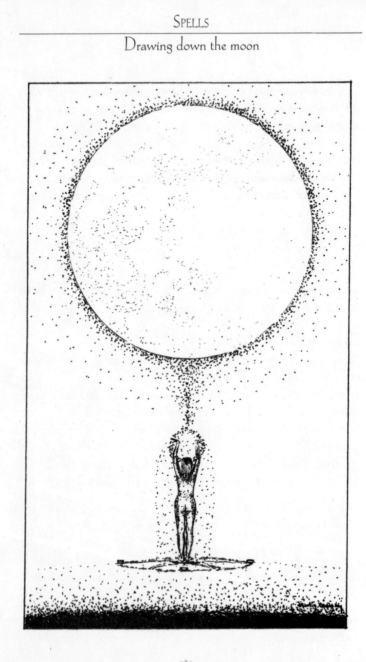

Goddess, restoring our vitality and strengthening our purpose.

Pick up the cup of juice, wine or water and hold it high above your head allowing the energy and the blessings of the moon to charge this liquid. Place the cup on the table, raise the second athame or crystal wand high above your head, and allow the energy and the blessings of the moon to charge it too. Now lower the athame or crystal wand into the cup to symbolise the joining of male and female aspects of deity, of man and of life. Say these words:

> May man and woman be joined for eternal joy and happiness. May the plants that sustain us be fruitful and may we all be blessed with abundance.

Remove the athame from the cup and lay it to one side.

Your circle is now fully charged and you are ready to begin whatever task you have chosen to do.

You can now begin to perform any of the spells contained in this book or any other work that you have decided to do. When you have finished, give the water and salt back to the earth by pouring it into the ground just before you close your circle. If you are working inside your home, you can save this until you have finished and then go outside and pour this sacred liquid on to the soil in your circle or special place. Before you close your circle, say these words:

> Lord and Lady thank you for assisting me with my tasks. We have met in love and friendship, let us part the same way. May the love that has been in this circle be shared with all. Merry we meet, merry we part, merry may we meet again. The temple will now be closed.

> May the watchtower of the east, element of air take for your use any powers that have not been used.

Drawing down the moon

May the watchtower of the south, element of fire, take for your use any powers that have not been used.

May the watchtower of the west, element of water, take for your use any powers that have not been used.

May the watchtower of the north, element of earth, take for your use any powers that have not been used.

And it harm none so mote it be.

Go back to the centre of your circle and begin to clean and clear away your magickal tools. Take the incense stick and touch it to the liquid to put it out and give thanks to the element of air for its blessings. If you are outside, give the sacred liquid back to the earth by pouring it on the ground. As you do so give thanks to the elements of water and earth for their blessings.

Using a candle snuff, put out the candles on your altar and, as you do so, give thanks to the element of fire for its blessings.

Move to the edge of your circle and, using the candle snuff, put out your candles, one by one, starting at the east quarter, then the south, the west and lastly the north.

If you have placed your athame in the ground, pick it up now, thank it for guarding the entrance to your sacred space, and place it with the rest of your tools.

Rituals or ceremonies are times for celebration and if you are working in a coven you will find that the atmosphere is friendly and happy. There may be feasting, dancing, singing and storytelling. Obviously this is not possible if you are working on your own.

Part Two:

Making the Magick Happen

Making the Magick Happen ... or ...

Singed Knees and Waxy Fingers

THIS chapter heading came directly from the subject line in an e-mail from one of my students. She was at that time quite worried and depressed about the way things were going in her life and I suggested that she conjure up a few changes. I instructed her on how to cast a circle and do a simple candle magick spell. The e-mail in question was sent to me after her first attempt. She had set out her favourite rug in the middle of the floor in her lounge, set up her candles and began to work her magick. She told me in her e-mail that apart from getting covered in melted wax and singeing both her knees and her favourite rug, she felt much better. Even though the spell had not had time to take effect she felt as though she had done something positive ... but she was lucky that she didn't burn the house down.

Bear this in mind when you begin to practise and remember that, in more ways than one, you can burn your fingers when playing with fire.

Now that you know a little of the background it is time to get down to the nitty gritty. The good news is that magick can be performed anywhere and at any time without too much bother. You can set up a circle around yourself in your mind by visualising your circle around you, complete with all the elements in place and just silently declare the words that are necessary for your chosen spell. This is not as much fun but it is very effective in emergencies or when you are away from home.

All rituals are basically the same, however, the oils, herbs, symbols or colours used for specific spells will be different. There is nothing worse though when preparing to work a spell than having the scene set, complete with your book open at the appropriate page, and then being told to follow the instructions on a different page. So, in this book, my spells include details of everything you will need to gather around you, say and do in each case.

Before you begin to work with your chosen spell you must prepare all your ingredients. Have everything that you need on your workspace or altar and you will feel more confident. This confidence will help you to have successful outcomes to all your spells.

There are spells for every conceivable situation but most people are at some time or another concerned about:

Health
When you or a loved one is ill.

Love
When you or someone close to you feels lonely and unloved. Remember when you are using love spells that you should never try to force a relationship with a particular person.

Career
When you are looking for promotion or securing the best job. Of course there is no point in performing a spell if you do not intend to scan the employment pages and apply for positions! Magic will assist your efforts but you must make that effort in the first place.

Finances

When you need to improve or encourage financial security. No matter how well off you are, at certain times money just seems to stop flowing. There could be a delay, for any number of reasons, in money coming to you that you expect or depend on and an appropriate spell will speed up the arrival and help you to meet your financial obligations.

Protection

When we are affected by negative energies caused by abusive people, situations or even stalkers, a protection spell can act like the knight in shining armour that is so vital to make us feel safe and secure.

> Never under any circumstances
> interfere with someone's will.

Magickal ingredients

Decide first on the spell that you are planning to create and then choose from the lists of ingredients at the beginning of each chapter those items that are easily accessible to you. Remember that you do not need every single item but the more you have the better.

You can vary the times, dates and Goddesses and use your favourites. This list is only a guide to help you initially. Later your magick will become spontaneous and much more fun.

The methods and rituals are explained step by step for each spell. Everything you need to know about each particular spell is contained within each chapter so that you don't have to refer back and forth to other sections.

Now let's make some magick happen!

1

Good Luck

Day of the week: The best day of the week is Thursday

Time of day: The best time of day is 5am. Also noon, 7pm or at any time in the evening when the moon is waxing or full but not when it is waning

God: Quirinus

Goddess: Gamelia

Planet: Jupiter

Guardian Angel: Zadkiel

Star sign: Sagittarius

Metal: Tin, silver or gold

Colour: Blue

Rune: Daeg (also known as Dagaz)

Symbol: Two=sided objects such as coins

Number: Your own birth number. Add together the day, month and year of your birth. [e.g., my date of birth is 25/12/1947 and my birth number is 4.

$2+5+1+2+1+9+4+7 = 31$, then $(3+1) = 4$.]

Crystal: Citrine or amber

Flower: White heather

Essential oil: Sandalwood

Herb: Clover

Tree: Cedar

Sagittarius	Jupiter	Daeg

Good Luck

Good luck spell 1

Prepare yourself and decorate your work surface or altar space with all your chosen ingredients such as:

One blue taper candle
One white taper candle
A candle snuff
Several two=sided objects such as coins
A sprig of white heather
A sprig of clover (plants available in garden centres)
An item of silver or gold jewellery
A piece of citrine or amber
A piece of paper with a drawing of the symbol Daeg and the number that represents your date of birth.
An ashtray or a small fireproof dish for spent matches or any paper that you may light during your spell and some matches or a lighter.

When everything is in place, close your eyes and, as you breathe in, visualise positive, white, light energy filling your body. As you breathe out, breathe away all negative energy. After some minutes, you will feel all tension flowing away from your mind and body. Allow pure light energy to flow into and through your entire body filling your sacred space, filling your room. When you are completely relaxed, stand up and move quietly to the east quarter of your circle or room.

Light the east candle and say:
   May the element of air bless this space with light, love and air and grant me good fortune.

Light the south candle and say:
   May the element of fire bless this space with light, love and fire and grant me good fortune.

Good Luck

Light the west candle and say:
May the element of water bless this space with light, love and water and grant me good fortune.

Light the north candle and say:
May the element of earth bless this space with light, love and earth and grant me good fortune.

Move quietly back to your workspace and kneel in front of your table. Light your white altar candle and meditate quietly on your heart's desire and visualise before you your wish coming true. In your mind, focus on your desire and ask Quirinus and Gamelia to grant you their blessings for good luck. Visualise the Guardian Angel Zadkiel protecting you and surrounding you with good fortune.

Light your blue candle and take your piece of paper and light it from the altar candle and let it burn in the ashtray or small dish.

As it burns say these words:

> Good luck be with me every day.
> Quirinus and Gamelia, hear me pray.
> Zadkiel bring good news,
> Change my fortune that I may not lose.
> And it harm none so be it.

Spend some quiet time in your circle focusing your mind on your luck changing and improving. If you can, allow your altar candle to burn through to the end, but, if you must put it out, do so with a candle snuff or pinch the wick between dampened fingertips.

When you are finished working move quietly to the left of your circle.

Good Luck

Extinguish the east candle and say:
I thank the element of air for blessing me with good fortune.

Extinguish the south candle and say:
I thank the element of fire for blessing me with good fortune.

Extinguish the west candle and say:
I thank the element of water for blessing me with good fortune.

Extinguish the north candle and say:
I thank the element of earth for blessing me with good fortune.

Close your circle by saying:
May the four powers give back to the universe any powers and energies that have not been used.
The work is now done and the circle is closed.
So mote it be.

Good luck spell 2

10 mls base oil (sunflower, jojoba or almond)
Sandalwood pure essential oil
A bottle for your oil mixture
A small face cloth or some tissues (to clean your hands after working with the oil)
An ornament or picture of a black cat
Some citrine or amber, or your favourite crystal
Any items that you consider to be your lucky charms
One tall blue taper candle and holder
One tall white taper candle and holder
One small pointed knife

Good Luck

A small fireproof dish or an ashtray for spent matches or any paper that you may light during your spell and some matches or a lighter

Prepare a blend of oil using 10 mls of base oil and add three drops of sandalwood pure essential oil. Hold the bottle of oil in your hands in the prayer position and rub the bottle vigorously between the palms of your hands and as you do so visualise the oil being empowered with good fortune. When you feel as though the oil has been charged, place it on your altar or work surface ready for use along with the other ingredients.

Place four small candles at the east, south, west and north, in that order. When everything is in place, sit or kneel comfortably in front of your table.

Close your eyes and, as you breathe in, picture positive, white, light energy filling your body. As you breathe out, breathe away all negative energy. After some minutes, you will feel all tension flowing away from your mind and body.

Allow pure light energy to flow into and through your entire body filling your sacred space, filling your room. When you are completely relaxed stand up and move quietly to the east quarter of your room.

Light the east candle and say:
   May the element of air bless this space with light, love and air and grant me good fortune.

Light the south candle and say:
   May the element of fire bless this space with light, love and fire and grant me good fortune.

Good Luck

Light the west candle and say:
May the element of water bless this space with light, love and water and grant me good fortune.

Light the north candle and say:
May the element of earth bless this space with light, love and earth and grant me good fortune.

Move quietly back to your workspace and kneel in front of your table. Light your white altar candle and meditate quietly on your heart's desire and visualise your wish coming true. Take your blue spell candle and the small pointed knife and inscribe your lucky number and the rune symbol Daeg at the top of the candle.

Place the candle back in the holder and, taking the bottle of empowered oil, place some in the palm of your hands. Rub your hands together and visualise that you are charging the energy in the oil and in your hands. Your hands will begin to feel very warm.

At this point take the blue spell candle and spread the oil from middle to top and middle to bottom of the candle until the candle is completely covered in oil. While you are doing this visualise that you are empowering the candle with your desire. Keep thinking about your heartfelt desire and whilst doing this rub your hands vigorously together with the candle still held between the palms of your hands. After a few minutes, place your candle back in its holder and light the flame and say these words:

> Candle burning, burning bright,
> Change my luck this very night.
> Bring to me my heart's desire,
> Powered by this magick fire.
> And it harm none so be it.

Good Luck

Allow your candle to burn for as long as possible but if you must put it out do not blow it out otherwise you will reverse or negate your spell. You can use a candle-snuff or pinch the flame between your thumb and finger. You may light your candle again but, each time you do so, visualise your wish as though it has already begun to happen. When you are finished working, clean your hands on the cloth and move quietly to the left of your room.

Extinguish the east candle and say:
I thank the element of air for blessing me with good fortune.

Extinguish the south candle and say:
I thank the element of fire for blessing me with good fortune.

Extinguish the west candle and say:
I thank the element of water for blessing me with good fortune.

Extinguish the north candle and say:
I thank the element of earth for blessing me with good fortune.

Close your circle by saying:
May the four powers give back to the universe any powers and energies that have not been used.
The work is now done and the circle is closed.
So mote it be.

2

Prosperity

Day of the week: The best day
of the week is Sunday

Time of day: The best time of
day is 5am. Also noon, 7pm
or at any time in the evening
when the moon is waxing or
full but not when it is
waning

Goddess: Aditi

Planet: The sun

Guardian Angel: Michael

Star sign: Leo

Metal: Gold

Colour: Yellow

Rune: Feoh (also known as
Fehu)

Symbol: Coal, salt, money or
keys

Number: Nine

Crystal: Diamond, jade or
ruby

Flower: Sunflower

Essential oil: Rose otto

Herb: Bay

Tree: Cherry

The Sun

Leo

Feoh

Prosperity

Prosperity spell 1

Prepare yourself and decorate your work surface or altar space with all your chosen ingredients such as:

Items of gold and silver
One yellow taper candle
One white taper candle
One piece of coal
A dish of salt
A dish of coins
A key or bunch of keys
Diamond, jade or ruby jewellery
Your purse, wallet or bankbook, even if they are empty
A piece of paper and a pen or pencil
An ashtray or a small fireproof dish for spent matches or any paper
    that you may light during your spell and some matches or a lighter

First bathe in a warm luxurious bath to which you have added three drops of rose otto essential oil. Dry yourself with your favourite towel and dab a little of your desired scent on your wrists, behind your ears and over your heart. Dress in your best clothes and, when you are ready and everything is in place, stand at the edge of your circle. Close your eyes and breathe in, visualising light energy filling your body. Breathe out and breathe away all negative energy.

When you are completely relaxed, stand up and move quietly to the east quarter of your circle or room.

Light the east candle and say:
    May the element of air bless this space with light, love and air
    and grant me prosperity.

Light the south candle and say:
   May the element of fire bless this space with light, love and fire and grant me prosperity.

Light the west candle and say:
   May the element of water bless this space with light, love and water and grant me prosperity.

Light the north candle and say:
   May the element of earth bless this space with light, love and earth and grant me prosperity.

Move quietly back to your workspace and kneel in front of your table. Light your white altar candle and meditate quietly on your financial situation as it is now. In your mind see yourself depositing money in your savings account. Your vision should be a happy one where anyone you see is smiling warmly at you. Now see yourself paying all your bills one by one. Having paid all your bills, see yourself buying a special treat for yourself or someone that you care for.

Light your yellow taper candle and as the flame grows write down a sensible sum of money that will make all these things possible. Do not be greedy by asking for the impossible.

Take your piece of paper and light it from the yellow taper candle placing it in the ashtray to burn through. See the smoke from your burning paper carry your wishes to the Goddess Aditi.

In your mind's eye see the rays of the sun surrounding you with abundance and say a prayer in your own words to the Guardian Angel Michael. Stand in front of your altar, raise your hands high above your head and say these words:

Prosperity

Coins that sparkle in the sun
Come to me when work is done.
Make me richer by the day,
Wealth aplenty comes my way.
And it harm none so be it.

Spend some quiet time in your circle focusing your mind on your situation improving. If you can, allow your altar candle to burn through to the end but if you must put it out do so with a candle snuff or pinch the wick between dampened fingertips. When you are finished working move quietly to the left of your circle.

Extinguish the east candle and say:
I thank the element of air for blessing me with prosperity.

Extinguish the south candle and say:
I thank the element of fire for blessing me with prosperity.

Extinguish the west candle and say:
I thank the element of water for blessing me with prosperity.

Extinguish the north candle and say:
I thank the element of earth for blessing me with prosperity.

Close your circle by saying:
May the four powers give back to the universe any powers and energies that have not been used.
The work is now done and the circle is closed.
So mote it be.

Prosperity spell 2

10 mls base oil (such as sunflower, jojoba, or almond)
Rose essential oil
A bottle for your oil mixture
A small face cloth or some tissues (to clean your hands)
A precious ornament or picture
Your favourite crystal or most valuable piece of
    jewellery
Any items of gold or silver
One tall white candle and one gold or silver taper candle and holder
One small pointed knife
An ashtray or a small fireproof dish for spent matches or any paper that you
    may light during your spell and some matches or a lighter.

Prepare a blend of oils using 10 mls of sunflower oil and add three drops of rose essential oil. Hold the bottle of oil in your hands in the prayer position, rub the bottle vigorously between the palms of your hands and as you do so visualise the oil being empowered with good fortune. When you feel as though the oil has been charged, place it on your altar or work surface ready for use along with the other ingredients.

When everything is in place, put four small candles at the east, south, west and north in that order. Sit or kneel comfortably in front of your table.

Close your eyes and, as you breathe in, picture positive, white light energy filling your body. When you are completely relaxed, stand up and move quietly to the east quarter of your room.

Light the east candle and say:
    May the element of air bless this space with light, love and air
    and grant me abundance.

Prosperity

Light the south candle and say:
  May the element of fire bless this space with light, love and fire and grant me abundance.

Light the west candle and say:
  May the element of water bless this space with light, love and water and grant me abundance.

Light the north candle and say:
  May the element of earth bless this space with light, love and earth and grant me abundance.

Move quietly back to your workspace and kneel in front of your table. Light your white altar candle and meditate quietly on your heart's desire and visualise your wish coming true.

Take your gold or silver spell candle and the small pointed knife and inscribe the number nine and the rune symbol Feoh at the top of the candle.

Place the candle back in the holder and, taking the bottle of empowered oil, place some in the palm of your hands. Rub your hands together and visualise that you are charging the energy in the oil and in your hands. Your hands will begin to feel very warm. Take the spell candle and spread the oil from middle to top and middle to bottom of the candle until the candle is completely covered in oil.

Visualise that you are empowering the candle with your desire. Rub your hands vigorously together with the candle still held between the palms of your hands. After a few minutes, place your candle back in its holder, light the flame and say these words:

Prosperity

As sure as the cherry blossoms in spring
Aditi and Geb to me wealth bring.
No more struggle, no more strife,
By your power enrich my life.
And it harm none so be it.

Allow your candle to burn for as long as possible, but, if you must put it out, do not blow it out otherwise you will reverse or negate your spell. You can use a candle snuff or pinch the flame between your thumb and finger. You may light your candle again but, each time you do so, visualise your wish as though it has already begun to happen. When you are finished working, clean your hands on the cloth and move quietly to the left of your room.

Extinguish the east candle and say:
    I thank the element of air for blessing me with abundance.

Extinguish the south candle and say:
    I thank the element of fire for blessing me with abundance.

Extinguish the west candle and say:
    I thank the element of water for blessing me with abundance.

Extinguish the north candle and say:
    I thank the element of earth for blessing me with abundance.

Close your circle by saying:
    May the four powers give back to the universe any powers and energies that have not been used.
    The work is now done and the circle is closed.
    So mote it be.

3

Gratitude

Day of the week: The best day of
the week is Monday
Time of day: The best time of
day is 5am. Also noon, 7pm
or at any time in the evening
when the moon is waxing or
full but not when it is
waning
Goddess: Rangda
Planet: Moon
Guardian Angel: Gabriel
Star sign: Pisces
Metal: Silver
Colour: White
Rune: Ken (sometimes known
as Kano or Kenaz)
Symbol: Circular objects and
fruit
Number: Three
Crystal: Snow quartz or opal
Flower: Hibiscus
Essential oil: Bergamot
Herb: Saffron
Tree: Birch

Moon

Pisces

Ken

Gratitude spell 1

Prepare yourself and decorate your work surface or altar space with all your chosen ingredients such as:

Any silver items
One silver and one white taper candle
A posy of white flowers
A bowl of fruits
A dish of coins
A piece of snow quartz

When you are ready and everything is in place, stand at the edge of your circle. Close your eyes and breathe in, visualising light energy filling your body. Breathe out and breathe away all negative energy. When you are completely relaxed stand up and move quietly to the east quarter of your circle or room.

Light the east candle and say:

> May the element of air bless this space with light, love and air and accept my gratitude for those gifts that I have been given.

Light the south candle and say:

> May the element of fire bless this space with light, love and fire and accept my gratitude for those gifts that I have been given.

Light the west candle and say:

> May the element of water bless this space with light, love and water and accept my gratitude for those gifts that I have been given.

Light the north candle and say:

> May the element of earth bless this space with light, love and

earth and accept my gratitude for those gifts that I have been given.

Move quietly back to your workspace and kneel in front of your table. Light your white altar candle and meditate quietly on the Goddess Rangda. In your mind give thanks for the gifts that you are showing gratitude for.

See the abundance that you have been blessed with and say a prayer in your own words to the Guardian Angel Gabriel.

Light your silver candle and, standing in front of your altar, raise your hands high above your head and say these words:

> I thank the Goddess for her blessings.
> I thank the Goddess for her gifts.
> For bringing me my heart's desire
> By the power of sacred fire.
> And it harm none so be it.

Spend some quiet time in your circle and allow your altar candle to burn through to the end but if you must put it out do so with a candle snuff or pinch the wick between dampened fingertips.

When you are finished working move quietly to the left of your circle.

Extinguish the east candle and say:

> I thank the element of air for blessing me with the gifts I have been given.

Extinguish the south candle and say:

> I thank the element of fire for blessing me with the gifts I have been given.

Gratitude

Extinguish the west candle and say:

I thank the element of water for blessing me with the gifts I have been given.

Extinguish the north candle and say:

I thank the element of earth for blessing me with the gifts I have been given.

Close your circle by saying:

May the four powers give back to the universe any powers and energies that have not been used.

The work is now done and the circle is closed.

So mote it be.

Gratitude spell 2

10 mls of almond oil

Bergamot pure essential oil

A bottle for your oil mixture

A small face cloth or some tissues (to clean your hands after working with the oil)

Any item that you are grateful for or something that represents gratitude (For instance if you are showing gratitude for the birth of a child or the recovery of someone who has been ill you could use a photograph of that person)

Your favourite crystal or a piece of moonstone

Any silver items

One tall silver taper candle and holder

One tall white taper candle and holder

One small pointed knife

An ashtray or a small fireproof dish for spent matches or any paper that you may light during your spell and some matches or a lighter

Gratitude

Prepare a blend of oils using 10 mls of almond oil and add three drops of bergamot pure essential oil. Hold the bottle of oil in your hands in the prayer position and rub the bottle vigorously between the palms of your hands and, as you do so, visualise the oil being empowered with gratitude. When you feel as though the oil has been charged, place it on your altar or work surface ready for use along with the other ingredients.

Place four small candles at the east, south, west and north in that order. Sit or kneel comfortably in front of your table. Close your eyes and as you breathe in, picture positive, white, light energy filling your body.

When you are completely relaxed stand up and move quietly to the east quarter of your room.

Light the east candle and say:
    May the element of air bless this space with light, love and air and accept my gratitude for those gifts that I have been given.

Light the south candle and say:
    May the element of fire bless this space with light, love and fire and accept my gratitude for those gifts that I have been given.

Light the west candle and say:
    May the element of water bless this space with light, love and water and accept my gratitude for those gifts that I have been given.

Light the north candle and say:
    May the element of earth bless this space with light, love and earth and accept my gratitude for those gifts that I have been given.

Gratitude

Move quietly back to your workspace and kneel in front of your table. Light your white altar candle and meditate quietly on those aspects that you are grateful for. Take your silver spell candle and the small pointed knife and inscribe the number three and the rune symbol Ken at the top of the candle.

Place the candle back in the holder and, taking the bottle of empowered oil, place some in the palms of your hands. Rub your hands together and visualise that you are charging the energy in the oil and in your hands. Your hands will begin to feel very warm. Take the spell candle and spread the oil from middle to top and middle to bottom of the candle until the candle is completely covered in oil. Visualise that you are empowering the candle with your gratitude. Rub your hands vigorously together with the candle still held between the palms of your hands. After a few minutes, place your candle back in its holder and light the flame and say these words:

> The Goddess to me has been kind,
> And brought to me some peace of mind.
> I now give thanks for those gifts given,
> And bless each day the sun has arisen.
> So mote it be.

Allow your candle to burn for as long as possible but if you must put it out do not blow it out otherwise you will reverse or negate your spell. You can use a candle snuff or pinch the flame between your thumb and finger. You may light your candle again but, each time you do so, visualise your wish as though it has already begun to happen. When you are finished working clean your hands on the cloth and move quietly to the left of your room.

Gratitude

Extinguish the east candle and say:
I thank the element of air for blessing me with the gifts I have been given.

Extinguish the south candle and say:
I thank the element of fire for blessing me with the gifts I have been given.

Extinguish the west candle and say:
I thank the element of water for blessing me with the gifts I have been given.

Extinguish the north candle and say:
I thank the element of earth for blessing me with the gifts I have been given.

Close your circle by saying:
May the four powers give back to the universe any powers and energies that have not been used.
The work is now done and the circle is closed.
So mote it be.

4

Communication

Day of the week: The best day
   of the week is Wednesday
Time of day: The best time of
   day is 5am. Also noon, 7pm
   or at any time in the evening
   when the moon is waxing or
   full but not when it is
   waning
Goddess: Shakti
Planet: Mercury
Guardian Angel: Raphael
Star sign: Scorpio
Metal: Silver
Colour: Green
Rune: Ansur (also known as
   Ansuz)
Symbol: Writing materials
Number: Six
Crystal: Malachite
Flower: White lotus or
   chrysanthemum
Essential oil: Geranium
Herb: Parsley
Tree: Rowan

Mercury

Scorpio

Ansur

Communication

Communication spell 1

Prepare yourself and decorate your work surface or altar space with all your chosen ingredients such as:

White flowers
One white and one green taper candle and candle holders
A silver pen or a pen with silver ink and a piece of writing paper
A piece of malachite
An ashtray or a small fireproof dish for spent matches or any paper that you may light during your spell and some matches or a lighter

When you are ready and everything is in place, stand at the edge of your circle. Close your eyes and breathe in, visualising light energy filling your body. Breathe out and breathe away all negative energy. When you are completely relaxed stand up and move quietly to the east quarter of your circle or room.

Light the east candle and say:
May the element of air bless this space with light, love and air and grant me the ability to listen with understanding and speak with wisdom.

Light the south candle and say:
May the element of fire bless this space with light, love and fire and grant me the ability to listen with understanding and speak with wisdom.

Light the west candle and say:
May the element of water bless this space with light, love and water and grant me the ability to listen with understanding and speak with wisdom.

Communication

Light the north candle and say:

> May the element of earth bless this space with light, love and earth and grant me the ability to listen with understanding and speak with wisdom.

Move quietly back to your workspace and kneel in front of your table and light your white altar candle.

Using your pen and paper, write your favourite verse or prayer. Hold the malachite crystal in your left hand and meditate quietly on the God Amotken and the Goddess Shakti. In your mind ask for the blessings of communication so that you may listen with understanding and speak with wisdom. Ask the Guardian Angel Raphael to bless your mouth, ears, nose and throat. Light your green candle, and using this candle, set light to the paper on which you have written your prayer or verse. Allow the burning paper to burn to ash in the fireproof dish.

Stand in front of your altar, raise your hands high above your head and say these words:

> Amotken, Shakti hear me pray,
> Listen to the words I say.
> May wisdom bless my tongue, my lips
> Your guidance at my fingertips.
> And it harm none so be it.

Spend some quiet time in your circle and allow your candles to burn through to the end but if you must put them out do so with a candle snuff or pinch the wick between dampened fingertips. When you are finished working move quietly to the left of your circle.

Communication

Extinguish the east candle and say:

I thank the element of air for blessing me with the ability to listen with understanding and speak with wisdom.

Extinguish the south candle and say:

I thank the element of fire for blessing me with the ability to listen with understanding and speak with wisdom.

Extinguish the west candle and say:

I thank the element of water for blessing me with the ability to listen with understanding and speak with wisdom.

Extinguish the north candle and say:

I thank the element of earth for blessing me with the ability to listen with understanding and speak with wisdom.

Close your circle by saying:

May the four powers give back to the universe any powers and energies that have not been used.
The work is now done and the circle is closed.
So mote it be.

Communication spell 2

10 mls almond oil
Geranium pure essential oil
A bottle for your oil mixture
A small face cloth or some tissues (to clean your hands after working with the oil)
A malachite crystal
Any silver items
Any items representing communication such as a telephone, pens, or paper

Communication

One tall green candle and one tall white candle and holder
One small pointed knife
An ashtray or a small fireproof dish for spent matches or any paper
    that you may light during your spell and some matches or a lighter.

Prepare a blend of oils using 10 mls of almond oil and add three drops of geranium pure essential oil. Hold the bottle of oil in your hands in the prayer position and rub the bottle vigorously between the palms of your hands and, as you do so, visualise the oil being empowered with gratitude. When you feel as though the oil has been charged place it on your altar or work surface ready for use along with the other ingredients.

Place four small candles at the east, south, west and north in that order. Sit or kneel comfortably in front of your table. Close your eyes and as you breathe in, picture positive white light energy filling your body. When you are completely relaxed stand up and move quietly to the east quarter of your room.

Light the east candle and say:
    May the element of air bless this space with light, love and air
    and grant me the ability to listen with understanding and speak
    with wisdom.

Light the south candle and say:
    May the element of fire bless this space with light, love and fire
    and grant me the ability to listen with understanding and speak
    with wisdom.

Light the west candle and say:
    May the element of water bless this space with light, love and
    water and grant me the ability to listen with understanding and
    speak with wisdom.

Communication

Light the north candle and say:

> May the element of earth bless this space with light, love and
> earth and grant me the ability to listen with understanding and
> speak with wisdom.

Move quietly back to your workspace and kneel in front of
your table. Light your white altar candle and meditate quietly
on the qualities that you wish to be blessed with. Take your
green spell candle and the small pointed knife and inscribe the
number six and the rune symbol Ansur at the top of the candle.
Place the candle back in the holder and taking the bottle of
empowered oil place some in the palm of your hands. Rub
your hands together and visualise that you are charging the
energy in the oil and in your hands. Your hands will begin to
feel very warm. Take the spell candle again and spread the oil
from middle to top and middle to bottom of the candle until
the candle is completely covered in oil. Visualise that you are
empowering the candle with communication. Rub your hands
vigorously together with the candle still held between the palms
of your hands.

After a few minutes, place your candle back in its holder and
light the flame and say these words:

> Candle burning precious light,
> Bring to me this very night
> Messages from far and near.
> Help me listen help me hear.
> And it harm none so mote it be.

Allow your candle to burn for as long as possible but if you
must put it out do not blow it out otherwise you will reverse

or negate your spell. You can use a candle snuff or pinch the flame between your thumb and finger. You may light your candle again but each time you do so visualise your wish as though it has already begun to happen. When you are finished working, clean your hands on the cloth and move quietly to the left of your room.

Extinguish the east candle and say:
I thank the element of air for blessing me with the ability to listen with understanding and speak with wisdom.

Extinguish the south candle and say:
I thank the element of fire for blessing me with the ability to listen with understanding and speak with wisdom.

Extinguish the west candle and say:
I thank the element of water for blessing me with the ability to listen with understanding and speak with wisdom.

Extinguish the north candle and say:
I thank the element of earth for blessing me with the ability to listen with understanding and speak with wisdom.

Close your circle by saying:
May the four powers give back to the universe any powers and energies that have not been used.
The work is now done and the circle is closed.
So mote it be.

5

Courage

Day of the week: The best day
of the week is Tuesday

Time of Day: The best time of
day is 5am. Also noon, 7pm
or at any time in the evening
when the moon is waxing or
full but not when it is
waning.

God: Bes

Goddess: Lillith

Planet: Mars

Guardian Angel: Samael

Star Sign: Aries

Metal: Iron

Colour: Red

Rune: Tir (also known as
Tiwaz, or Tiewaz)

Symbol: Sword

Number: Four

Crystal: Jade, bloodstone or
malachite

Flower: Honeysuckle

Essential oil: Lavender

Herb: Pepper

Tree: Holly

Mars

Aries

Tir

Courage

Courage spell 1

Prepare yourself and decorate your work surface or altar space with all your chosen ingredients such as:

A red cloth
Some honeysuckle or holly
Some jade, bloodstone or malachite crystals
One red taper candle and
One white taper candle
An oil burner to which you have added some lavender essential oil
  and a pinch of black pepper

When you are ready and everything is in place, stand at the edge of your circle. Close your eyes and breathe in, visualising light energy filling your body. Breathe out and breathe away all negative energy. When you are completely relaxed, stand up and move quietly to the east quarter of your circle or room.

Light the east candle and say:
  May the element of air bless this space with light, love and air
  and grant me courage.

Light the south candle and say:
  May the element of fire bless this space with light, love and fire
  and grant me courage.

Light the west candle and say:
  May the element of water bless this space with light, love and
  water and grant me courage.

Light the north candle and say:

May the element of earth bless this space with light, love and earth and grant me courage.

Move quietly back to your workspace and kneel in front of your table. Light your white altar candle and meditate quietly on the God Bes and the Goddess Lillith asking for courage for the challenge, which lies ahead.

See yourself in triumph as though the victory is already yours and say a prayer in your own words to the Guardian Angel Samael.

Light your red candle and standing in front of your altar, raise your hands high above your head and say these words:

Courage and strength I possess
Given to me by Lillith and Bes.
Samael he blesses me,
So that everyone can see.
And it harm none so be it.

Spend some quiet time in your circle and allow your candles to burn through to the end. If you must put your candles out use a candle snuff or pinch the wick between a dampened finger and thumb. When you are finished working move quietly to the left of your circle.

Extinguish the east candle and say:

I thank the element of air for blessing me with courage.

Courage

Extinguish the south candle and say:
I thank the element of fire for blessing me with courage.

Extinguish the west candle and say:
I thank the element of water for blessing me with courage.

Extinguish the north candle and say:
I thank the element of earth for blessing me with courage.

Close your circle by saying:
May the four powers give back to the universe any powers and energies that have not been used.
The work is now done and the circle is closed.
So mote it be.

Courage spell 2

10 mls almond oil
Lavender pure essential oil
A bottle for your oil mixture
A small face cloth or some tissues (to clean your hands after working with the oil)
An item that represents victory, for instance, a medal or trophy would be ideal
Something made of iron or steel
A sword or dagger
A piece of jade, bloodstone or malachite
One tall red taper candle and holder
One tall white taper candle and holder
One small pointed knife

Prepare a blend of oils using 10 mls of almond oil and add

three drops of lavender pure essential oil. Hold the bottle of oil in your hands in the prayer position and rub the bottle vigorously between the palms of your hands and as you do so visualise the oil being empowered with courage. When you feel as though the oil has been charged, place it on your altar or work surface ready for use along with the other ingredients.

Place four small candles at the east, south, west and north in that order. Sit or kneel comfortably in front of your table.

Close your eyes and, as you breathe in, picture positive, white light energy filling your body. When you are completely relaxed stand up and move quietly to the east quarter of your room.

Light the east candle and say:
  May the element of air bless this space with light, love and air and grant me courage.

Light the south candle and say:
  May the element of fire bless this space with light, love and fire and grant me courage.

Light the west candle and say:
  May the element of water bless this space with light, love and water and grant me courage.

Light the north candle and say:
  May the element of earth bless this space with light, love and earth and grant me courage.

Move quietly back to your workspace and kneel in front of your table. Light your white altar candle and meditate quietly on the challenge that requires courage and victory. Take your red spell candle and the small pointed knife and inscribe the number eight and the rune symbol Tir at the top of the candle. Place the candle back in the holder and, taking the bottle of empowered oil, place some in the palm of your hands. Rub your hands together and visualise that you are charging the energy in the oil and in your hands. Your hands will begin to feel very warm. Take the spell candle and spread the oil from middle to top and middle to bottom of the candle until the candle is completely covered in oil.

Visualise that you are empowering the candle with your courage and victory. Rub your hands vigorously together with the candle still held between the palms of your hands.

After a few minutes, place your candle back in its holder and light the flame and say these words:

> Burning flame that burns so true
> Bring to me the courage to
> Make me strong both day and night
> To meet this challenge with my might.
> Victory it shall be mine.
> Blessed be the powers that shine.
> And it harm none so mote it be.

Allow your candle to burn for as long as possible, but if you must put it out do not blow it out otherwise you will reverse or negate your spell. You can use a candle snuff or pinch the flame between your thumb and finger. You may light your candle again but, each time you do so, visualise your wish as though it has already begun to happen. When you are finished working, clean your hands on the cloth and move quietly to the left of your room.

Courage

Extinguish the east candle and say:
    I thank the element of air for blessing me with courage.

Extinguish the south candle and say:
    I thank the element of fire for blessing me with courage.

Extinguish the west candle and say:
    I thank the element of water for blessing me with courage.

Extinguish the north candle and say:
    I thank the element of earth for blessing me with courage.

Close your circle by saying:
    May the four powers give back to the universe any powers and
    energies that have not been used.
    The work is now done and the circle is closed.
    So mote it be.

6

Forgiveness

Day of the week: The best day
  of the week is Wednesday
Time of day: The best time of
  day is 5am. Also noon, 7pm
  or at any time in the evening
  when the moon is waxing or
  full but not when it is
  waning
God: Zeus
Goddess: Hera
Planet: Neptune
Guardian Angel: Sabbathi
Star sign: Pisces
Metal: Platinum
Colour: Violet
Rune Symbol: Eolh (also
  known as Elhaz or
  Algiz)
Number: Six
Crystal: Apache teardrop
Flower: Daffodil
Essential oil: Cedarwood
Herb: Angelica
Tree: Ash

Neptune

Pisces

Eolh

Forgiveness spell 1

Prepare yourself and decorate your work surface or altar space with all your chosen ingredients such as:

A purple= or violet=coloured cloth
A bowl of daffodils
A piece of writing paper
A pen
Any silver or platinum items
One violet purple or silver taper candle
One white taper candle
A piece of angelica
A piece of apache teardrop
A small twig of an ash tree

When you are ready and everything is in place, stand at the edge of your circle. Close your eyes and breathe in, visualising light energy filling your body. Breathe out and breathe away all negative energy. When you are completely relaxed stand up and move quietly to the east quarter of your circle or room.

Light the east candle and say:
> May the element of air bless this space with light, love and air and grant me the ability to forgive (or grant me forgiveness).

Light the south candle and say:
> May the element of fire bless this space with light, love and fire and grant me the ability to forgive (or grant me forgiveness).

Light the west candle and say:
> May the element of water bless this space with light, love and water and grant me the ability to forgive (or grant me forgiveness).

Forgiveness

Light the north candle and say:
May the element of earth bless this space with light, love and earth and grant me the ability to forgive (or grant me forgiveness).

Move quietly back to your workspace and kneel in front of your table. Light your white altar candle and meditate quietly on the God Zeus and or the Goddess Hera. In your mind ask that you be granted forgiveness or ask that you have the ability to forgive. Write down a brief outline of the situation that requires forgiveness. This could be something that you want to be forgiven for or it could be something that you want to forgive another for.

Say a prayer in your own words to the Guardian Angel Sabbathi.

Light your violet, purple or silver taper candle and taking your paper light it from the coloured candle. Let it burn through in the fireproof dish. Stand in front of your altar.

Raise your hands high above your head and say these words:

Zeus and Hera hear me pray.
Hurts to me are now forgiven
'Sorry', be the word I say
Love restored my joy has risen
And it harm none so be it.

Spend some quiet time in your circle and allow your altar candle to burn through to the end but if you must put it out do so with a candle snuff or pinch the wick between dampened fingertips. When you are finished working move quietly to the left of your circle.

Forgiveness

Extinguish the east candle and say:
I thank the element of air for blessing me with the ability to forgive (or granting me forgiveness).

Extinguish the south candle and say:
I thank the element of fire for blessing me with the ability to forgive (or granting me forgiveness).

Extinguish the west candle and say:
I thank the element of water for blessing me with the ability to forgive (or granting me forgiveness).

Extinguish the north candle and say:
I thank the element of earth for blessing me with the ability to forgive (or granting me forgiveness).

Close your circle by saying:
May the four powers give back to the universe any powers and energies that have not been used.
The work is now done and the circle is closed.
So mote it be.

Forgiveness spell 2

10 mls almond oil
Cedarwood pure essential oil
A bottle for your oil mixture
A small face cloth or some tissues (to clean your hands after working with the oil)
A piece of apache teardrop
A vase of violets or daffodils or any other yellow or violet coloured flower

Forgiveness

One tall violet or purple taper candle and holder
One small pointed knife
An ashtray or a small fireproof dish for spent matches or any paper
that you may light during your spell and some matches or a lighter.

Prepare a blend of oils using 10 mls of almond oil and add three drops of cedarwood pure essential oil. Hold the bottle of oil in your hands in the prayer position and rub the bottle vigorously between the palms of your hands and, as you do so, visualise the oil being empowered with gratitude. When you feel as though the oil has been charged place it on your altar or work surface ready for use along with the other ingredients.

Place four small candles at the east, south, west and north in that order.

Sit or kneel comfortably in front of your table. Close your eyes and, as you breathe in, picture positive, white light energy filling your body. When you are completely relaxed stand up and move quietly to the east quarter of your room.

Light the east candle and say:
May the element of air bless this space with light, love and air and grant me the ability to forgive (or grant me forgiveness).

Light the south candle and say:
May the element of fire bless this space with light, love and fire and grant me the ability to forgive (or grant me forgiveness).

Light the west candle and say:
May the element of water bless this space with light, love and water and grant me the ability to forgive (or grant me forgiveness).

Forgiveness

Light the north candle and say:
> May the element of earth bless this space with light, love and
> earth and grant me the ability to forgive (or grant me forgiveness).

Move quietly back to your workspace and kneel in front of your table. Light your white altar candle and meditate quietly on being forgiven or giving forgiveness.

Take your violet spell candle and the small pointed knife and inscribe the number six and the rune symbol Eolh at the top of the candle. Place the candle back in the holder and, taking the bottle of empowered oil, place some in the palm of your hands. Rub your hands together and visualise that you are charging the energy in the oil and in your hands. Your hands will begin to feel very warm. Take the spell candle and spread the oil from middle to top and middle to bottom of the candle until the candle is completely covered in oil. Visualise that you are empowering the spell candle with forgiveness. Rub your hands vigorously together with the candle still held between the palms of your hands.

After a few minutes, place your candle back in its holder and light the flame and say these words:

> Life's too short to hold a grudge,
> Deeds forgotten do not judge,
> Forgiveness now I pray this day,
> Let love return and sorrow away.
> And it harm none so mote it be.

Allow your candle to burn for as long as possible but, if you must put it out, do not blow it out otherwise you will reverse or negate your spell. You can use a candle snuff or pinch the flame between your thumb and finger. You may light your candle again but each time you do so visualise your wish as though it has already begun to happen. When you are finished working clean your hands on the cloth and move quietly to the left of your room.

Extinguish the east candle and say:
I thank the element of air for blessing me with the ability to forgive (or for granting me forgiveness).

Extinguish the south candle and say:
I thank the element of fire for blessing me with the ability to forgive (or for granting me forgiveness).

Extinguish the west candle and say:
I thank the element of water for blessing me with the ability to forgive (or for granting me forgiveness).

Extinguish the north candle and say:
I thank the element of earth for blessing me with the ability to forgive (or for granting me forgiveness).

Close your circle by saying:
May the four powers give back to the universe any powers and energies that have not been used.
The work is now done and the circle is closed.
So mote it be.

7

Inspiration

Day of the week: The best day
of the week is Saturday
Time of day: The best time of
day is 5am. Also noon, 7pm
or at any time in the evening
when the moon is waxing or
full but not when it is
waning
God: Telesphoros
Goddess: Ostara
Planet: Uranus
Guardian Angel: Arvath
Star sign: Aquarius
Metal: Aluminium
Colour: Indigo
Rune: Ansur (also
known as Ansuz)
Symbol: Key
Number: One
Crystal: Amethyst
Flower: Anemones
Essential oil: Peppermint
Herb: Sage
Tree: Hazel

Uranus

Aquarius

Ansur

Inspiration

Inspiration spell 1

Prepare yourself and decorate your work surface or altar space with all your chosen ingredients such as:

Keys
Any book that inspires you
Any aluminium items
    (for instance you could cover your favourite vase or candle holder
    with aluminium foil)
One indigo taper candle
One white taper candle
A vase of anemones
A sprig or pinch of sage
A twig from a hazel tree
A piece of amethyst crystal
An ashtray or a small fireproof dish for spent matches or any paper
    that you may light during your spell and some matches or a lighter

When you are ready and everything is in place, stand at the edge of your circle. Close your eyes and breathe in, visualising light energy filling your body. Breathe out and breathe away all negative energy.

When you are completely relaxed stand up and move quietly to the east quarter of your circle or room.

Light the east candle and say:
    May the element of air bless this space with light, love and air
    and grant me inspiration.

Light the south candle and say:
    May the element of fire bless this space with light, love and fire
    and grant me inspiration.

Inspiration

Light the west candle and say:
> May the element of water bless this space with light, love and water and grant me inspiration.

Light the north candle and say:
> May the element of earth bless this space with light, love and earth and grant me inspiration.

Move quietly back to your workspace and kneel in front of your table. Light your white altar candle and holding your crystal in your left hand meditate quietly on the God Telesphoros and the Goddess Ostara. In your mind and heart, begin to feel excitement and motivation build. Say a prayer in your own words to the Guardian Angel Arvath.

Light your indigo candle, stand in front of your altar, raise your hands high above your head and say these words:

> May the light of inspiration
> Motivate and guide my way.
> To Telesphoros and Ostara
> These sacred words I pray.
> And it harm none so be it.

Spend some quiet time in your circle and allow your altar candle to burn through to the end but if you must put it out do so with a candle snuff or pinch the wick between dampened fingertips. When you are finished working move quietly to the left of your circle.

Extinguish the east candle and say:
> I thank the element of air for blessing me with inspiration.

Extinguish the south candle and say:
I thank the element of fire for blessing me with inspiration.

Extinguish the west candle and say:
I thank the element of water for blessing me with inspiration.

Extinguish the north candle and say:
I thank the element of earth for blessing me with inspiration.

Close your circle by saying:
May the four powers give back to the universe any powers and
energies that have not been used.
The work is now done and the circle is closed.
So mote it be.

**Place your crystal under your pillow and keep it there for the
next seven nights. During the daytime when you are working
hold your crystal in your left hand from time to time allowing
inspiration to grow within you.**

Inspiration spell 2

10 mls almond oil
Peppermint pure essential oil
A bottle for the oil mixture
A small face cloth or some tissues (to clean your hands after working
    with the oil)
A set of keys and a dictionary or thesaurus
An amethyst crystal
An oil burner to which you have added some water
    some sage and one drop of lemon pure essential oils
One tall indigo taper candle and holder

Inspiration

One tall white taper candle and holder
One small pointed knife

Prepare a blend of oils using 10 mls of almond oil and add three drops of peppermint pure essential oil. Hold the bottle of oil in your hands in the prayer position and rub the bottle vigorously between the palms of your hands and as you do so visualise the oil being empowered with gratitude. When you feel as though the oil has been charged, place it on your altar or work surface ready for use along with the other ingredients.

Place four small candles at the east, south, west and north in that order.

Sit or kneel comfortably in front of your table. Close your eyes and as you breathe in, picture positive, white light energy filling your body. When you are completely relaxed stand up and move quietly to the east quarter of your room.

Light the east candle and say:
May the element of air bless this space with light, love and air and grant me inspiration.

Light the south candle and say:
May the element of fire bless this space with light, love and fire and grant me inspiration.

Light the west candle and say:
May the element of water bless this space with light, love and water and grant me inspiration.

Light the north candle and say:
May the element of earth bless this space with light, love and earth and grant me inspiration.

Move quietly back to your workspace and kneel in front of your table and light your white altar candle.

Meditate quietly on the area of your life that requires inspiration. Take your indigo spell candle and the small pointed knife and inscribe the number one and the rune symbol Ansur at the top of the candle. Place the candle back in the holder and, taking the bottle of empowered oil, place some in the palm of your hands. Rub your hands together and visualise that you are charging the energy in the oil and in your hands. Your hands will begin to feel very warm. Take the spell candle and spread the oil from middle to top and middle to bottom of the candle until the candle is completely covered in oil. Visualise that you are empowering the candle with your inspiration. Rub your hands vigorously together with the candle still held between the palms of your hands.

After a few minutes, place your candle back in its holder and light the flame and say these words:

> Angel Arvath, hear my plea,
> Inspiration send to me,
> Make ideas flow thick and fast,
> Projects planned to thrive and last.
> And it harm none so mote it be.

Allow your candle to burn for as long as possible but, if you must put it out, do not blow it out otherwise you will reverse or negate your spell. You can use a candle snuff or pinch the flame between your thumb and finger. You may light your candle again but each time you do so visualise your wish as though it has already begun to happen. When you are finished working clean your hands on the cloth and move quietly to the left of your room.

Inspiration

Extinguish the east candle and say:
I thank the element of air for blessing me with inspiration.

Extinguish the south candle and say:
I thank the element of fire for blessing me with inspiration.

Extinguish the west candle and say:
I thank the element of water for blessing me with inspiration.

Extinguish the north candle and say:
I thank the element of earth for blessing me with inspiration.

Close your circle by saying:
May the four powers give back to the universe any powers and energies that have not been used.
The work is now done and the circle is closed.
So mote it be.

8

Peace

Day of the week: The best day
   of the week is Friday
Time of day: The best time of
   day is 5am. Also noon, 7pm
   or at any time in the evening
   when the moon is waxing or
   full but not when it is
   waning
God: Wakantanka
Goddess: Pax
Planet: Venus
Guardian Angel: Arnad
Star sign: Taurus
Metal: Copper or rose gold
Colour: White
Rune: Othel (also known as
   Othala)
Symbol: Cone shaped items
Number: Two
Crystal: Rhodochrosite
Flower: White lily
Essential oil: Marjoram
Herb: Chamomile
Tree: Olive

Venus

Taurus

Othel

Peace spell 1

Prepare yourself and decorate your work surface or altar space with all your chosen ingredients such as:

Two white taper candles
Items made of copper or rose gold
A vase of lilies or chamomile
A piece of rhodochrosite crystal
Shells or funnel=shaped items, which could possibly be made from paper
Photographs or pictures of doves
An ashtray or a small fireproof dish for spent matches or any paper
   that you may light during your spell and some matches or a lighter

When you are ready and everything is in place, stand at the edge of your circle. Close your eyes and breathe in, visualising light energy filling your body. Breathe out and breathe away all negative energy. When you are completely relaxed, stand up and move quietly to the east quarter of your circle or room.

Light the east candle and say:
   May the element of air bless this space with light, love and air
   and grant me peace.

Light the south candle and say:
   May the element of fire bless this space with light, love and fire
   and grant me peace.

Light the west candle and say:
   May the element of water bless this space with light, love and
   water and grant me peace.

Light the north candle and say:
   May the element of earth bless this space with light, love and
   earth and grant me peace.

Peace

Move quietly back to your workspace and kneel in front of your table. Light your white altar candle and, holding your crystal in your left hand, meditate quietly on the God Wakantanka and the Goddess Pax. In your mind and heart begin to feel a sense of peace and harmony filling your body and spirit. Say a prayer in your own words to the Guardian Angel Arnad.

Light your second candle, stand in front of your altar, raise your hands high above your head and say these words:

> Let peace be felt upon the land
> No weapons lifted by any hand
> Let us prosper as animals graze
> And Pax be with us to hear our praise
> And it harm none so be it.

When you have finished, put one silver coin into one of the shells. If it is possible, let the large white candle burn until it is finished.

Extinguish the east candle and say:
I thank the element of air for blessing me with peace.

Extinguish the south candle and say:
I thank the element of fire for blessing me with peace.

Extinguish the west candle and say:
I thank the element of water for blessing me with peace.

Extinguish the north candle and say:
I thank the element of earth for blessing me with peace.

Close your circle by saying:

May the four powers give back to the universe any powers and energies
that have not been used.
The work is now done and the circle is closed.
So mote it be

Each day, for thirty days, add one silver coin. This spell will
work best if it is begun on the first day of the new moon. At
the end of the thirty days give the coins you have collected to
a charity or to a worthwhile cause.

Peace spell 2

10 mls almond oil
Marjoram pure essential oil
A bottle for your oil mixture
A small face cloth or some tissues (to clean your hands after working with the
   oil)
An item that represents peace to you
A rhodochrosite crystal
Two tall, white taper candle and holders
One small pointed knife

Prepare a blend of oils using 10 mls of almond oil and add
three drops of marjoram essential oil. Hold the bottle of oil in
your hands in the prayer position and rub the bottle vigorously
between the palms of your hands and as you do so visualise the
oil being empowered with gratitude. When you feel as though
the oil has been charged place it on your altar or work surface
ready for use along with the other ingredients.

Place four small candles at the east, south, west and north in
that order. Sit or kneel comfortably in front of your table. Close

Peace

your eyes and, as you breathe in, picture positive, white light energy filling your body.

When you are completely relaxed stand up and move quietly to the east quarter of your room.

Light the east candle and say:
May the element of air bless this space with light, love and air and grant me peace.

Light the south candle and say:
May the element of fire bless this space with light, love and fire and grant me peace.

Light the west candle and say:
May the element of water bless this space with light, love and water and grant me peace.

Light the north candle and say:
May the element of earth bless this space with light, love and earth and grant me peace.

Move quietly back to your workspace and kneel in front of your table. Light your white altar candle and meditate quietly on Wakantanka, the supreme being. Take your second white candle and the small pointed knife and inscribe the number two and the rune symbol Othel at the top of the candle. Place the candle back in the holder and taking the bottle of empowered oil place some in the palm of your hands. Rub your hands together and visualise that you are charging the energy in the oil and in your hands. Your hands will begin to feel very warm. Take the spell candle and spread the oil from middle to top and middle to bottom of the candle until the candle is completely covered in oil. Visualise that you are empowering the candle with peace. Rub your hands vigorously together with the candle still held between the palms of your hands. After a few minutes, place your candle back in its holder and light the flame and say these words:

> Wakantanka hear me pray,
> Let peace be with us on this day.
> No more trouble, no more strife,
> Peace and harmony fill my life.
> And it harm none so mote it be.

Allow your candle to burn for as long as possible but, if you must put it out, do not blow it out otherwise you will reverse or negate your spell. You can use a candle snuff or pinch the flame between your thumb and finger. You may light your candle again but, each time you do so, visualise your wish as though it has already begun to happen. When you are finished working, clean your hands on the cloth and move quietly to the left of your room.

Extinguish the east candle and say:
  I thank the element of air for blessing me with peace.

Extinguish the south candle and say:
  I thank the element of fire for blessing me with peace.

Extinguish the west candle and say:
  I thank the element of water for blessing me with peace.

Extinguish the north candle and say:
  I thank the element of earth for blessing me with peace.

Peace

Close your circle by saying:
May the four powers give back to the universe any powers and energies that have not been used.

The work is now done and the circle is closed.

So mote it be.

10

Health

Day of the week: The best day of
the week is Sunday

Time of day: The best time of day
is 5am. Also noon, 7pm or at
any time in the evening when
the moon is waxing or full but
not when it is waning

Goddess: Brigit

Planet: Neptune

Guardian Angel: Germaine

Star sign: Pisces

Metal: Gold

Colour: Green yellow or violet

Rune: Beork

Symbol: Fish

Number: Three

Crystal: Clear quartz

Flower: Marigold, daffodil or
sunflower

Essential oil: Sandalwood

Herb: Lavender

Tree: Ash

Neptune

Pisces

Beork

Health spell 1

Prepare yourself and decorate your work surface or altar space with all your chosen ingredients such as:

A green, yellow or violet cloth
Any items made of gold
One green and one white taper candle and holders
A spray of marigolds, daffodils or sunflowers
A piece of clear quartz crystal

When you are ready and everything is in place, stand at the edge of your circle. Close your eyes and breathe in, visualising light energy filling your body. Breathe out and breathe away all negative energy. When you are completely relaxed, stand up and move quietly to the east quarter of your circle or room.

Light the east candle and say:
    May the element of air bless this space with light, love and air and grant good health.

Light the south candle and say:
    May the element of fire bless this space with light, love and fire and grant me good health.

Light the west candle and say:
    May the element of water bless this space with light, love and water and grant me good health.

Light the north candle and say:
    May the element of earth bless this space with light, love and earth and grant me good health.

Health

Move quietly back to your workspace and kneel in front of your table. Light your white altar candle and meditate quietly on the Goddess Brigit. In your mind, visualise yourself or the person who you wish to be well in good health. Say a prayer in your own words to the Guardian Angel Germaine.

Light your green candle and as the flame grows in strength visualise health improving.

Stand in front of your altar, raise your hands high above your head and say these words:

> Flesh be healthy, spirit strong,
> Dancing feet and joyful song,
> Health restored, revitalised,
> (Name) recovered before my eyes.
> And it harm none so be it.

Spend some quiet time in your circle and allow your altar candle to burn through to the end but if you must put it out do so with a candle snuff or pinch the wick between dampened fingertips.

When you are finished working move quietly to the left of your circle.

Extinguish the east candle and say:
  I thank the element of air for blessing me with good health.

Extinguish the south candle and say:
  I thank the element of fire for blessing me with good health.

Extinguish the west candle and say:
  I thank the element of water for blessing me with good health.

Extinguish the north candle and say:
I thank the element of earth for blessing me with good health.

Close your circle by saying:
May the four powers give back to the universe any powers and energies that have not been used.

The work is now done and the circle is closed.
So mote it be.

Health spell 2

10 mls almond oil
Sandalwood pure essential oil
A bottle for your oil mixture
A small face cloth or some tissues (to clean your hands after working with the oil)
A goldfish bowl and goldfish
A clear quartz crystal
A sprig of lavender or a pinch of dried lavender added to a burner
One tall green, yellow or violet taper candle
One white candle
Candle holders
One small pointed knife

Prepare a blend of oils using 10 mls of almond oil and add the three drops of sandalwood essential oil. Hold the bottle of oil in your hands in the prayer position and rub the bottle vigorously between the palms of your hands and as you do so visualise the oil being empowered with gratitude.

When you feel as though the oil has been charged place it on your altar or work surface ready for use along with the other ingredients.

Place four small candles at the east, south, west and north in that order. Sit or kneel comfortably in front of your table. Close your eyes and as you breathe in, picture positive, white light energy filling your body.

When you are completely relaxed stand up and move quietly to the east quarter of your room.

Light the east candle and say:
May the element of air bless this space with light, love and air and grant good health.

Light the south candle and say:
May the element of fire bless this space with light, love and fire and grant me good health.

Light the west candle and say:
May the element of water bless this space with light, love and water and grant me good health.

Light the north candle and say:
May the element of earth bless this space with light, love and earth and grant me good health.

Move quietly back to your workspace and kneel in front of your table. Light your white altar candle and meditate quietly on all the things that would be possible with good health.

Take your coloured spell candle and the small pointed knife and inscribe the number three and the rune symbol Beork at the top of the candle. Place the candle back in the holder and taking the bottle of empowered oil place some in the palm of your hands. Rub your hands together and visualise that you are charging the energy in the oil and in your hands. Your hands will begin to feel very warm. Take the spell candle and spread the oil from middle to top and middle to bottom of the candle until the candle is completely covered in oil.

Visualise that you are empowering the candle with good health. Rub your hands vigorously together with the candle still held between the palms of your hands. After a few minutes, place your candle back in its holder and light the flame and say these words:

> Swift and sure let healing come
> To us all the work is done
> Blessed be the guardians who
> Work to heal both me and you
> And it harm none so mote it be

Allow your candle to burn for as long as possible but, if you must put it out, do not blow it out otherwise you will reverse or negate your spell. You can use a candle snuff or pinch the flame between your thumb and finger. You may light your candle again but each time you do so visualise your wish as though it has already begun to happen. When you are finished working, clean your hands on the cloth and move quietly to the left of your room.

Extinguish the east candle and say:
  I thank the element of air for blessing me with good health.

Extinguish the south candle and say:
  I thank the element of fire for blessing me with good health.

Extinguish the west candle and say:
  I thank the element of water for blessing me with good health.

Peace

Extinguish the north candle and say:

I thank the element of earth for blessing me with good health.

Close your circle by saying:

May the four powers give back to the universe any powers and energies that have not been used.

The work is now done and the circle is closed.

So mote it be.

11

Love

Day of the week: The best day
of the week is Friday
Time of day: The best time of
day is 5am. Also noon,
7pm or at any time in the
evening when the moon is
waxing or full but not when
it is waning
Goddess: Freya
Planets: Venus, Mars
Guardian Angel: Arnad
Star sign: Taurus
Metal: Copper or brass
Colour: Pink, red or orange
Rune: Ing (or Inguz), Mann
Symbol: Hearts
Number: Two
Crystal: Rose quartz, emerald
or sapphire
Flower: Lavender, lilac, red,
rose or jasmine
Essential oil: Rose Bulgar, rose
Maroc, ylang ylang,
geranium or jasmine
Herb: Rose
Tree: Apple

Venus   Mars

Taurus

Ing   Mann

Love

Love spell 1

Prepare yourself and decorate your work surface or altar space with all your chosen ingredients such as:

Hearts, rings and symbols of love and romance
Items made of copper or brass
A piece of rose quartz
Two red roses
An apple
Some pictures of happy couples holding hands or kissing (ideally, close family or friends whom you know have happy relationships)
One white and one pink taper candle and holders
An oil burner to which you have added essential oil of ylang ylang or patchouli
A small flowerpot filled with potting compost
A sharp knife
A small glass of water

When you are ready and everything is in place, stand at the edge of your circle. Close your eyes and breathe in, visualising light energy filling your body. Breathe out and breathe away all negative energy. When you are completely relaxed, stand up and move quietly to the east quarter of your circle or room.

Light the east candle and say:
    May the element of air bless this space with light, love and air and grant true love given and returned alike.

Light the south candle and say:
    May the element of fire bless this space with light, love and fire and grant true love given and returned alike.

Love

Light the west candle and say:
> May the element of water bless this space with light, love and water and grant true love given and returned alike.

Light the north candle and say:
> May the element of earth bless this space with light, love and earth and grant true love given and returned alike.

Move quietly back to your workspace and kneel in front of your table. Light your white altar candle and meditate quietly on the Goddess Venus. In your mind see yourself in a loving relationship. Say a prayer in your own words to the Guardian Angel Arnad. Light your pink candle and, standing in front of your altar, raise your hands high above your head and say these words.

> Venus shining in the night,
> Bless my heart with love and light.
> Loved in truth I wish to be,
> Listen to my prayer, my plea.
> May I love and be loved too,
> Blessed be the love that's true.
> And it harm none so be it.

Spend some quiet time in your circle and allow your pink candle to burn through to the end.

While your candle is burning, peel and core your apple, carefully removing the pips and place them in the small flowerpot. Pour some water over the pips that you have planted and say:

> As the seeds I have planted begin to grow,
> May the love that I have begin to show.

When you are finished move quietly to the left of your circle.

Extinguish the east candle and say:

I thank the element of air for blessing me with a loving and happy relationship.

Extinguish the south candle and say:

I thank the element of fire for blessing me with a loving and happy relationship.

Extinguish the west candle and say:

I thank the element of water for blessing me with a loving and happy relationship.

Extinguish the north candle and say:

I thank the element of earth for blessing me with a loving and happy relationship.

Close your circle by saying:
May the four powers give back to the universe any powers and energies that have not been used.
The work is now done and the circle is closed.
So mote it be.

Set your planted seeds in an area where they will be blessed by light and nourish them with water and love.

Love spell 2

A piece of rose quartz, jade, aventurine or moonstone.

A small dish of the herbs chamomile, sorrel or bay

A small posy of gardenias, tansies or roses

A small bottle of 'romance blend' oil: 10 mls of sunflower oil, one
   drop of rose absolute, Bulgar, Maroc or Egyptian. (These oils are
   expensive so you can substitute three drops of patchouli, jasmine,
   ylang ylang or geranium)

A small face cloth or some tissues

A small fireproof dish for matches or burning herbs or paper

Any items that you consider to be symbolic of love or romance

One white, and two pink, tall taper candles and holders

One small pointed knife

A small fireproof dish or an ashtray for spent matches or any paper
   that you may light during your spell and some matches or a lighter

Place four small candles at the east, south, west, and north in
that order. When everything is in place, sit or kneel comfortably
in front of your table. Close your eyes and as you breathe in,
picture positive, white light energy filling your body. As you
breathe out, breathe away all negative energy. After some
minutes, you will feel all tension flowing away from your mind
and body. Allow pure light energy to flow into and through
your entire body filling your sacred space, filling your room.
When you are completely relaxed stand up and move quietly
to the east quarter of your room.

Light the east candle and say:
   May the element of air bless this space with light, love and air
   and grant me the love that I desire. As I give love so shall I receive
   love.

Love

Light the south candle and say:

May the element of fire bless this space with light, love and fire and grant me the love that I desire. As I give love so shall I receive love.

Light the west candle and say:

May the element of water bless this space with light, love and water and grant me the love that I desire. As I give love so shall I receive love.

Light the north candle and say:

May the element of earth bless this space with light, love and earth and grant me the love that I desire. As I give love so shall I receive love.

Move quietly back to your workspace and kneel in front of your table. Light your white altar candle and meditate quietly on your hearts desire and see your wish come true.

Take one of your pink spell candles and the small pointed knife and inscribe the symbol for Venus at the top of the candle. Place the candle back in the holder and taking the bottle of empowered oil place some in the palm of your hands. Rub your hands together and visualise that you are charging the energy in the oil and in your hands. Your hands will begin to feel very warm. At this point take the first pink spell candle and spread the oil from middle to top and middle to bottom of the candle until the candle is completely covered in oil.

While you are doing this visualise that you are empowering the candle with your desire. Keep thinking about your heartfelt desire and whilst doing this rub your hands vigorously together with the candle still held between the palms of your hands. After a few minutes, place your candle back in its holder. Now take the second pink candle and the small knife and inscribe the symbol for Mars and the rune symbols Mann and Ing.

Anoint your candle as before and put it into the candle holder. Light both pink candles and say these words:

> Love to me I pray you bring
> By the power of love so true.
> Fill my heart so it may sing,
> Rejoice and let me love anew.
> And it harm none so be it.

Allow your altar candle to burn for as long as possible but if you must put it out do not blow it. You may light your candle again but each time you do so visualise your wish as though it has already begun to happen. When you are finished working clean your hands on the cloth and move quietly to the left of your room.

Extinguish the east candle and say:
   I thank the element of air for blessing me with a loving and happy relationship.

Extinguish the south candle and say:
   I thank the element of fire for blessing me with a loving and happy relationship.

Extinguish the west candle and say:
   I thank the element of water for blessing me with a loving and happy relationship.

Extinguish the north candle and say:
I thank the element of earth for blessing me with a loving and happy relationship.

Close your circle by saying
May the four powers give back to the universe any powers and energies that have not been used.
The work is now done and the circle is closed.
So mote it be.

The following day, set two candles at opposite ends of your room and light them repeating the words:

> Love to me I pray you bring
> By the power of love so true.
> Fill my heart so it may sing,
> Rejoice and let me love anew.
> And it harm none so be it.

Do this every day for thirty days, moving the candles closer and closer together until they sit side by side. Let your candles burn for as long as possible or put them out with a candle snuff.

12

Career

Day of the week: The best day
of the week is Sunday
Time of day: The best time of
day is 5am. Also noon, 7pm
or at any time in the evening
when the moon is waxing or
full but not when it is
waning.
Goddess: Oshion
Planet: Sun
Guardian Angel: Michael
Star sign: Leo
Metal: Gold
Colour: Yellow or orange
Rune: Tir (also known as
Tiwaz)
Symbol: Keys
Number: Five
Crystal: Citrine, tiger's eye,
sunstone
Flower: Marigold
Essential oil: Bergamot
Herb: Chamomile
Tree: Hazel

Sun

Leo

Tir

Career spell 1

Prepare yourself and decorate your work surface or altar space with all your chosen ingredients such as:

Any gold items
One gold and one white taper candle and holders
A vase of marigolds
Some keys
A piece of citrine, tiger's eye or sunstone

When you are ready and everything is in place, stand at the edge of your circle. Close your eyes and breathe in, visualising light energy filling your body. Breathe out and breathe away all negative energy.

When you are completely relaxed stand up and move quietly to the east quarter of your circle or room.

Light the east candle and say:
> May the element of air bless this space with light, love and air and grant me the position I desire.

Light the south candle and say:
> May the element of fire bless this space with light, love and fire and grant me the position I desire.

Light the west candle and say:
> May the element of water bless this space with light, love and water and grant me the position I desire.

Light the north candle and say:
> May the element of Earth bless this space with light, love and Earth and grant me the position I desire.

Move quietly back to your workspace and kneel in front of your table. Light your white altar candle and meditate quietly on the Goddess Oshion.

See yourself in a worthwhile, well-paid position that you enjoy, and where you feel happy and content. Also visualise that you and your new work colleagues enjoy harmonious working relationships together and say a prayer in your own words to the Guardian Angel Michael.

Light your gold candle and, standing in front of your altar, raise your hands high above your head and say these words:

> Keys to open doors for me,
> Chances come to set me free,
> Ambitions reached and realised,
> Seen before my very eyes.
> And it harm none so be it.

Spend some quiet time in your circle and allow your candles to burn through to the end or put them out using a candle snuff. When you are finished working move quietly to the left of your circle.

Extinguish the east candle and say:
  I thank the element of air for blessing me with a new career.

Extinguish the south candle and say:
  I thank the element of fire for blessing me with a new career.

Extinguish the west candle and say:
  I thank the element of water for blessing me with a new career.

Extinguish the north candle and say:
I thank the element of earth for blessing me with a new career.

Close your circle by saying:
May the four powers give back to the universe any powers and energies that have not been used.
The work is now done and the circle is closed.
So mote it be.

Career spell 2

10 mls almond oil
3 drops of bergamot pure essential oil
A bottle for your oil mixture
A small face cloth or some tissues
A small fireproof dish for matches or burning herbs or paper
Your current CV or job applications
A piece of tiger's eye crystal
A sprig of hazel
One white and one orange gold or yellow taper candle and holders
One small pointed knife

Prepare a blend of oils using 10 mls of almond oil and add three drops of bergamot pure essential oil. Hold the bottle of oil in your hands in the prayer position and rub the bottle vigorously between the palms of your hands and as you do so visualise the oil being empowered with gratitude. When you feel as though the oil has been charged place it on your altar or work surface ready for use along with the other items. Place four small candles at the east, south, west, and north in that order. Sit or kneel comfortably in front of your table. Close your eyes and as you breathe in, picture positive white light energy filling your body.

When you are completely relaxed stand up and move quietly to the east quarter of your room.

Light the east candle and say:
> May the element of air bless this space with light, love and air and grant me the position I desire.

Light the south candle and say:
> May the element of fire bless this space with light, love and fire and grant me the position I desire.

Light the west candle and say:
> May the element of water bless this space with light, love and water and grant me the position I desire.

Light the north candle and say:
> May the element of earth bless this space with light, love and earth and grant me the position I desire.

Move quietly back to your workspace and kneel in front of your table. Light your white altar candle and meditate quietly on the Goddess Oshion. Take your coloured spell candle and the small pointed knife and inscribe the number five and the rune symbol Tir at the top of the candle.

Place the candle back in the holder and taking the bottle of empowered oil place some in the palm of your hands. Rub your hands together and visualise that you are charging the energy in the oil and in your hands. Your hands will begin to feel very warm. Take the spell candle and spread the oil from middle to top and middle to bottom of the candle until the candle is completely covered in oil. Visualise that you are empowering the candle with career opportunities. Rub your hands vigorously together with the candle still held between the palms of your hands.

After a few minutes, place your candle back in its holder and light the flame and say these words:

> Work success will come to me —
> Successful now, fulfilled and free.
> I am happy and content
> With this position heaven sent.
> And it harm none so mote it be.

Allow your candle to burn for as long as possible but, if you must put it out, use a candle snuff or pinch the flame between your thumb and finger. You may light your candle again but each time you do so visualise your wish as though it has already begun to happen. When you are finished working clean your hands on the cloth and move quietly to the left of your room.

Extinguish the east candle and say:
    I thank the element of air for blessing me with a new career.

Extinguish the south candle and say:
    I thank the element of fire for blessing me with a new career.

Extinguish the west candle and say:
    I thank the element of water for blessing me with a new career.

Extinguish the north candle and say:
    I thank the element of earth for blessing me with a new career.

Close your circle by saying:

May the four powers give back to the universe any powers and energies that have not been used.

The work is now done and the circle is closed.

So mote it be.

13

Interviews

Day of the week: The best day of the week is Wednesday

Time of day: The best time of day is 5am. Also noon, 7pm or at any time in the evening when the moon is waxing or full but not when it is waning

Goddess: Kali

Guardian Angel: Raphael

Planet: Mercury

Star sign: Gemini or Virgo

Metal: Quicksilver

Colour: Silver or indigo

Rune: Wynn (also known as Wunjo)

Symbol: Papers certificates or official documents

Number: Four, five or seven

Crystal: Amethyst tiger's eye

Flower: Almond blossom

Herb: Dill

Essential Oil: Lemongrass

Tree: Hazel

Mercury

Virgo   Gemini

Wynn

Interviews

Interviews spell 1

Prepare yourself and decorate your work surface or altar space with all your chosen ingredients such as:

A silver=coloured cloth
A vase of almond blossom
Leaves' that have a silver sheen
Your CV
Job adverts or applications
One silver or white taper candle
A piece of amethyst or tiger's eye
One white and one silver taper candle and holders

When you are ready and everything is in place, stand at the edge of your circle. Close your eyes and breathe in, visualising light energy filling your body. Breathe out and breathe away all negative energy. When you are completely relaxed stand up and move quietly to the east quarter of your circle or room.

Light the east candle and say:
> May the element of air bless this space with light, love and air, knowledge and wisdom, so that I may have a successful interview.

Light the south candle and say:
> May the element of fire bless this space with light, love and fire, knowledge and wisdom, so that I may have a successful interview.

Light the west candle and say:
> May the element of water bless this space with light, love and water, knowledge and wisdom, so that I may have a successful interview.

Interviews

Light the north candle and say:

May the element of earth bless this space with light, love and earth, knowledge and wisdom, so that I may have a successful interview.

Move quietly back to your workspace and kneel in front of your table. Light your white altar candle and meditate quietly on the Goddess Kali. In your mind see yourself being offered a new position.

Say a prayer in your own words to the Guardian Angel Raphael and stand in front of your altar. Raise your hands high above your head and say these words:

Letters dropping on the floor,
Many offers are in store.
The perfect job's within my sight,
My talents, strengths and skills unite.
And it harm none so be it.

Spend some quiet time in your circle and allow your altar candle to burn through to the end or put it out with a candle snuff. When you are finished working move quietly to the left of your circle.

Extinguish the east candle and say:

I thank the element of air for blessing me so that I may have a successful interview.

Extinguish the south candle and say:

I thank the element of fire for blessing me so that I may have a successful interview.

Extinguish the west candle and say:
> I thank the element of water for blessing me so that I may have a successful interview.

Extinguish the north candle and say:
> I thank the element of earth for blessing me so that I may have a successful interview.

Close your circle by saying:
> May the four powers give back to the universe any powers and energies that have not been used.
> The work is now done and the circle is closed.
> So mote it be.

Interviews spell 2

10 mls almond oil
Lemongrass pure essential oil
A bottle for your oil mixture
An indigo tablecloth
A small face cloth or some tissues and a small fireproof dish for matches or burning herbs or paper
Some amethyst crystals
Certificates or qualifications that you have achieved
One white and one silver taper candle and holders
One small pointed knife

Prepare a blend of oils using 10 mls of almond oil and add three drops of lemongrass pure essential oil. Hold the bottle of oil in your hands in the prayer position and rub the bottle vigorously between the palms of your hands and as you do so visualise the oil being empowered with gratitude. When you feel as though the oil has been charged place it on your altar or work surface ready for use along with the other items.

Place four small candles at the east, south, west and north in that order. Sit or kneel comfortably in front of your table. Close your eyes and as you breathe in, picture positive, white light energy filling your body. When you are completely relaxed stand up and move quietly to the east quarter of your room.

Light the east candle and say:
> May the element of air bless this space with light, love and air, knowledge and wisdom, so that I may have a successful interview

Light the south candle and say:
> May the element of fire bless this space with light, love and fire, knowledge and wisdom, so that I may have a successful interview.

Light the west candle and say:
> May the element of water bless this space with light love water, knowledge and wisdom, so that I may have a successful interview.

Light the north candle and say:
> May the element of earth bless this space with light, love and earth, knowledge and wisdom, so that I may have a successful interview.

Move quietly back to your workspace and kneel in front of your table. Light your white altar candle and meditate quietly on the Goddess Kali. Take your silver spell candle and the small pointed knife and inscribe the number three and the rune symbol Wynn at the top of the candle. Place the candle back in the holder and taking the bottle of empowered oil place some in the palm of your hands. Rub your hands together and visualise that you are charging the energy in the oil and in your hands. Your hands will begin to feel very warm. Take the spell candle and spread the oil from middle to top and middle to bottom of the candle until the candle is completely covered in oil. Visualise that you are empowering the candle with your desire. Rub your hands vigorously together with the candle still held between the palms of your hands. After a few minutes, place your candle back in its holder and light the flame and say these words:

> Candle bring to me the news
> Of successful interviews.
> Happy am I to receive
> Blessings given on this eve.
> And it harm none so mote it be.

Allow your altar candle to burn through to the end or put it out with a candle snuff. You may light your candle again but each time you do so visualise your wish as though it has already begun to happen. When you are finished working, clean your hands on the cloth and move quietly to the left of your room.

Extinguish the east candle and say:
I thank the element of air for blessing me so that I may have a successful interview.

Extinguish the south candle and say:
I thank the element of fire for blessing me so that I may have a successful interview.

Interviews

Extinguish the west candle and say:
I thank the element of water for blessing me so that I may have a successful interview.

Extinguish the north candle and say:
I thank the element of earth for blessing me so that I may have a successful interview.

Close your circle by saying:
May the four powers give back to the universe any powers and energies that have not been used.
The work is now done and the circle is closed.
So mote it be.

14

Protection

Day of the week: The best day
of the week is Thursday

Time of day: The best time of
day 5am. Also noon, 7pm
or at any time in the evening
when the moon is waxing or
full but not when it is
waning

Goddess: Callisto

Planet: Jupiter

Guardian angel: Zadkiel

Star sign: Sagittarius

Metal: Tin

Colour: Blue

Rune: Eohl

Symbol: Ankh or crucifix

Number: Eight

Crystal: Turquoise

Flower: Lilac and apple
blossom

Essential oil: Frankincense

Herb: Garlic, mint or feverfew

Tree: Rowan

Jupiter

Sagittarius

An Egyptian ankh

Eohl

Protection spell 1
Prepare yourself and decorate your work surface or altar space with all your chosen ingredients such as:

An ankh, or a crucifix
One white and one blue taper candle and holders
A clove of garlic
A vase of lilac flowers
A dish of salt and a small bowl of water
A dish containing some dried or fresh mint
A sprig of rowan
A piece of turquoise

When you are ready and everything is in place, stand at the edge of your circle. Close your eyes and breathe in, visualising light energy filling your body. Breathe out and breathe away all negative energy. When you are completely relaxed stand up and move quietly to the east quarter of your circle or room.

Light the east candle and say:
    May the element of air bless this space with light, love and air and grant me protection in everything I do and anywhere I go.

Light the south candle and say:
    May the element of fire bless this space with light, love and fire and grant me protection in everything I do and anywhere I go.

Light the west candle and say:
    May the element of water bless this space with light, love and water and grant me protection in everything I do and anywhere I go.

Light the north candle and say:

> May the element of earth bless this space with light, love and earth and grant me protection in everything I do and anywhere I go.

Move quietly back to your workspace, kneel in front of your table and light your white altar candle.

Place the dish of water in front of you and take three pinches of salt and add this to the water dish. Raise your dominant hand high above your head pointing your index finger to the sky above you. Visualise white light connecting with your index finger and flowing through your body.

Now place your index finger into the dish of salted water and say these words:

> Water be healing and salt be pure
> Keep me safe and protected sure.
> Guard me and mine from any harm,
> Whilst I keep this sacred charm.
> Bad energy please turn from me
> Send it back so none need flee.
> And it harm none so mote it be.

Dip the ankh or crucifix once in the salted water.

Spend some time meditating quietly on the Goddess Callisto and allow your altar candle to burn through to the end, or put it out with a candle snuff or pinch the wick between dampened fingertips.

When you are finished working move quietly to the left of your circle.

Extinguish the east candle and say:

I thank the element of air for blessing me with protection, making me and mine safe in everything that we do or anywhere that we go.

Extinguish the south candle and say:

I thank the element of fire for blessing me with protection, making me and mine safe in everything that we do or anywhere that we go.

Extinguish the west candle and say:

I thank the element of water for blessing me with protection, making me and mine safe in everything that we do or anywhere that we go.

Extinguish the north candle and say:

I thank the element of earth for blessing me with protection, making me and mine safe in everything that we do or anywhere that we go.

Close your circle by saying:

May the four powers give back to the universe any powers and energies that have not been used.
The work is now done and the circle is closed.
So mote it be.

Wear the ankh or crucifix round your neck or keep it safe on your person. Take your dish of water and salt and go to your front door. Holding the dish in your non-dominant hand place the fingers of your dominant hand in the dish and flick the salted water around your door. Do this round the walls and the windows and, if you have a garden, sprinkle the water round the perimeter of your garden. This can also be done on your car. Do not forget to sprinkle some on your letterbox and your telephone. As you sprinkle be sure to repeat the words:

> Water be healing and salt be pure
> Keep me safe and protected sure.
> Guard me and mine from any harm
> Whilst I keep this sacred charm.
> Bad energy please turn from me
> Send it back so none need flee.
> And it harm none so mote it be.

If you run out of water and salt make some more. You do not have to cast a circle to do this but you should visualise the connection to the pure energy from infinity above you before you begin.

Protection spell 2

10 mls almond oil
Frankincense pure essential oil
A bottle for your oil mixture
A small face cloth or some tissues
A small fireproof dish for matches or burning herbs or paper
An ankh or crucifix
A vase of apple blossom
A piece of turquoise
One tall blue and one tall white taper candle and holders
One small pointed knife

Prepare a blend of oils using 10 mls of almond oil and add three drops of frankincense pure essential oil. Hold the bottle of oil in your hands in the prayer position and rub the bottle vigorously between the palms of your hands and as you do so visualise the oil being empowered with the power of protection. When you feel as though the oil has been charged, place it on your altar or work surface, ready for use along with the other items.

Place four small candles at the east, south, west, and north in that order.

Sit or kneel comfortably in front of your table. Close your eyes and as you breathe in, picture positive, white light energy filling your body. When you are completely relaxed, stand up and move quietly to the east quarter of your room.

Light the east candle and say:
> May the element of air bless this space with light, love and air and grant me protection in everything I do and anywhere I go.

Light the south candle and say:
> May the element of fire bless this space with light, love and fire and grant me protection in everything I do and anywhere I go.

Light the west candle and say:
> May the element of water bless this space with light, love and water and grant me protection in everything I do and anywhere I go.

Light the north candle and say:
> May the element of earth bless this space with light, love and earth and grant me protection in everything I do and anywhere I go.

Move quietly back to your workspace and kneel in front of your table. Light your white altar candle and meditate quietly on the Goddess Callisto. Take your blue spell candle and the small pointed knife and inscribe the number eight and the rune symbol Eohl at the top of the candle. Place the candle back in the holder and, taking the bottle of empowered oil, place some in the palm of your hands.

Rub your hands together and visualise that you are charging the energy in the oil and in your hands. Your hands will begin to feel very warm. Take the spell candle and spread the oil from middle to top and middle to bottom of the candle until the candle is completely covered in oil. Visualise that you are empowering the candle with the power of protection. Rub your hands vigorously together with the candle still held between the palms of your hands. After a few minutes, place your candle back in its holder and light the flame and say these words:

> Flame that burns and brings me light
> Keep me safe both day and night.
> Even when the flame is done
> Let no harm come from any one.
> And it harm none so mote it be.

Allow your candle to burn for as long as possible or use a candle snuff to put it out. You may light your candle again but each time you do so visualise your wish as though it has already begun to happen. When you are finished working, clean your hands on the cloth and move quietly to the left of your room.

Extinguish the east candle and say:
I thank the element of air for blessing me with protection, making me and mine safe in everything that we do or anywhere that we go.

Protection

Extinguish the south candle and say:
I thank the element of fire for blessing me with protection, making me and mine safe in everything that we do or anywhere that we go.

Extinguish the west candle and say:
I thank the element of water for blessing me with protection, making me and mine safe in everything that we do or anywhere that we go.

Extinguish the north candle and say:
I thank the element of earth for blessing me with protection, making me and mine safe in everything that we do or anywhere that we go.

Close your circle by saying:
May the four powers give back to the universe any powers and energies that have not been used.
The work is now done and the circle is closed.
So mote it be.

For as long as you feel threatened, each day or night, continue to light a candle that you have dedicated to your protection. Prepare yourself and your workspace as you would normally do and as you light the flame say the words:

Flame that burns and brings me light
Keep me safe both day and night.
Even when the flame is done
Let no harm come from anyone.
And it harm none so mote it be.

15

Opportunities

Day of the week: The best day
of the week is Sunday
Time of day: The best time of
day 5am. Also noon, 7pm
or at any time in the evening
when the moon is waxing or
full but not when it is
waning
Goddess: Carna
Planet: Sun
Star sign: Leo
Metal: Gold
Colour: Yellow
Rune: Ken (also known as
Kano), Daeg (also known
as Dagaz)
Symbol: Keys and doors
Number: Seven
Crystal: Diamond, ruby, sun
stone or citrine
Flower: Jasmine
Essential oil: Neroli
Tree: Cherry

Sun

Leo

Ken   Dagaz

Opportunity

Opportunity spell 1
Prepare yourself and decorate your work surface or altar space with all your chosen ingredients such as:

Yellow and gold coloured cloths
A letter addressed to yourself or for whomever you are
    preparing the spell.
    [In the letter write the words:
'We would like to offer you (insert your own words here)']
Diamond or ruby jewellery, citrine or sunstone crystals
Circular shaped discs covered with gold foil to represent the sun
One gold and one white taper candle and holders
An ashtray or a small fireproof dish
Some matches or a lighter
A vase of jasmine blossoms

When you are ready and everything is in place, stand at the edge of your circle. Close your eyes and breathe in, visualising light energy filling your body. Breathe out and breathe away all negative energy. When you are completely relaxed stand up and move quietly to the east quarter of your circle or room.

Light the east candle and say:
    May the element of air bless this space with light, love and air
    and grant me the opportunity to change my life for the better.

Light the south candle and say:
    May the element of fire bless this space with light, love and fire
    and grant me the opportunity to change my life for the better.

Opportunity

Light the west candle and say:
   May the element of water bless this space with light, love and water and grant me the opportunity to change my life for the better.

Light the north candle and say:
   May the element of earth bless this space with light, love and earth and grant me the opportunity to change my life for the better.

Move quietly back to your workspace and kneel in front of your table. Light your white altar candle and meditate quietly on the Goddess Carna. In your mind give thanks for the gifts that you have been given.

Open your letter and read aloud the words that you have written and in your mind visualise this coming true. Light your gold candle and light the letter from the gold candle and allow it to burn through in the fireproof dish.

Stand in front of your altar, raise your hands high above your head and say these words:

> Carna hear me when I say
> I give thanks to you today
> Chances offered I will take
> And my future I shall make
> And it harm none so be it.

Spend some quiet time in your circle and allow your altar candle to burn through to the end or put it out with a candle snuff. When you are finished working, move quietly to the left of your circle.

Opportunity

Extinguish the east candle and say:
I thank the element of air for blessing me with the opportunity to change my life.

Extinguish the south candle and say:
I thank the element of fire for blessing me with the opportunity to change my life.

Extinguish the west candle and say:
I thank the element of water for blessing me with the opportunity to change my life.

Extinguish the north candle and say:
I thank the element of earth for blessing me with the opportunity to change my life.

Close your circle by saying:
May the four powers give back to the universe any powers and energies that have not been used.
The work is now done and the circle is closed.
So mote it be.

Opportunity spell 2

10 mls almond oil
Neroli pure essential oil
A bottle for your oil mixture
A small face cloth or some tissues
A small fireproof dish for matches or burning herbs or paper
An incense burner to which you have added yellow or gold coloured
    potpourri and a few drops of your favourite oil
A piece of sun stone
One tall white and one tall yellow or gold taper candles and holders
One small pointed knife

Prepare a blend of oils using 10 mls of almond oil and add
three drops of neroli pure essential oil. Hold the bottle of oil in
your hands in the prayer position and rub the bottle vigorously
between the palms of your hands and as you do so visualise the
oil being empowered with gratitude. When you feel as though
the oil has been charged place it on your altar or work surface
ready for use along with the other items.

Place four small candles at the east, south, west and north in
that order. Sit or kneel comfortably in front of your table. Close
your eyes and, as you breathe in, picture positive white light
energy filling your body. When you are completely relaxed
stand up and move quietly to the east quarter of your room.

Light the east candle and say:
    May the element of air bless this space with light, love and air
    and grant me the opportunity to change my life for the better.

Opportunity

Light the south candle and say:
   May the element of fire bless this space with light, love and fire
   and grant me the opportunity to change my life for the better.

Light the west candle and say:
   May the element of water bless this space with light, love and
   water and grant me the opportunity to change my life for the
   better.

Light the north candle and say:
   May the element of earth bless this space with light, love and
   earth and grant me the opportunity to change my life for the better.

Move quietly back to your workspace and kneel in front of
your table. Light your white altar candle and meditate quietly
on the opportunities that you would like to see come your
way. Take your yellow or gold spell candle and the small
pointed knife and inscribe the number seven and the rune
symbol Daeg at the top of the candle. Place the candle back
in the holder and, taking the bottle of empowered oil, place
some in the palm of your hands. Rub your hands together
and visualise that you are charging the energy in the oil and
in your hands. Your hands will begin to feel very warm. Take
the spell candle and spread the oil from middle to top and
middle to bottom of the candle until the candle is completely
covered in oil. Visualise that you are empowering the candle
with exciting new opportunities. Rub your hands vigorously
together with the candle still held between the palms of your
hands.

   After a few minutes, place your spell candle back in its holder
and light the flame and say these words:

Opportunity

Chances now have come my way,
Blessed be this special day.
My life is changed, improving ever,
Chances now do come together.
And it harm none so mote it be.

Allow your altar candle to burn through to the end or put it out with a candle snuff. You may light your candle again but each time you do so visualise your wish as though it has already begun to happen. When you are finished working clean your hands on the cloth and move quietly to the left of your room.

Extinguish the east candle and say:
I thank the element of air for blessing me with the opportunity to change my life.

Extinguish the south candle and say:
I thank the element of fire for blessing me with the opportunity to change my life.

Extinguish the west candle and say:
I thank the element of water for blessing me with the opportunity to change my life.

Extinguish the north candle and say:
I thank the element of earth for blessing me with the opportunity to change my life.

Close your circle by saying:
May the four powers give back to the universe any powers and energies that have not been used.
The work is now done and the circle is closed.
So mote it be.

16

Marriage

Day of the week: The best day of the week is Friday

Time of day: The best time of day is 5am. Also noon, 7pm or at any time in the evening when the moon is waxing or full but not when it is waning

Goddess: Freya

Planet: Venus

Guardian Angel: Adonai

Star sign: Taurus and Libra

Metal: Rose, gold and copper

Colour: Red, pink or green

Rune: Geofu (also known as Gefu), Ing (also known as Ingux, Ingwaz), Mann (also known as Manaz)

Symbol: Rings

Number: Two, four and six

Crystal: Rose quartz

Flower: Rose

Essential Oil: Rose otto

Tree: Apple

Herb: Ylang ylang

Venus

Taurus

Libra

Geofu

Ing

Mann

Marriage spell 1
Prepare yourself and decorate your work surface or altar space with all your chosen ingredients such as:

Cloths, which are coloured red, pink and green
Place on your table pieces of paper on which you have written the
    numbers two, four and six
Several pieces of rose quartz
A dish in which you have placed some rings
One white and one pink taper candle and holders
A small posy of pink roses

When you are ready and everything is in place, stand at the edge of your circle. Close your eyes and breathe in, visualising light energy filling your body. Breathe out and breathe away all negative energy.

When you are completely relaxed, stand up and move quietly to the east quarter of your circle or room.

Light the east candle and say:
    May the element of air bless this space with light, love and air
    and bless our sacred union so that we may live long and happy
    together.

Light the south candle and say:
    May the element of fire bless this space with light, love and fire
    and bless our sacred union so that we may live long and happy
    together.

Light the west candle and say:
    May the element of water bless this space with light, love and
    water and bless our sacred union so that we may live long and
    happy together.

Marriage

Light the north candle and say:
May the element of earth bless this space with light, love and earth and bless our sacred union so that we may live long and happy together.

Move quietly back to your workspace and kneel in front of your table. Light your white altar candle and meditate quietly on the Goddess Venus. Say a prayer in your own words to the Guardian Angel Adonai. Light your pink candle and stand in front of your altar, raise your hands high above your head and say these words:

Marriage is a sacred way.
None shall come between us
Blessed with love every day
This our gift from Venus.
And it harm none so be it.

Spend some quiet time in your circle and allow your altar candle to burn through to the end or put it out with a candle snuff. When you are finished working move quietly to the left of your circle.

Extinguish the east candle and say:
I thank the element of air for blessing our union so that we may live long and happy together.

Extinguish the south candle and say:
I thank the element of fire for blessing our union so that we may live long and happy together.

Marriage

Extinguish the west candle and say:
I thank the element of water for blessing our union so that we may live long and happy together.

Extinguish the north candle and say:
I thank the element of earth for blessing our union so that we may live long and happy together.

Close your circle by saying
May the four powers give back to the universe any powers and energies that have not been used.
The work is now done and the circle is closed.
So mote it be.

Marriage spell 2

10 mls almond oil
Rose otto pure essential oil
A bottle for your oil mixture
A small face cloth or some tissues
A small fireproof dish for matches or burning herbs or paper
Write on a piece of paper the words: 'May (name) and I live long and happy lives together blessed with perfect love, perfect truth and perfect happiness'
Photographs of happily married couples
(You could use photographs that are personal to you such as parents or grandparents)
Some rose quartz
One white and one pink candles and holders
One small pointed knife

Prepare a blend of oils using 10 mls of almond oil and add three drops of rose otto pure essential oil. Hold the bottle of oil in your hands in the prayer position and rub the bottle vigorously between the palms of your hands and as you do so visualise the oil being empowered with gratitude. When you feel as though the oil has been charged, place it on your altar or work surface ready for use along with the other items.

Place four small candles at the east, south, west and north in that order.

Sit or kneel comfortably in front of your table. Close your eyes and as you breathe in, picture positive, white light energy filling your body. When you are completely relaxed stand up and move quietly to the east quarter of your room.

Light the east candle and say:
May the element of air bless this space with light, love and air and bless our sacred union so that we may live long and happy together.

Light the south candle and say:
May the element of fire bless this space with light, love and fire and bless our sacred union so that we may live long and happy together.

Light the west candle and say:
May the element of water bless this space with light, love and water and bless our sacred union so that we may live long and happy together.

Light the north candle and say:
May the element of earth bless this space with light, love and earth and bless our sacred union so that we may live long and happy together.

Move quietly back to your workspace and kneel in front of your table. Light your white altar candle and meditate quietly on you and your partner and the life that you see ahead of you. Take your pink spell candle and the small pointed knife and inscribe the numbers two, four and six and the rune symbol Geofu and Ing at the top of the candle. Place the candle back in the holder and, taking the bottle of empowered oil, place some in the palms of your hands. Rub your hands together and visualise that you are charging the energy in the oil and in your hands. Your hands will begin to feel very warm. Take the spell candle and spread the oil from middle to top and middle to bottom of the candle until the candle is completely covered in oil. Visualise that you are empowering the candle with stability and security in your marriage. Rub your hands vigorously together with the candle still held between the palms of your hands. After a few minutes, place your candle back in its holder and light the flame and say these words:

> I give myself to you in love,
> Promises we make forever.
> Blessed by all the stars above,
> Remembered always — forgotten never.
> And it harm none so mote it be.

Take the paper that you have written on and light it with the pink candle. Let it burn through in the fireproof dish. Allow your altar candles to burn through to the end or put them out with a candle snuff. You may light your candles again but each time you do so visualise your wish as though

Marriage

it has already begun to happen. When you are finished working, clean your hands on the cloth and move quietly to the left of your room.

Extinguish the east candle and say:
I thank the element of air for blessing our union so that we may live long and happily together.

Extinguish the south candle and say:
I thank the element of fire for blessing our union so that we may live long and happily together.

Extinguish the west candle and say:
I thank the element of water for blessing our union so that we may live long and happily together.

Extinguish the north candle and say:
I thank the element of earth for blessing our union so that we may live long and happily together.

Close your circle by saying;
May the four powers give back to the universe any powers and energies that have not been used.
The work is now done and the circle is closed.
So mote it be.

17

Harvest

Day of the week: The best day
  of the week is Saturday
Time of day: The best time of
  day is 5am. Also noon, 7pm
  or at any time in the evening
  when the moon is waxing or
  full but not when it is
  waning
Goddess: Ceres
Planet: Saturn
Star sign: Capricorn
Metal: Lead
Colour: Deep blue
Rune: Jara (also known as
  Jera)
Symbol: Autumn leaves,
  wheat sheaves, grains or
  bread
Number: Nine
Crystal: Lapis or amber
Flower: Violet
Essential oil: Sage
Tree: Bamboo

Saturn

Capricorn

Jara

Harvest spell 1

Prepare yourself and decorate your work surface or altar space with all your chosen ingredients such as:

A deep blue cloth
Some autumn coloured leaves and a small bamboo plant (available from most garden stores)
A piece of amber or lapis
One gold and white taper candle and holders
Some crusty bread
A dish of grains or cereals

When you are ready and everything is in place, stand at the edge of your circle. Close your eyes and breathe in, visualising light energy filling your body. Breathe out and breathe away all negative energy. When you are completely relaxed stand up and move quietly to the east quarter of your circle or room.

Light the east candle and say:

May the element of air bless this space with light, love and air and bless the work that I have done so that I may reap the rewards for my efforts.

Light the south candle and say:

May the element of fire bless this space with light, love and fire and bless the work that I have done so that I may reap the rewards for my efforts.

Light the west candle and say:

May the element of water bless this space with light, love and water and bless the work that I have done so that I may reap the rewards for my efforts.

Harvest

Light the north candle and say:
> May the element of earth bless this space with light, love and earth and bless the work that I have done so that I may reap the rewards for my efforts.

Move quietly back to your workspace and kneel in front of your table. Light your white altar candle and meditate quietly on the Goddess Ceres. In your mind give thanks for the ability to work and see your rewards grow before you. Break a piece from the crusty bread and eat it, enjoying the taste and savouring every mouthful. Think about how this piece of bread came to be, starting with the planting of the seed. See the seed growing and dancing in a gentle breeze. Say a prayer in your own words to your Guardian Angel. Stand in front of your altar, raise your hands high above your head and say these words:

> Seeds where planted now they grow,
> Rewards to me begin to flow,
> Harvest time comes round again
> Blessed by sun and wind and rain.
> And it harm none so be it.

Spend some quiet time in your circle and allow your altar candle to burn through to the end or put it out with a candle snuff. When you are finished working, move quietly to the left of your circle.

Extinguish the east candle and say:
> I thank the element of air for blessing the work that I have done so that I may reap the rewards for my efforts.

Extinguish the south candle and say:
I thank the element of fire for blessing the work that I have done so that I may reap the rewards for my efforts.

Extinguish the west candle and say:
I thank the element of water for blessing the work that I have done so that I may reap the rewards for my efforts.

Extinguish the north candle and say:
I thank the element of earth for blessing the work that I have done so that I may reap the rewards for my efforts.

Close your circle by saying:
May the four powers give back to the universe any powers and energies that have not been used.
The work is now done and the circle is closed.
So mote it be.

Harvest spell 2

10 mls almond oil
Sage pure essential oil
A bottle for your oil mixture
A small face cloth or some tissues and a small fireproof dish for matches or burning herbs or paper.
A golden cloth
A vase of violets
A piece of lead
One white and one deep blue candle and holders

Prepare a blend of oils using 10 mls of almond oil and add

three drops of sage pure essential oil. Hold the bottle of oil in your hands in the prayer position and rub the bottle vigorously between the palms of your hands and as you do so visualise the oil being empowered with gratitude. When you feel as though the oil has been charged place it on your altar or work surface ready for use along with the other items.

Place four small candles at the east, south, west and north in that order. Sit or kneel comfortably in front of your table. Close your eyes and, as you breathe in, picture positive white light energy filling your body. When you are completely relaxed, stand up and move quietly to the east quarter of your room.

Light the east candle and say:

May the element of air bless this space with light, love and air and bless the work that I have done so that I may reap the rewards for my efforts.

Light the south candle and say:

May the element of fire bless this space with light, love and fire and bless the work that I have done so that I may reap the rewards for my efforts.

Light the west candle and say:

May the element of water bless this space with light, love and water and bless the work that I have done so that I may reap the rewards for my efforts.

Light the north candle and say:

May the element of earth bless this space with light, love and earth and bless the work that I have done so that I may reap the rewards for my efforts.

Harvest

Move quietly back to your workspace and kneel in front of your table. Light your white altar candle and meditate quietly on the work that you have done and the rewards that you are hoping to achieve. Take your blue spell candle and the small pointed knife and inscribe the number nine and the rune symbol Jara at the top of the candle. Place the candle back in the holder and taking the bottle of empowered oil place some in the palm of your hands. Rub your hands together and visualise that you are charging the energy in the oil and in your hands. Your hands will begin to feel very warm. Take the spell candle and spread the oil from middle to top and middle to bottom of the candle until the candle is completely covered in oil. Visualise that you are empowering the candle with a bountiful harvest. Rub your hands vigorously together with the candle still held between the palms of your hands. After a few minutes, place your candle back in its holder and light the flame and say these words.

Candle burning clear and bright,
I have worked from day till night,
The fruits of work begin to show,
Make them golden, let them grow.
And it harm none so mote it be.

Allow your altar candles to burn through to the end or put them out with a candle snuff. You may light your candles again but each time you do so visualise your wish as though it has already begun to happen. When you are finished working, clean your hands on the cloth and move quietly to the left of your room.

Harvest

Extinguish the east candle and say:

I thank the element of air for blessing the work that I have done so that I may reap the rewards for my efforts.

Extinguish the south candle and say:

I thank the element of fire for blessing the work that I have done so that I may reap the rewards for my efforts.

Extinguish the west candle and say:

I thank the element of water for blessing the work that I have done so that I may reap the rewards for my efforts.

Extinguish the north candle and say:

I thank the element of earth for blessing the work that I have done so that I may reap the rewards for my efforts.

Close your circle by saying:

May the four powers give back to the universe any powers and energies that have not been used.
The work is now done and the circle is closed.
So mote it be.

Secrets

Day of the week: The best day
    of the week is Tuesday
Time of day: The best time of
    day is 5am. Also noon, 7pm
    or at any time in the evening
    when the moon is waxing or
    full but not when it is
    waning
Goddess: Meretsegar
Guardian Angel: Masleh
Planet: Pluto
Star sign: Scorpio
Metal: Tungsten or tutonium
Colour: Black
Rune: Peorth
Symbol: Diaries, puzzles or
    boxes
Number: Two
Crystal: Beryl or sardonyx
Flower: Begonia
Essential oil: Geranium
Herb: Coriander
Tree: Cedar

Pluto

Scorpio

Peorth

Secrets spell 1
Prepare yourself and decorate your work surface or altar space with all your chosen ingredients such as:

A black silk or velvet cloth
On your table place an incense burner to which you have added some water and a pinch of dried coriander and some geranium or cedar essential oil
A piece of beryl, sardonyx, jet or obsidian
Your diary and some puzzles
One white and one black tall taper candle and holders

When you are ready and everything is in place, stand at the edge of your circle. Close your eyes and breathe in, visualising light energy filling your body. Breathe out and breathe away all negative energy. When you are completely relaxed stand up and move quietly to the east quarter of your circle or room.

Light the east candle and say:
   May the element of air bless this space with light, love and air and keep my secret so that none may share.

Light the south candle and say:
   May the element of fire bless this space with light, love and fire and keep my secret so that none may share.

Light the west candle and say:
   May the element of water bless this space with light, love and water and keep my secret so that none may share.

Light the north candle and say:
> May the element of earth bless this space with light, love and earth and keep my secret so that none may share.

Move quietly back to your workspace and kneel in front of your table. Light your white altar candle and meditate quietly on the Goddess Meretsegar. In your mind, visualise your secret being locked into a small black box. Say a prayer in your own words to the Guardian Angel Masleh and stand in front of your altar. Raise your hands high above your head and say these words:

> In my heart I hold the key
> To the secret none should see.
> Never will it be revealed
> Blessed be the powers that be.
> And it harm none so be it.

Light your black candle and meditate as the candle burns. See in your mind the secret being consumed by the flame. Spend some quiet time in your circle and allow your altar candles to burn through to the end or put them out with a candle snuff. When you are finished working, move quietly to the left of your circle.

Extinguish the east candle and say:
> I thank the element of air for blessing and keeping my secret so that none may share.

Extinguish the south candle and say:
> I thank the element of fire for blessing and keeping my secret so that none may share.

Extinguish the west candle and say:
  I thank the element of water for blessing and keeping my secret so that none may share.

Extinguish the north candle and say:
  I thank the element of earth for blessing and keeping my secret so that none may share.

Close your circle by saying:
  May the four powers give back to the universe any powers and energies that have not been used.
  The work is now done and the circle is closed.
  So mote it be.

Secrets spell 2

10 mls almond oil
Geranium pure essential oil
A bottle for your oil mixture
A small face cloth or some tissues
A small fireproof dish for matches or burning herbs or paper
A black silk or velvet cloth to cover your table with
A single begonia in a black vase
Some black coloured crystals
One white and one black taper candle and holders
A small sharp knife

Prepare a blend of oils using 10 mls of almond oil and add three drops of geranium pure essential oil. Hold the bottle of oil in your hands in the prayer position and rub the bottle vigorously between the palms of your hands and as you do so visualise the oil being empowered with gratitude. When you feel as though the oil has been charged place it on your altar or work surface ready for use along with the other items.

Place four small candles at the east, south, west and north in that order. Sit or kneel comfortably in front of your table. Close your eyes and as you breathe in, picture positive white light energy filling your body. When you are completely relaxed stand up and move quietly to the east quarter of your room.

Light the east candle and say:
   May the element of air bless this space with light, love and air and keep my secret so that none may share.

Light the south candle and say:
   May the element of fire bless this space with light, love and fire and keep my secret so that none may share.

Light the west candle and say:
   May the element of water bless this space with light, love and water and keep my secret so that none may share.

Light the north candle and say:
   May the element of earth bless this space with light, love and earth and keep my secret so that none may share.

Move quietly back to your workspace and kneel in front of your table. Light your white altar candle and meditate quietly on your secret. Take your black spell candle and the small pointed knife and inscribe the number two and the rune symbol Peorth at the top of the candle. Place the candle back in the holder and taking the bottle of empowered oil place some in the palm of your hands. Rub your hands together and visualise that you are charging the energy in the oil and in your hands. Your hands will begin to feel very warm.

Take the spell candle and spread the oil from middle to top and middle to bottom of the candle until the candle is completely covered in oil. Visualise that you are empowering the candle with hidden information. Rub your hands vigorously together with the candle still held between the palms of your hands.

After a few minutes, place your candle back in its holder and light the flame and say these words:

> To the candle burning bright
> I give my secret here tonight.
> None shall listen, none shall see,
> Just the candle, flame and me.
> And it harm none so mote it be.

Allow your altar candle to burn through to the end or put it out with a candle snuff. You may light your candles again but each time you do so, visualise your wish as though it has already begun to happen. When you are finished working, clean your hands on the cloth and move quietly to the left of your room.

Extinguish the east candle and say:
I thank the element of air for blessing and keeping my secret so that none may share.

Extinguish the south candle and say:
I thank the element of fire for blessing and keeping my secret so that none may share.

Extinguish the west candle and say:
I thank the element of water for blessing and keeping my secret so that none may share.

Extinguish the north candle and say:
I thank the element of earth for blessing and keeping my secret so that none may share.

Close your circle by saying:
May the four powers give back to the universe any powers and energies that have not been used.
The work is now done and the circle is closed.
So mote it be.

19

Home

Day of the week: The best day
of the week is Monday
Time of day: The best time of
day is 5am. Also noon, 7pm
or at any time in the evening
when the moon is waxing or
full but not when it is
waning

Moon

Goddess: Heket
Planet: Moon
Guardian Angel: Haniel
Star sign: Cancer or Taurus
Metal: Silver or gold
Colour: Green or gold or
silver

Taurus   Cancer

Rune: Othel
Symbol: Hand=knitted or
hand=sewn items, cakes and
breads
Number: Four
Crystal: Rhodochrosite
Flower: Honeysuckle
Essential oil: Jasmine
Tree: Rowan
Herb: Myrrh

Othel

Home spell 1

Prepare yourself and decorate your work surface or altar space with all your chosen ingredients such as:

A green cloth and some small frog ornaments
Some small kitchen tools
Hand=sewn or hand=knitted items
A piece of rhodochrosite
One green and one white taper candle and holder
A vase of honeysuckle
A bowl of fruit
A sprig of rowan
A piece of rhodochrosite crystal

When you are ready and everything is in place, stand at the edge of your circle. Close your eyes and breathe in, visualising light energy filling your body. Breathe out and breathe away all negative energy. When you are completely relaxed stand up and move quietly to the east quarter of your circle or room.

Light the east candle and say:
    May the element of air bless this space with light, love and air and keep my home safe and happy.

Light the south candle and say:
    May the element of fire bless this space with light, love and fire and keep my home safe and happy.

Light the west candle and say:
    May the element of water bless this space with light, love and water and keep my home safe and happy.

Light the north candle and say:
May the element of earth bless this space with light, love and earth and keep my home safe and happy.

Move quietly back to your workspace and kneel in front of your table. Light your white altar candle and meditate quietly on the Goddess Heket. In your mind, see your home happy, contended and safe and blessed with abundance. Say a prayer in your own words to the Guardian Angel Haniel. Stand in front of your altar, raise your hands high above your head and say these words:

Happy is the home I have,
Contented is the life I live,
Blessed is the joy I share,
Blessed by Heket who doth care.
And it harm none so be it.

Spend some quiet time in your circle and allow your altar candle to burn through to the end but if you must put it out do so with a candle snuff or pinch the wick between dampened fingertips.
When you are finished working move quietly to the left of your circle.

Extinguish the east candle and say:
I thank the element of air for blessing me so that I may have a happy home.

Extinguish the south candle and say:
I thank the element of fire for blessing me so that I may have a happy home.

Extinguish the west candle and say:
I thank the element of water for blessing me so that I may have a happy home.

Extinguish the north candle and say:
I thank the element of earth for blessing me so that I may have a happy home.

Close your circle by saying:
May the four powers give back to the universe any powers and energies that have not been used.
The work is now done and the circle is closed.
So mote it be.

Home spell 2

10 mls almond oil
Myrrh pure essential oil
A bottle for your oil mixture
A green tablecloth
A small face cloth or some tissues
A small fireproof dish for matches or burning herbs or paper.
One white and one green taper candle and holders
One small pointed knife
Some small, favourite household items
A rhodochrosite crystal
A small dish containing some dried basil

Prepare a blend of oils using 10 mls of almond oil and add three drops of myrrh pure essential oil. Hold the bottle of oil in your hands in the prayer position and rub the bottle vigorously between the palms of your hands and as you do so visualise the oil being

238

empowered with gratitude. When you feel as though the oil has been charged place it on your altar or work surface ready for use along with the other items. Place four small candles at the east, south, west and north in that order.

Sit or kneel comfortably in front of your table. Close your eyes and as you breathe in, picture positive white light energy filling your body. When you are completely relaxed stand up and move quietly to the east quarter of your room.

Light the east candle and say:
> May the element of air bless this space with light, love and air and keep my home safe and happy.

Light the south candle and say:
> May the element of fire bless this space with light, love and fire and keep my home safe and happy.

Light the west candle and say:
> May the element of water bless this space with light, love and water and keep my home safe and happy.

Light the north candle and say:
> May the element of earth bless this space with light, love and earth and keep my home safe and happy.

Move quietly back to your workspace and kneel in front of your table. Light your white altar candle and meditate quietly on your home. Take your green spell candle and the small pointed knife and inscribe the number four and the rune symbol Othel at the top of the candle. Place the candle back in the holder and taking the bottle of empowered oil place some in the palm of your hands. Rub your hands together and visualise that you are charging the energy in the oil and in your hands. Your hands will begin to feel very warm.

Take the spell candle and spread the oil from middle to top and middle to bottom of the candle until the candle is completely covered in oil. Visualise that you are empowering your candle with a happy and contented home.

Rub your hands vigorously together with the candle still held between the palms of your hands. After a few minutes, place your candle back in its holder and light the flame and say these words:

> Enter here within my home,
> Witness here the love that's shown.
> Content and happy, safe and warm,
> Safe from any outside harm.
> And it harm none so mote it be.

Allow your altar candle to burn through to the end or put it out with a candle snuff. You may light your candle again but, each time you do so, visualise your wish as though it has already begun to happen. When you are finished working clean your hands on the cloth and move quietly to the left of your room.

Extinguish the east candle and say:
   I thank the element of air for blessing me so that I may have a happy home.

Extinguish the south candle and say:
   I thank the element of fire for blessing me so that I may have a happy home.

Home

Extinguish the west candle and say:

I thank the element of water for blessing me so that I may have a happy home.

Extinguish the north candle and say:

I thank the element of earth for blessing me so that I may have a happy home.

Close your circle by saying:

May the four powers give back to the universe any powers and energies that have not been used.

The work is now done and the circle is closed.

So mote it be.

20

Fertility

Day of the week: The best day
of the week is Friday
Time of day: The best time of
day is 5am. Also noon, 7pm
or at any time in the evening
when the moon is waxing or
full but not when it is
waning

Mars   Venus

Goddess: Vesta
Planet: Mars or Venus
Guardian Angel: Raziel
Star sign: Scorpio
Metal: Iron
Colour: Red
Rune: Beork, Wynn (also
known as Wunjo)
Symbol: Eggs
Number: One and three
Crystal: Moonstone and
carnelian
Flower: Hyacinth
Essential oil: Frankincense
Herb: Mint
Tree: Birch

Scorpio

Beork   Wynn

Fertility spell

Prepare yourself and decorate your work surface or altar space with all your chosen ingredients such as:

A red coloured cloth
A bowl of wooden or marble eggs
One red and one white taper candle and holders
A vase of hyacinth flowers
A bowl of apples
Some moonstone or carnelian crystals
A piece of iron

When you are ready and everything is in place, stand at the edge of your circle. Close your eyes and breathe in, visualising light energy filling your body. Breathe out and breathe away all negative energy. When you are completely relaxed, stand up and move quietly to the east quarter of your circle or room.

Light the east candle and say:
    May the element of air bless this space with light, love and air and make me fertile

Light the south candle and say:
    May the element of fire bless this space with light, love and fire and make me fertile

Light the west candle and say:
    May the element of water bless this space with light, love and water and make me fertile.

Fertility

Light the north candle and say:
   May the element of earth bless this space with light, love and
   earth and make me fertile.

Move quietly back to your workspace and kneel in front of
your table. Light your white altar candle and meditate quietly
on the Goddess Vesta. In your mind see yourself holding in
your arms the child that you have just given birth to and say a
prayer in your own words to the Guardian Angel Raziel. Stand
in front of your altar, raise your hands high above your head
and say these words:

> Vesta, Vesta hear my plea,
> Let my own child come to me,
> Let my child of good health be.
> Vesta, Vesta hear my plea.
> And it harm none so be it.

Allow your candles to burn through to the end or put them
out with a candle snuff. When you are finished working, move
quietly to the left of your circle.

Extinguish the east candle and say:
   I thank the element of air for blessing me with fertility.

Extinguish the south candle and say:
   I thank the element of fire for blessing me with fertility.

Extinguish the west candle and say:
   I thank the element of water for blessing me with fertility.

Extinguish the north candle and say:

I thank the element of earth for blessing me with fertility.

Close your circle by saying:

May the four powers give back to the universe any powers and
energies that have not been used.
The work is now done and the circle is closed.
So mote it be.

Fertility spell 2

10 mls almond oil
Frankincense pure essential oil
A bottle for your oil mixture
A small face cloth or some tissues
A small fireproof dish for matches or burning herbs or paper
A red tablecloth
Some pieces of moonstone
A sprig of birch
One white and one red taper candle and holders
One small pointed knife
A small dish to which you have added a pinch of dried basil

Prepare a blend of oils using 10 mls of almond oil and add
three drops of frankincense pure essential oil. Hold the bottle
of oil in your hands in the prayer position and rub the bottle
vigorously between the palms of your hands and as you do so
visualise the oil being empowered with gratitude.

When you feel as though the oil has been charged place it on
your altar or work surface ready for use along with the other
items.

Place four small candles at the east, south, west and north

in that order. Sit or kneel comfortably in front of your table. Close your eyes and as you breathe in, picture positive white light energy filling your body. When you are completely relaxed stand up and move quietly to the east quarter of your room.

Light the east candle and say:
> May the element of air bless this space with light, love and air and make me fertile.

Light the south candle and say:
> May the element of fire bless this space with light, love and fire and make me fertile.

Light the west candle and say:
> May the element of water bless this space with light, love and water and make me fertile.

Light the north candle and say:
> May the element of earth bless this space with light, love and earth and make me fertile.

Move quietly back to your workspace and kneel in front of your table. Light your white altar candle and meditate quietly on Goddess Vesta. Take your red spell candle and the small pointed knife and inscribe the numbers one and three and the rune symbols Beork and Wynn at the top of the candle. Place the candle back in the holder and taking the bottle of empowered oil place some in the palm of your hands. Rub your hands together and visualise that you are charging the energy in the oil and in your hands. Your hands will begin to feel very warm. Take the spell candle and spread the oil from middle to top and middle to bottom of the candle until the candle is completely covered in oil. Visualise that you are empowering the candle with fertility. Rub your hands vigorously together with the candle still held between the palms of your hands. After a few minutes, place your candle back in its holder and light the flame and say these words:

> Ripe as seeds grow blessed with life
> Fertile be my love, my life,
> Sacred be this spell this day,
> Fertility to come my way.
> And it harm none so mote it be.

Allow your candle to burn for as long as possible but, if you must put it out, do not blow it out otherwise you will reverse or negate your spell. You can use a candle snuff or pinch the flame between your thumb and finger. You may light your candle again but each time you do so visualise your wish as though it has already begun to happen. When you are finished working, clean your hands on the cloth and move quietly to the left of your room.

Extinguish the east candle and say:
    I thank the element of air for blessing me with fertility.

Extinguish the south candle and say:
    I thank the element of fire for blessing me with fertility.

Extinguish the west candle and say:
    I thank the element of water for blessing me so that I may have happy home.

Extinguish the north candle and say:
I thank the element of earth for blessing me so that I may have happy home.

Close your circle by saying:
May the four powers give back to the universe any powers and energies that have not been used.
The work is now done and the circle is closed.
So mote it be.

21

Friendship

Day of the week: The best day
   of the week is Monday
Time of day: The best time of
   day is 5am. Also noon, 7pm
   or at any time in the evening
   when the moon is waxing or
   full but not when it is
   waning

Moon

Goddess: Luna
Planet: Moon
Guardian Angel: Gabriel
Star Sign: Cancer
Metal: Silver
Colour: White, silver, orange
   and yellow
Rune: Geofu (also known as
   Gefu), Eolh
Symbol: Pairs of things
Number: Any even number
   (2, 4, 6, 8 ...)
Crystal: Moonstone
Flower: Freesia
Essential oil: Patchouli
Tree: Silver birch
Herb: Fennel

Cancer

Geofu   Eohl

Friendship

Friendship spell 1
Prepare yourself and decorate your work surface or altar space with all your chosen ingredients such as:

A cloth coloured white, silver orange or yellow
Some pieces of silver or silver friendship rings or
    tokens
Any suitable items that come in pairs
A piece of moonstone
A vase of freesia
A sprig of birch

When you are ready and everything is in place, stand at the edge of your circle. Close your eyes and breathe in, visualising light energy filling your body. Breathe out and breathe away all negative energy. When you are completely relaxed stand up and move quietly to the east quarter of your circle or room.

Light the east candle and say:
  May the element of air bless this space with light, love and air and grant me true friendship.

Light the south candle and say:
  May the element of fire bless this space with light, love and fire and grant me true friendship.

Light the west candle and say:
  May the element of water bless this space with light, love and water and grant me true friendship.

Friendship

Light the north candle and say:
   May the element of earth bless this space with light, love and earth and grant me true friendship.

Move quietly back to your workspace and kneel in front of your table. Light your white altar candle and meditate quietly on the Goddess Luna. In your mind see yourself among true friends, laughing, happy and content, well liked by all who know you.

   Say a prayer in your own words to your Guardian Angel and, standing in front of your altar, raise your hands high above your head and say these words:

> Friends may come and friends may go
> But true friends stay forever.
> Merry we meet and merry we part,
> Happy when we're together.
> And it harm none so mote it be.

Spend some quiet time in your circle and allow your candles to burn through to the end or put them out with a candle snuff. When you are finished working move quietly to the left of your circle.

Extinguish the east candle and say:
   I thank the element of air for blessing me with loyal, loving friends.

Extinguish the south candle and say:
   I thank the element of fire for blessing me with loyal, loving friends.

Friendship

Extinguish the west candle and say:
I thank the element of water for blessing me with loyal, loving friends.

Extinguish the north candle and say:
I thank the element of earth for blessing me with loyal, loving friends.

Close your circle by saying:
May the four powers give back to the universe any powers and energies that have not been used.
The work is now done and the circle is closed.
So mote it be.

Friendship spell 2

10 mls almond oil
Patchouli pure essential oil
A bottle for your oil mixture
A white tablecloth
A small face cloth or some tissues
A small fireproof dish for matches or burning herbs or paper
One white and one pink taper candle and holders
One small pointed knife
A sprig of silver birch
A small dish of dried fennel
A piece of moonstone

Prepare a blend of oils using 10 mls of almond oil and add three drops of patchouli pure essential oil. Hold the bottle of

oil in your hands in the prayer position and rub the bottle vigorously between the palms of your hands and as you do so visualise the oil being empowered with friendship. When you feel as though the oil has been charged place it on your altar or work surface ready for use along with the other items.

Place four small candles at the east, south, west and north in that order. Sit or kneel comfortably in front of your table. Close your eyes and as you breathe in, picture positive white light energy filling your body. When you are completely relaxed stand up and move quietly to the east quarter of your room.

Light the east candle and say:
 May the element of air bless this space with light, love and air, and loyal friends.

Light the south candle and say:
 May the element of fire bless this space with light, love and fire, and loyal friends.

Light the west candle and say:
 May the element of water bless this space with light, love and water, and loyal friends.

Light the north candle and say:
 May the element of earth bless this space with light, love and earth, and loyal friends.

Move quietly back to your workspace and kneel in front of your table. Light your white altar candle and meditate quietly on the Goddess Luna. Take your pink spell candle and the small pointed knife and inscribe even numbers and the rune symbols Geofu and Eolh at the top of the candle. Place the candle back in the holder and taking the bottle of empowered oil place some in the palms of your hands. Rub your hands together and visualise that you are charging the energy in the oil and in your hands. Your hands will begin to feel very warm. Take the spell candle and spread the oil from middle to top and middle to bottom of the candle until the candle is completely covered in oil. Visualise that you are empowering your candle with friendship. Rub your hands vigorously together with the candle still held between the palms of your hands.

After a few minutes, place your candle back in its holder and light the flame and say these words:

> Luna, Goddess of the moon,
> Let my friends come to me soon.
> May they be loyal and be kind,
> And may they be of like mind.
> And it harm none so mote it be.

Allow your altar candle to burn through to the end or put it out with a candle snuff. You may light your candle again but each time you do so visualise your wish as though it has already begun to happen. When you are finished working clean your hands on the cloth and move quietly to the left of your room.

Extinguish the east candle and say:
I thank the element of air for blessing me with loyal and loving friends.

Extinguish the south candle and say:
I thank the element of fire for blessing me with loyal and loving friends.

Friendship

Extinguish the west candle and say:

I thank the element of water for blessing me with loyal and loving friends.

Extinguish the north candle and say:

I thank the element of earth for blessing me with loyal and loving friends.

Close your circle by saying:

May the four powers give back to the universe any powers and energies that have not been used.

The work is now done and the circle is closed.

So mote it be.

22

Passion

Day of the week: The best day of the week is Tuesday

Time of Day: The best time of day is 5am. Also noon, 7pm or at any time in the evening when the moon is waxing or full but not when it is waning

Goddess: Lillith

Planet: Venus

Guardian Angel: Gamelie

Star Sign: Scorpio, Taurus and Libra

Metal: Copper and brass

Colour: Red, orange and green

Rune: Ing (also known as Ingux)

Symbol: Fire

Number: One

Crystal: Emerald and sapphire

Flower: Poppy and tiger lily

Essential oil: Patchouli

Tree: Pine

Herb: Fennel

Venus

Scorpio

Taurus

Libra

Ing

Passion spell 1

Prepare yourself and decorate your work surface or altar space with all your chosen ingredients such as:

A red cloth
A piece of emerald, sapphire or ruby jewellery
Small items made of copper or brass
One white and one red taper candle and holders
A vase of poppies or tiger lilies
A sprig of pine

When you are ready and everything is in place, stand at the edge of your circle. Close your eyes and breathe in, visualising light energy filling your body. Breathe out and breathe away all negative energy. When you are completely relaxed stand up and move quietly to the east quarter of your circle or room.

Light the east candle and say:
  May the element of air bless this space with light, love and air and bring passion into my life.

Light the south candle and say:
  May the element of fire bless this space with light, love and fire and bring passion into my life.

Light the west candle and say:
  May the element of water bless this space with light, love and water and bring passion into my life.

Passion

Light the north candle and say:
   May the element of earth bless this space with light, love and earth and bring passion into my life.

Move quietly back to your workspace and kneel in front of your table. Light your white altar candle and meditate quietly on the Goddess Lilith.

Say a prayer in your own words to the Guardian Angel Gamelie and, standing in front of your altar, raise your hands high above your head and say these words:

>Passion burns within my loins —
>My heart, my soul, a-fire.
>Lillith bring to me this night
>The passion I desire.
>And it harm none so be it.

Spend some quiet time in your circle and allow your altar candles to burn through to the end or put them out with a candle snuff. When you are finished working, move quietly to the left of your circle.

Extinguish the east candle and say:
   I thank the element of air for blessing me with passion.

Extinguish the south candle and say:
   I thank the element of fire for blessing me with passion.

Extinguish the west candle and say:
   I thank the element of water for blessing me with passion.

Extinguish the north candle and say:
> I thank the element of earth for blessing me with passion.

Close your circle by saying:
> May the four powers give back to the universe any powers and energies that have not been used.
> The work is now done and the circle is closed.
> So mote it be.

Passion spell 2

10 mls almond oil
Patchouli pure essential oil
A bottle for your oil mixture
A red tablecloth
A small face cloth or some tissues
A small fireproof dish for matches or burning herbs or paper
One white and one red taper candle and holders
One small pointed knife
A deep red crystal or some ruby emerald or sapphire jewellery
A vase of poppies
A small dish containing some hazelnuts

Prepare a blend of oils using 10 mls of almond oil and add three drops of patchouli pure essential oil. Hold the bottle of oil in your hands in the prayer position and rub the bottle vigorously between the palms of your hands and as you do so visualise the oil being empowered with passion. When you feel as though the oil has been charged, place it on your altar or work surface ready for use along with the other items.

Passion

Place four small candles at the east, south, west and north in that order. Sit or kneel comfortably in front of your table. Close your eyes and as you breathe in, picture positive white light energy filling your body. When you are completely relaxed stand up and move quietly to the east quarter of your room.

Light the east candle and say:
  May the element of air bless this space with light, love and air and bring passion into my life.

Light the south candle and say:
  May the element of fire bless this space with light, love and fire and bring passion into my life.

Light the west candle and say:
  May the element of water bless this space with light, love and water and bring passion into my life.

Light the north candle and say:
  May the element of earth bless this space with light, love and earth and bring passion into my life.

Move quietly back to your workspace and kneel in front of your table. Light your white altar candle and meditate quietly on the Goddess Lillith. Take your red spell candle and the small pointed knife and inscribe the number one and the rune symbol Ing at the top of the candle. Place the candle back in the holder and, taking the bottle of empowered oil, place some in the palms of your hands. Rub your hands together and visualise that you are charging the energy in the oil and in your hands. Your hands will begin to feel very warm.

Passion

Take the spell candle and spread the oil from middle to top and middle to bottom of the candle until the candle is completely covered in oil. Visualise that you are empowering your candle with passion. Rub your hands vigorously together with the candle still held between the palms of your hands. After a few minutes, place your candle back in its holder and light the flame and say these words:

> Strong in me doth passion burn
> Bliss is what my soul doth yearn
> Candle take this wish of mine
> Blessed above, from the Divine.
> And it harm none so mote it be.

Allow your altar candle to burn through to the end or put it out with a candle snuff. You may light your candle again but each time you do so visualise your wish as though it has already begun to happen. When you are finished working clean your hands on the cloth and move quietly to the left of your room.

Extinguish the east candle and say:
    I thank the element of air for blessing me with passion.

Extinguish the south candle and say:
    I thank the element of fire for blessing me with passion.

Extinguish the west candle and say:
    I thank the element of water for blessing me with passion.

Extinguish the north candle and say:
    I thank the element of earth for blessing me with passion.

Passion

Close your circle by saying:

May the four powers give back to the universe any powers and energies that have not been used.

The work is now done and the circle is closed.

So mote it be.

23

Answers

Day of the week: The best day
of the week is Wednesday

Time of day: The best time of
day is 5am. Also noon, 7pm
or at any time in the evening
when the moon is waxing or
full but not when it is
waning

Goddess: Themis

Planet: Mercury

Star sign: Gemini or Virgo

Metal: Quicksilver

Colour: Orange, yellow or
green

Rune: Ansur (also known as
Ansuz)

Symbol: Books or calculators

Number: Nine

Crystal: Opal, aquamarine,
hematite or jet

Flower: Lavender

Herb: Angelica

Essential oil: Marjoram

Tree: Oak

Mercury

Gemini   Virgo

Ansur

Answers spell 1

Prepare yourself and decorate your work surface or altar space with all your chosen ingredients such as:

A yellow or green cloth
A vase of lavender
A dictionary
A thesaurus
A calculator
A piece of opal or aquamarine
One yellow and one white taper candle and holder

When you are ready and everything is in place, stand at the edge of your circle. Close your eyes and breathe in, visualising light energy filling your body. Breathe out and breathe away all negative energy. When you are completely relaxed, stand up and move quietly to the east quarter of your circle or room.

Light the east candle and say:
  May the element of air bless this space with light, love and air and help me find the answers to my question.

Light the south candle and say:
  May the element of fire bless this space with light, love and fire and help me find the answers to my question.

Light the west candle and say:
  May the element of water bless this space with light, love and water and help me find the answers to my question.

Answers

Light the north candle and say:
  May the element of earth bless this space with light, love and
  earth and help me find the answers to my question.

Move quietly back to your workspace and kneel in front of
your table. Light your white altar candle and meditate quietly
on the Goddess Themis. In your mind see your answers coming
to you. Say a prayer in your own words your Guardian Angel
and ask for guidance.
  Stand in front of your altar, raise your hands high above your
head and say these words:

> Answers come to me in sleep
> So they can be mine to keep.
> They give me guidance, clear and true
> So that I may know what's sure.
> And it harm none so be it.

Spend some quiet time in your circle and allow your altar
candles to burn through to the end or put them out with a
candle snuff. When you are finished working move quietly to
the left of your circle.

Extinguish the east candle and say:
  I thank the element of air for blessing me with the answers that
  make things clear.

Extinguish the south candle and say:
  I thank the element of fire for blessing me with the answers that
  make things clear.

Extinguish the west candle and say:

> I thank the element of water for blessing me with the answers that
> make things clear.

Extinguish the north candle and say:

> I thank the element of earth for blessing me with the answers that
> make things clear.

Close your circle by saying:

> May the four powers give back to the universe any powers and
> energies that have not been used.
> The work is now done and the circle is closed.
> So mote it be.

Answers spell 2

10mls almond oil
Marjoram pure essential oil
A bottle for your oil mixture
A orange yellow or green tablecloth
A small face cloth or some tissues and a small fireproof dish for
   matches or burning herbs or paper.
One white and one green taper candle and holders
One small pointed knife
A piece of hematite or jet
A sprig of oak
A small dish containing some angelica

Prepare a blend of oils using 10 mls of almond oil and add
three drops of marjoram pure essential oil. Hold the bottle of
oil in your hands in the prayer position and rub the bottle

vigorously between the palms of your hands and as you do so visualise the oil being empowered with the answers to your questions. When you feel as though the oil has been charged place it on your altar or work surface ready for use along with the other items.

Place four small candles at the east, south, west and north in that order. Sit or kneel comfortably in front of your table. Close your eyes and as you breathe in, picture positive white light energy filling your body. When you are completely relaxed stand up and move quietly to the east quarter of your room.

Light the east candle and say:
   May the element of air bless this space with light, love and air and help me find the answers to my question.

Light the south candle and say:
   May the element of fire bless this space with light, love and fire and help me find the answers to my question.

Light the west candle and say:
   May the element of water bless this space with light, love and Water and help me find the answers to my question.

Light the north candle and say:
   May the element of earth bless this space with light, love and earth and help me find the answers to my question.

Move quietly back to your workspace and kneel in front of your table. Light your white altar candle and meditate quietly on the problem that perplexes you. Take your green spell candle and the small pointed knife and inscribe the number nine and the rune symbol Ansur at the top of the candle. Place the candle back in the holder and, taking the bottle of empowered oil, place some in the palm of your hands. Rub your hands together and visualise that you are charging the energy in the oil and in your hands. Your hands will begin to feel very warm. Take the spell candle and spread the oil from middle to top and middle to bottom of the candle until the candle is completely covered in oil. Visualise that you are empowering your candle with the answers that you are looking for. Rub your hands vigorously together with the candle still held between the palms of your hands.

After a few minutes, place your candle back in its holder and light the flame and say these words:

> Answers, may they come to me
> So that I may clearly see
> What is hidden from me now
> Will be shown to me somehow.
> And it harm none so mote it be.

Allow your altar candle to burn through to the end or put it out with a candle snuff. You may light your candle again but, each time you do so, visualise your wish as though it has already begun to happen. When you are finished working, clean your hands on the cloth and move quietly to the left of your room.

Extinguish the east candle and say:
   I thank the element of air for granting me the answers I require.

Extinguish the south candle and say:
   I thank the element of fire for granting me the answers I require.

Answers

Extinguish the west candle and say:

I thank the element of water for granting me the answers I require.

Extinguish the north candle and say:

I thank the element of earth for granting me the answers I require.

Close your circle by saying:

May the four powers give back to the universe any powers and energies that have not been used.

The work is now done and the circle is closed.

So mote it be.

24

Travel

Day of the week: The best day
    of the week is Tuesday
Time of day: The best time of
    day is 5am. Also noon, 7pm
    or at any time in the evening
    when the moon is waxing or
    full but not when it is
    waning
Goddess: Dag
Planet: Uranus
Guardian Angel: Michael
Star sign: Sagittarius
Metal: Radium
Colour: Pale blue
Rune: Rad
Symbol: Passports, tickets,
    maps, wheels or spheres
Number: 19
Crystal: Turquoise or chrysolite
Flower: Yellow daisy
Essential oil: Basil
Herb: Caraway
Tree: Oak

Uranus

Sagittarius

Rad

Travel spell 1

Prepare yourself and decorate your work surface or altar space with all your chosen ingredients such as:

A blue cloth and a vase of yellow daisies
A piece of chrysolite
One blue and one white taper candle and holders
A sprig of oak
Some maps, a passport or tickets

When you are ready and everything is in place, stand at the edge of your circle. Close your eyes and breathe in, visualising light energy filling your body. Breathe out and breathe away all negative energy. When you are completely relaxed stand up and move quietly to the east quarter of your circle or room.

Light the east candle and say:
   May the element of air bless this space with light, love and air and fulfil my desire to travel in safety to . . .

Light the south candle and say:
   May the element of fire bless this space with light, love and fire and fulfil my desire to travel in safety to . . .

Light the west candle and say:
   May the element of water bless this space with light, love and water and fulfil my desire to travel in safety to . . .

Light the north candle and say:
   May the element of earth bless this space with light, love and earth and fulfil my desire to travel in safety to . . .

Travel

Move quietly back to your workspace and kneel in front of your table. Light your white altar candle and meditate quietly on the Goddess Dag. In your mind see your journey being planned, undertaken and visualise that you are arriving at your destination safely. Say a prayer in your own words to the Guardian Angel Michael. Stand in front of your altar, raise your hands high above your head and say these words:

> A journey to (place) I plan to make
> Precious things with me I take
> Safe and sure my trip will be
> Dag I thank you, blessed be
> And it harm none so be it.

Spend some quiet time in your circle and allow your altar candles to burn through to the end or put them out with a candle snuff. When you are finished working move quietly to the left of your circle.

Extinguish the east candle and say:
  I thank the element of air for blessing me with a safe journey.

Extinguish the south candle and say:
  I thank the element of fire for blessing me with a safe journey.

Extinguish the west candle and say:
  I thank the element of water for blessing me with a safe journey.

Extinguish the north candle and say:
  I thank the element of earth for blessing me with a safe journey.

Close your circle by saying:
> May the four powers give back to the universe any powers and
> energies that have not been used.
> The work is now done and the circle is closed.
> So mote it be.

Travel spell 2

10 mls almond oil
Basil pure essential oil
A bottle or your oil mixture
A pale blue tablecloth
Passports, tickets, maps, wheels or spheres
A small face cloth or some tissues
A small fireproof dish for matches or burning herbs or paper.
One white and one pale blue taper candle and holders
One small pointed knife
A piece of turquoise or chrysolite
A vase or posy of yellow daisies
A small dish containing some dried caraway

Prepare a blend of oils using 10 mls of almond oil and add
three drops of basil pure essential oil. Hold the bottle of oil in
your hands in the prayer position and rub the bottle vigorously
between the palms of your hands and as you do so visualise the
oil being empowered with safe travel. When you feel as though
the oil has been charged, place it on your altar or work surface
ready for use along with the other items.

Place four small candles at the east, south, west and north
in that order. Sit or kneel comfortably in front of your table.
Close your eyes and as you breathe in, picture positive white
light energy filling your body. When you are completely

relaxed, stand up and move quietly to the east quarter of your room.

Light the east candle and say:
> May the element of air bless this space with light, love and air and fulfil my desire to travel in safety to . . .

Light the south candle and say:
> May the element of fire bless this space with light, love and fire and fulfil my desire to travel in safety to . . .

Light the west candle and say:
> May the element of water bless this space with light, love and water and fulfil my desire to travel in safety to . . .

Light the north candle and say:
> May the element of earth bless this space with light, love and earth and fulfil my desire to travel in safety to . . .

Move quietly back to your workspace and kneel in front of your table. Light your white altar candle and meditate quietly on the Goddess Dag. Take your pale blue spell candle and the small pointed knife and inscribe the number 19 and the rune symbol Rad at the top of the candle.

Place the candle back in the holder and taking the bottle of empowered oil place some in the palm, of your hands. Rub your hands together and visualise that you are charging the energy in the oil and in your hands. Your hands will begin to feel very warm.

Take the spell candle and spread the oil from middle to top and middle to bottom of the candle until the candle is completely covered in oil. Visualise that you are empowering your candle with a safe journey. Rub your hands vigorously together with the candle still held between the palms of your hands.

After a few minutes, place your candle back in its holder and light the flame and say these words:

> Keep me safe and free from harm
> On this journey I do plan.
> Day or night I will get there,
> Dag, my plan with you I share.
> And it harm none so be it.

Allow your altar candle to burn through to the end or put it out with a candle snuff. You may light your candle again but each time you do so visualise your wish as though it has already begun to happen. When you are finished working, clean your hands on the cloth and move quietly to the left of your room.

Extinguish the east candle and say:
I thank the element of air for blessing me with a safe journey.

Extinguish the south candle and say:
I thank the element of fire for blessing me with a safe journey.

Extinguish the west candle and say:
I thank the element of water for blessing me with a safe journey.

Extinguish the north candle and say:
I thank the element of earth for blessing me with a safe journey.

Close your circle by saying:
May the four powers give back to the universe any powers and
energies that have not been used.
The work is now done and the circle is closed.
So mote it be.

Runes

THE RUNES are an ancient Nordic form of script used before the emergence of written language, taking the form of straight lines which were easily cut into wood or stone. It is not known exactly how old they are but they may originate as early as the Bronze Age.

'Runa' means 'mystery' or 'secret proceedings' and runes are a marvellous aid to magic because the symbols are easy to draw or inscribe and each rune has its own significance.

Feoh
Sometimes called: Fehu
Meaning: Cattle
Its significance in magick: For wealth, property, power and status.

Ur
Sometimes called: Uruz
Meaning: Aurochs, ox=like
beasts
Its significance in magick:
Overcoming challenges,
passing tests and anything
that requires effort on your
part.

Thorn
Sometimes called: Thurizas
Meaning: Thorn
Its significance in magick:
Could be used to help rid
yourself of a problem.

Ansur

Sometimes called: Ansuz
Meaning: A god
Its significance in magick: For
  communication.

Rad

Sometimes called: Rado and
  Raidho
Meaning: Riding
Its significance in magick: For
  travel plans or anything that
  is connected with movement.

Ken

Sometimes called: Kano, or
    Kenaz
Meaning: Torch
Its significance in magick: For
    openings and invitations.

Geofu

Sometimes called: Gefu and
    Gebo
Meaning: Gift
Its significance in magick: For
    partnerships and unions,
    marriages or engagements.

Wynn

Sometimes called: Wunjo
Meaning: Joy
Its significance in magick: For
joy, success and winning.

Hagall

Sometimes called: The Aett or
 Set of Hagalaz or Heimdall,
 Watcher of the Gods
Meaning: Hail
Its significance in magick: For
 projects or situations that
 demand sudden, unexpected
 changes.

Nied

Sometimes called: Naudhiz or
    Nauthiz
Meaning: Need
 Its significance in magick: To
    place restrictions on problem
    areas.

Is

Sometimes called: Isa
Meaning: Ice
Its significance in magick: For
    where caution is required and
    where you may be tempted to
    act in haste.

Yr

Sometimes known as: Eiwaz
Meaning: Yew
Its significance in magick: For
  projects that demand
  continuous effort.

Peorth

Sometimes called: Perth or
  Perthro
Meaning: Lot=cup
Its significance in magick: For
  secrets and hidden
  information.

Eolh
Sometimes called: Elhaz or
  Algiz
Meaning: Elk=Sedge
Its significance in magick: For
  friendship and protection.

Sigel
Sometimes called: Sowilo
Meaning: Sun
Its significance in magick: For
  victory.

Tir
Sometimes called: The Aett of
    Tiwaz, Tiwaz
Meaning: Star
Its significance in magick: For
    winning where competition is
    fierce.

Beork
Sometimes called: Berkano or
    Berkana
Meaning: Birch
Its significance in magick: For
    rebirth, new beginnings and
    fertility.

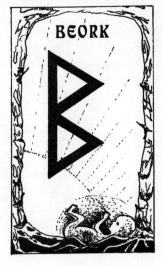

Eoh
Sometimes called: Ehwaz
Meaning: Horse
Its significance in magick: For
  stability and property.

Mann
Sometimes called: Manaz
Meaning: Man
Its significance in magick: For a
  helping hand or a true,
  sharing friendship.

Lagu
Sometimes called: Laguz
Meaning: Water
Its significance in magick: For
    water=related topics and the
    feminine element.

Ing
Sometimes called Inguz or
    Ingwaz
Meaning: The God Ing, God
    of the Hearth and the
    counterpart of Nerthus the
    Earth Mother
Its significance in magick: For
    fertility and bliss.

Daeg

Sometimes called: Dagaz
Meaning: Day
Its significance in magick: For
    hope and promise.

Othel

Sometimes called: Othillo or
    Othala
Meaning: Homestead
Its significance in magick: For the
    home, family and integrity.

Jara

Sometimes called: Gera

Meaning: Harvest

Its significance in magick: You will reap what you sow. Efforts made will be justly rewarded. The more effort put in, the greater the reward.

Wyrd

More difficult to represent on a candle is the Wyrd rune because it is blank and it stands for the inevitable. To use this rune it is important to be really focused, and to illustrate it, simply draw a square with the corners rounded off and visualise the inevitable.

Numerology

SOME people will say that they are typical of their astrological star sign whilst others will say that they are nothing like theirs. Why is that so? Did you know that the numbers in your date of birth play a very large part in forming your character? In fact these numbers will motivate and mould you, and their influence will be with you for the rest of your life.

Numbers are important because they have their own significance and power. Numerologists believe that the numbers one to nine have specific characteristics.

Numerology is the name given to the ancient method of studying numbers that has been in use for thousands of years. It gives insight into people's personalities and their motivation in life. It is an ancient practice that is used to analyse people's characters.

The most popular form of numerology in use today is based on the work of Pythagoras, the famous Greek mathematician and philosopher who lived during the sixth century BC.

Pythagoras believed that numbers were the first of all things in nature. It was his belief that numbers were the basis of everything, in the natural, spiritual and scientific world. He believed that everything could be reduced to mathematical terms and that everything had a numerical value. Pythagoras, who believed that numbers created order and beauty, founded a school for students to follow his philosophy, and this was known as the Italic or Pythagorean school.

As an avid numerologist I was amazed to discover recently that the age difference between myself and my husband Martin is seven years, seven months and seven days. Seven, which is a mystical number, is also my lucky number. In fact, the numbers in my name also add up to seven.

To find your birth number

Your birthday holds the key to the most significant number in your life.

To find it, you first need to write out your full date of birth in its numerical form.

For example:

21/04/1972

Add together the numbers in each section of your birth date:

$2 + 1 + 0 + 4 + 1 + 9 + 7 + 2 = 26$

Add these two numbers together to reduce the number to a single numeral within the range one to nine:

$2 + 6 = 8$

The birth number for this person is eight.

To find your name number

Name numbers are not tied to you in the way that birth numbers are. It is possible to change your name number. It is not possible to change your birth number.

Your name is a personal symbol. It has been chosen for you and you will react to it in your own individual way. The name that you choose to work with for the purposes of numerology is entirely up to you. It might include your middle name and your last name, or like me, you might just be known to most people by your first name.

The letters of the alphabet correspond to the numbers one to nine in the following way:

Name number

1	2	3	4	5	6	7	8	9
A	B	C	D	E	F	G	H	I
J	K	L	M	N	O	P	Q	R
S	T	U	V	W	X	Y	Z	

So the name number for 'Soraya' would be calculated in the following way:

S O R A Y A
$1 + 6 + 9 + 1 + 7 + 1 = 25$
$2 + 5 = 7$

My name number is seven.

Key words, which describe the numerical influences

One
Leadership, popularity, decisiveness, construction.

Two
Diplomacy, tactfulness, secrets, unions and partnerships.

Three
Caring, compassionate, tender, friends and celebration.

Four
Dependable, ambitious, property, stability and security.

Five
Keys, opportunities, religion, engineering and answers.

Six
Relationships, choices, loving, loyal.

Seven
Wisdom, control, transport,

Eight
Stubbornness, strength, persistence.

Nine
Completion, results, reunions, pregnancy.

Using Herbs and
Essential Oils

I F YOU plan to work with herbs for healing purposes begin
to prepare them on the new moon. Always use pure essential
oils and not blends unless you have blended them yourself.
Here are some helpful definitions, instructions and recipes.

Infusions

This process draws the properties you want out of the herb for
healing. An infusion is rather like a strong tea. The normal
mixture is 1 pint of water to half an ounce of herb. It takes
experience to learn how long each herb needs to steep, some
take longer than others. The average length of time is half an
hour but with practice you'll learn which take longer and which
take less time.

Decoctions

This is much the same as an infusion except you are working
with thick pieces of root or bark, which can't be ground up.

When you are working with several herbs, begin with the
toughest then work down. Start with cold water and, making
sure that no steam escapes or the vital oils will be lost, boil for
30 minutes to an hour then allow the blend to steep for the
same time.

Poultice

Pour boiling water over the herbs using just enough to dampen
them or evenly cover the plants. When they are all evenly wet,

remove them with a strainer and place between two pieces of fine cotton. Apply the poultice with the herbs inside to the affected area.

Ointments and salves

Heat some petroleum jelly or vegetable fat until it is quite warm and add the ground herbs to it. Strain and put into jars

Washes

Theses should be made in the same way as teas and when they are ready they can be applied externally.

Tinctures

These are used when long-term storage is required and vodka is perfect although I use brandy and malt whisky for chest infections and coughs.

1—4 ounces of the herb
8 ounces of vodka, brandy or whisky
4 ounces of water

Seal the jar and keep it safely out of the light for two weeks. Every day for the two weeks shake the jar lightly to blend the ingredients. At the end of the two-week period, strain the blend and store in a dark jar in the refrigerator.

There are many minor ailments that can be eased by the use of herbs and plants that grow in the garden but the first thing to do is to buy or borrow from your local library some reference books which show plant illustrations as well as text. There is nothing worse than not being able to identify a plant that you want to use as a spell or remedy. Some plants can be very dangerous.

Marigold syrup

Marigold is one of my favourites, however, it must be the old fashioned *Calendula officinalis* and not the African or any other variety. It is antiseptic, anti-fungal, antidepressant, anti-inflammatory and it also strengthens the immune system. For women, calendula is especially helpful during the menstrual cycle or the menopause and, as if that was not enough, it can be made into a cream and applied to cuts and grazes to aid the healing process. Aemilius Macer in the 13th century, said that gazing at the flowers strengthened the eyesight:

> 'The golden flower is good to be seen,
> it makes the sight bright and clean'.

My granddaughter Ashi calls the syrup I make from it 'Granny's Magick Syrup' and I use marigold petals in soups, salads and rice dishes as well as keeping a jar of the syrup in the fridge for any visitors who come and complain of a sore throat or a cold.

To make marigold syrup:
Marigold petals, enough to fill a two=pint pan
Boiling water
Brown or white sugar
Pure essential oil of calendula or pure essential oil of lavender

Fill a two-pint pan with marigold petals and add boiling water to reach almost to the top of the pan. Reduce the heat and allow the mixture to simmer until the volume has reduced by about two inches. Remove from the heat and allow to cool. When the mixture has cooled, strain the liquid through muslin cloth until the juices are extracted.

Using a cup or mug, measure the remaining marigold liquid. Put the liquid back into the pan and for each cup of liquid add

Marigold syrup

the equivalent amount of brown or white sugar. Bring to the boil and as before, reduce the heat and allow to simmer until the mixture has reduced by about two inches. Remove the mixture from the heat and add two drops of pure essential oil of calendula. I have used lavender before and it is also really lovely. When the mixture is cool enough put into jars and store in the fridge.

For depression
A teaspoonful of marigold syrup when you are feeling down will lift your spirits but, if you really have the blues, take it three to four times a day or make a tea with the petals.

Sore throat remedy
If you have a sore throat take one teaspoonful three times a day. Hold it in your mouth for a moment and let it slowly trickle down your throat.

Fever
Safe for children, marigold petals can be used as a tea to help to reduce fever especially if the neck glands are swollen.

Do not assume that this replaces medical treatment. It does not.

Dry cough mix
4 tablespoons of honey,
4 drops of pure essential oil of eucalyptus,
4 drops of pure essential oil of lemon
Brandy or whisky

Put the honey, essential oil of eucalyptus, essential oil of lemon and a good measure of brandy or whisky into a clean, dark

Marigold syrup

coloured medicine bottle. Shake the mixture thoroughly until all the ingredients are well mixed. One teaspoonful of this mixture can be diluted in a small glass of warm water and taken as and when it is required.

Remember that this remedy contains alcohol, and therefore you cannot drink a lot of this and drive, no matter how good it tastes!

The Kitchen
Goddess

WHEN I was a child I can remember going shopping with my mum and I don't believe I ever saw her buy a pre-cooked, pre-packed ready meal. Everything that we ate was cooked from scratch. If there were any cook-in sauces or pre-mixed bases in her store cupboard I certainly wasn't aware of them. I am sure that this was the case with my friends' families too. The result of this is that we can all cook – proper, healthy and hearty meals, from any kind of natural ingredients.

The 'ready=made' culture

Today when I go out for my shopping there are rows and rows of ready-mixed, pre-packed, pre-cooked meals. Take instant or 'straight-to-wok' noodles for example. For goodness sake, how long does it take to cook noodles? You just drop them into boiling water and leave them for four minutes. How hard is that?

The result of parents buying all this highly processed, pre-cooked food is that most young folk can't cook, don't know and don't care what they're eating and probably couldn't tell you that chips come from potatoes. When you only eat pre-packaged food you have no idea what good fresh food tastes

The 'ready=made' culture

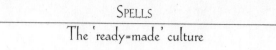

like and your palate is so dulled by fatty, sugary rubbish, full of salt, preservatives, MSG and other chemicals that when you are presented with healthy, tasty food made from fresh ingredients you turn your nose up at it!

Worse than that, when eating processed ready meals, you are eating food that was prepared by strangers and under unknown conditions and you have no real idea what you are eating or where the ingredients came from.

You have no way of knowing what kind of environment the food that you eat was prepared in. Suppose someone had an argument with their boss or was dissatisfied with their colleagues or working conditions or pay, what kind of mood are they in when preparing or packaging your food? We get our energy from the air that we breathe, the company that we keep, good or bad, and the food that we eat. If someone is angry and resentful when they are cooking then that is the kind of energy that they are giving to the food, and that is the energy that those who eat it are taking into their bodies.

I never, ever have ready-cooked foods in my fridge freezer or cupboard unless I have made them myself. I never eat food that has been cooked or heated in a microwave. I prefer to use unrefined golden sugar rather than white, although there are some recipes that require it. I don't like tea bags, they are full of dust! I much prefer real tea leaves and, of course, you can read tea leaves. You can't read a tea bag – well, at least I have never tried.

I never eat in restaurants unless I am absolutely certain that the food is good and fresh and that the staff are friendly. That, I must admit, is difficult to accomplish, but once I have found a suitable place to eat I seldom go anywhere else. I trust my instincts too and have walked out of restaurants because I felt unsure.

The 'ready=made' culture

The Sudan 1 dye scare of February 2005 revealed that this carcinogenic food colouring had found its way into over 500 food products. This Sudan 1 dye can cause cancer but we were told not to worry as the risk was small. If we didn't have to worry why was all the stock being recalled?

One slip up and over 500 commonly used products are contaminated with a highly dangerous substance. How easy it might be for this to happen again. How easy it might be for someone to deliberately introduce a dangerous substance into our food products in the guise of a harmless one. Think about it! And when you have thought about it start cooking for yourself!

I am just like everyone else, there are some days when I just can't be bothered cooking, so on the days that I do cook I tend to make much more than I need and then I stick the rest in a container and freeze it for my lazy or too-busy days. For me cooking is a magickal experience and when I am cooking that is when I feel most "witchy", combining all my fresh Goddess-given ingredients and concocting pure magick.

Traditionally, when working in a circle it is best to do so on an empty stomach, so eating something nice afterwards is an added blessing. When covens meet to work there is always a celebration afterwards so sharing good food is important, and generally the food chosen for the celebration will be appropriate to the festival.

Food at the Festivals
Samhain — October 31

Pronounced sow-en or sav-en, this holiday will be better known to you as Hallowe'en. It is the Wiccan equivalent of New Year and represents the last day of the harvest season.

It is a time to honour ancestors and many leave altar offerings in the form of food and wine in tribute to dead relatives, or set some extra places at the dinner table in case any late family member wants to join the feast.

This is traditionally the time for eating the last seasonal vegetables. Meat is traditional at this festival. This is the last opportunity for harvest, after this night, harvesting vegetables is thought to be bad luck. Apples are traditional so cider is the best accompaniment to the food.

Significance:	The last day of harvest, remembrance of and respect for the dead
Herbs:	Allspice, nutmeg, rosemary and sage.
Foods:	Root vegetables (carrots, parsnips, potatoes, turnips) apples, pumpkins and squashes, nuts, wines, cider, beef, lamb, pork and poultry.
Possible meal:	Pumpkin soup
	Roast pork with rosemary
	Honey-glazed roast vegetables
	Apple and blackberry crumble with nutmeg custard

Food at the Festivals

Yule — December 21 or 22

Yule, the winter solstice, falls on the shortest day of the year, either the 21st or the 22nd of the month of December. It is a time to think about and look forward to the coming summer and it is a time to think about and plan for the future

Meats are traditional as this would have been a time to slaughter animals for eating now, and for preserving, to see people through a long, lean winter period. Aromatic foods using spices like cinnamon and nutmeg or caraway are traditional, as is mulled wine. As well as smelling festive and warming, spices are good for helping to preserve foods. The essential oils of festive plants such as pine and cloves are good for warding off germs that the winter months can leave us prone to. Tea made from allspice is a traditional cold remedy. Turkey is a traditional meat to eat at Yule, but other poultry, roast pork or boiled ham would also be appropriate.

Significance:	The longest night, planning for the future.
Herbs:	Cinnamon, allspice, nutmeg, sage, thyme, tarragon and rosemary.
Foods:	Biscuits and shortbread, apples, nuts, pork and turkey, mulled wine, and fruit cake, recipes with preserved oranges and lemons.
Possible meal:	Mulled wine
	Chicken or turkey broth
	Tarragon turkey or chicken with sausagemeat stuffings and roast vegetables
	Spicy fruit pudding laced with sherry

Food at the Festivals

Imbolc — February 2

Imbolc, is a celebration of the first day of spring and the days finally becoming longer again. It is a time for turning the soil and preparing for new crops and it is a time for getting rid of the old and welcoming in the new, so spring cleaning is in order and so is a clear out of the larder in preparation for new produce. Seeds for planting would be blessed at this festival. Cooking ingredients should reflect foodstuffs that would have had to last the winter. Seeds, nuts, grains, dried fruit and flour would have survived. Seeded herb breads could be baked to celebrate the hope of the coming spring and the planting of new crops.

Significance: First day of spring, winter being swept away and hope for renewal.

Herbs: Angelica, basil, cinnamon and bay leaves

Foods: Seeds, nuts, bread, onions, garlic, cheese

Possible meal: Toasted herb bread topped with caramelised onions and grated cheese
Nut roast bound with egg and coated in breadcrumbs with onion gravy and green vegetables
Hot cinnamon and ginger cake with raisins and fresh cream

Food at the Festivals

Ostara — March 20 or 21

Another spring festival roughly equivalent to Easter time in the Christian calendar. Seeds blessed on Imbolc and at this festival would be ready for planting now. Aromatic cakes and fruity loaves could be baked and eaten at sunset. Fruit preserves could have lasted the winter and be ready to be spread on loaves and cakes. Salads of leafy vegetables strewn with wild flower petals would make an uplifting addition to Ostara food.

Significance:	The sowing of seeds and hope for a fruitful summer
Herbs:	Caraway, coriander seeds, cinnamon, allspice, preserved peel
Foods:	Leafy vegetables, wild flower petals (check they are edible!) dairy products, eggs, nuts, seeds, dried fruit.
Possible meal:	Spicy coleslaw of red cabbage, with honey, garlic and wine vinegar dressing, with carrots, nuts and seeds. Potato omelette, with fried shredded onions and green cabbage Pumpkinseed cake

Food at the Festivals

Beltane — April 30

The last day of spring, Beltane, is a fire festival representing the warming of the air and explosion of the environment into fertility and life. This is a time to celebrate reproduction, union and love.

Like the other spring festivals, seeded breads and cakes are traditional, and sweet varieties preferred. Flowers are gathered and worn in the hair and edible varieties such as dried lavender flowers would look attractive garnishing cakes.

Significance:	Fertility, sex, love
Herbs:	Lavender flowers, saffron, rose petals, lemon zest
Foods:	Breads and cakes made with seeds, nuts and dried fruit, garnished with fresh flowers
Possible meal:	Dandelion salad with wholemeal seed bread Sir fried vegetables with spicy saffron rice, with aromatic cauliflower salad Spongecake topped with almonds with lavender-scented whipped cream

Food at the Festivals

Litha — June 21 or 22

The summer solstice, midsummer's eve, Litha, pronounced lee-ta, does not have a set date each year but falls on the year's longest day. This is a powerful day and is an important time to connect with nature. Ripe seasonal fruits are best for this feast and food made from grains are traditional.

Significance:	The fruits of the sun, happiness, prosperity
Herbs:	Chamomile, thyme, oregano, marjoram
Foods:	Fruits and grains that have ripened under the sun
Possible meal:	Summer fruit and chamomile sorbet Courgette, tomato, celery and herb casserole with new boiled potatoes and fresh mange tout peas Fresh fruit salad

Food at the Festivals

Lammas — July 31

This is a harvest festival, also known as Lughnasadh, and is symbolic of the last day of summer and the year's first harvest. This is a time to make bread and as you do so give thanks for the crops of the summer as you knead the dough. Soup can be made with summer vegetables. As you make the soup give thanks for your home-grown yield or (modern equivalent) give thanks for the prosperity that allowed you to buy that food and for the conditions that allowed those vegetables to be grown. Orange and yellow foods that represent the sun would be appropriate and edible flowers such as nasturtium and marigold could be included with breads and salads.

Significance:	A harvest festival
Herbs:	Parsley, marjoram, flower petals, leafy salad herbs
Foods:	Breads, grains, summer fruits and vegetables
Possible meal:	Celery soup with home made bread
	Perfect Rice with cabbage and a side salad of herbs and wild flowers
	Summer pudding

Food at the Festivals

Mabon — September 21 or 22

The second harvest festival is Mabon, pronounced may-bon, it is also known as the Autumn Equinox. This is a time for reaping the crops and harvesting vegetables that grow under the earth and celebrating by making them into a delicious feast.

This is a feast in which the fine food must be matched by fine dress. Apples are symbolic of this festival so cider is the perfect drink. And corn on the cob eaten hot with butter or made into round cornbreads is a delicious golden representation of the sun.

Making preserves from the summer harvest – soft fruit jams and pickled vegetables – was at one time a wise occupation to take advantage of an abundance of food and make preparation for harder times during the winter.

Meaning:	The last harvest of the year, giving thanks for the yield, preparing for winter
Herbs:	Marigold, rose, sage.
Foods:	Breads, nuts, apples, corn on the cob and root vegetables (potatoes, parsnips, onions, beetroot and carrots).
Possible meal:	Parsnip soup with cornbread
	Mashed potato with sage and onion, roast root vegetables and carrot and beetroot salad
	Baked apples, with syrup and whipped cream

Recipes

I have included some of my favourite recipes and I hope that you will send me some of yours.

The following are recipes that my mum taught me how to make. Of course they are not as good as my mum's because she would never tell me or my sisters the full list of ingredients, always keeping that secret something to herself! So typical of a witch to do something like that but she never admitted that she was.

Enjoy them, experiment with them and improvise with your own ingredients.

Herb guide

In this book, each spell lists herbs that are recommended for that particular ritual. For handiness I will also list of some of them here to help you in choosing ingredients for a meal following a ritual.

Allspice	–	money, luck and healing
Angelica	–	protection, healing
Basil	–	money and riches, protection, love
Bay	–	divination, protection, purification
Caraway	–	travel
Chamomile	–	healing, prosperity, preparation for magick
Cinnamon	–	healing, love, passion and money.
Clove	–	wards off negative energies.
Coriander	–	love, fertility, protection, secrets
Dill	–	protection, interviews
Fennel	–	friendship and passion
Garlic	–	protection
Parsley	–	communication

Recipes

Pepper	–	courage
Rosemary	–	success, respect for family and ancestors
Sage	–	inspiration
Marjoram	–	peace and for answers
Mint	–	protection and fertility

Perfect Rice

I am going to give you my mum's way of making rice first and if you follow these directions it will always turn out perfectly. Always use basmati rice and never use boil in the bag or easy-cook rice.

Ingredients

1 lb (450 g) basmati rice
2 chicken stock cubes or fresh
   chicken stock

Method

Using stock cubes:
Put about a cup of water into a pot and add the stock cubes and bring it to the boil to melt the cubes.

Using fresh stock:
Bring your stock to the boil and have it standing by. Meanwhile, put your rice into a jug and stand the jug under running water from the hot tap. Let the water run on the rice for about five minutes and if you stir it once or twice you will see all the starch coming to the top.

  Now the tricky bit: strain the rice through a sieve and add it to the pot with the boiling stock. You can add a little boiling water or stock but there should only be an inch of liquid above the rice no matter what quantity you are cooking. So keep a kettle of boiling water or a pot of boiling stock standing by to add more if you need it. My mother's favourite trick when adding the rice was to stand a spoon in the middle of the pot of rice and stock. If the spoon fell over there was too much water. Bring the stock and rice back to the boil. Reduce the heat as low as possible and cover the pot with a tight-fitting lid.

Do not stir and do not touch for at least ten minutes.

Now lift the lid and there should be small air holes all over the surface of the rice. Now replace the lid, turn off the heat and leave the pot to stand for another ten minutes cooking in its own heat. It will then be ready to serve.

Rating: As perfect as it is easy and useful for so many recipes.

You can add cloves of garlic and fresh or dried herbs to the above basic rice to vary it. I love this rice served plain with a knob of butter.

Magickal benefits: For magickal working use a herb that is suitable for your spell. Traditionally, rice is used to cure digestive upsets and is an ideal food for someone recovering from a bout of sickness. Rice water is a natural remedy used to treat feverish and inflammatory conditions like urinary tract problems. One or two cloves added to basmati rice is a delicious ingredient and is also good for warding off negative influences.

Cauliflower Rice

Ingredients

1 fresh cauliflower
Buttermilk or fresh natural yogurt
Perfect Rice: follow the recipe up
until the rice is added to boiling
stock

Method

Break a fresh cauliflower into florets and shallow fry them until they are brown all over. In the meantime, prepare your rice as above. When you add the rice to the pot of boiling stock put the browned cauliflower on top, then cover with the lid and cook as before.

When serving this add a generous helping of buttermilk or natural yogurt to the top and garnish with your favourite herb or side salad.

Rating: A great way to make cauliflower tasty.

Magickal benefits: When not overcooked, cauliflower is a great source of vitamin C and has sulphur-containing compounds that protect against cancer.

Cabbage Rice

This is a lazy version of the Greek dish *dolmades* or the Arab dish my mother made called *mashie*. We used to stand over the pot waiting for it to be ready and, no matter how much she made, it was always finished that day. It is long and complicated to make but I will include the recipe and you can try it out for yourself. Anyway, this lazy version gives the same taste and is done in much less time.

Ingredients

Fresh cabbage
Perfect Rice
3 fresh lemons

Method

Shred cabbage finely as though you were preparing coleslaw. Add this to the top of the rice and cook as before. When it is ready, serve with fresh lemon halves and squeeze the lemon juice all over the rice and cabbage.

Rating: Healthy and tangy, this is a delicious side dish.

Magickal benefits: Cabbage has a long history of use in traditional medicine. The outside leaves of the cabbage can be wrapped around painful joints. Raw cabbage juice is used to encourage the healing of gastric ulcers. Lemon juice is high in vitamin C and helps protect against disease.

Ladies' Fingers

Ingredients

6 oz (170g) Okra
1 tin or tube of tomato purée
1 pound (450g) fresh tomatoes or 1
   tin of tomatoes
1 large onion
2 cloves garlic
1 tbsp olive oil for frying
Perfect Rice

Method

Top and tail the okra and chop into 1-inch pieces. Soak the okra in a bowl of water to allow the slimy juices to wash out.

Chop the onion and add to the frying pan along with the diced or crushed garlic and fry it slowly until it is opaque. Strain the okra and add this to the frying pan and allow this to cook while you are chopping the fresh tomatoes which you will add to the pan.

If you are using tinned tomatoes allow the okra to cook for about 5 to 10 minutes before adding the tinned tomatoes. Cook this mixture for about ten minutes then add the tomato pure. The quantity can be to your liking. Put a lid over the frying pan and allow this to simmer very gently while you cook your perfect rice. Check the thickness frequently and if required add water or stock to prevent the mixture from sticking or becoming too thick. Serve on top of your Perfect Rice and a dollop of natural yogurt or buttermilk can be added.

Ladies' Fingers

Rating: Delicious though unusual for Western tastes

Magickal benefits: Okra is the edible pod and seeds of a plant grown in hot countries and it is popular in eastern and African cuisine. It is an excellent source of fibre, vitamins, and minerals and promotes a healthy digestive system. It is also an antioxidant which may help prevent diseases such as cancers. In Turkey, the leaves are used in making a natural medicine to soothe or reduce inflammation. Because of it's healing qualities I would cook this to accompany spells for health, home and protection.

Green Lentils

This is a fantastic dish and is made up of three components. Part one is the rice and green lentils. Part two, onions, garlic and oil, is added to the rice and green lentils at the end of the cooking period. Part three is the salad traditionally served with this dish.

Put them all together and the result is wonderful so here goes:

Part One
Ingredients

Half a tea cup of green lentils (I
generally use a ramekin dish full)
Perfect Rice

Method

Put your green lentils into a pot and half fill the pot with water. Bring to the boil and allow them to simmer until they begin to swell round the edges but are not cooked through. You can be preparing your perfect rice while you are waiting for this to happen. Now take your lentils and rinse them under cold running water and strain them through a sieve. When you add your rice to the boiling stock add the part cooked green lentils too. Cook as usual for perfect rice. While this is happening you can prepare the next stage

Green Lentils

Part Two
Ingredients

3 large onions
3 cloves garlic
2 tsps sugar
1 tbsp olive oil for frying

Method

Cut the onions into halves and then slice finely. Crush or chop the garlic and add the onions, garlic and sugar to the frying pan and allow this mixture to cook slowly. The sugar will help to brown and caramelise the onions but if you cook this too fast and do not stir it enough you will end up with burnt onions and burnt garlic and ruin the dish so slowly does it and stir often. While this magick is happening you can make the salad.

Part Three
Ingredients

6 fresh tomatoes
2 onions
1 clove garlic
Some fresh or dried basil
Some fresh or dried oregano
Some fresh or dried mint
1 fresh lemon
1 tablespoon olive oil
Crusty bread

Green Lentils

Method

Chop the onions finely and cut the tomatoes into chunks and put this into a deep salad bowl to which you will add the crushed garlic and the fresh or dried herbs. Now add the olive oil and stir well. Half and squeeze the lemon and add a little at a time stirring and tasting until you achieve the taste you like. Put this to one side.

Putting it all together

When the rice is cooked add the fried onion mixture and stir once or twice. Serve on a nice plate and garnish with the tomato salad and some crusty bread. The juice from the salad is lovely for dipping the crusty bread in.

Rating: Difficult but worth the effort

Magickal benefits: Green lentils are an excellent source of protein and so aid tissue growth and repair. This is an excellent dish for diabetics (just miss out the sugar in caramelising the onions) because lentils are a slow-release carbohydrate food and won't cause blood sugar to rise too quickly. For this reason it's also a good dish for dieters as it will fill you up for many hours. Lentils are rich in soluble fibre which helps lower cholesterol. Use this recipe with spells for inspiration, travel, protection or fertility. Basil and mint will in combination be good for following a ritual for love, protection, fertility and prosperity. Oregano (or marjoram) can be involved in rituals for answers and for peace.

Aromatic Cauliflower Salad

I always came home from school at lunch time and this was always my favourite lunch dish. It is easy to make and even easier to eat.

Ingredients

1 cauliflower, broken into florets,
   boiled and cooled
1 clove garlic
1 fresh lemon
Olive oil to garnish
Crusty bread

Method

Break the cauliflower into florets and boil it until it is tender but firm. Strain through a colander and set to one side until it is cool. Next drizzle it with olive oil and squeeze the juice of a lemon over the top. Finish with some salt and ground black pepper and cover with a lid. Put this in the fridge and leave it for at least an hour until it is cold. Serve with crusty bread.

Rating: Really easy, really tasty, really healthy.

Magickal benefits: Add herbs to compliment your magickal working. For example parsley for communication, pepper for courage, marjoram for peace and for answers, garlic for protection, coriander for secrets, mint for fertility, caraway seeds for travel.

Tomato Salad

This is another of my favourites and is very similar to the salad accompanying the Green Lentils recipe

Ingredients

6 tomatoes
2 or 3 onions
1 tablespoon of olive oil
1 fresh lemon
1 clove of garlic
Some fresh or dried mint
Salt and black pepper to season

Method

For this basic tomato salad all you need to do is dice the onion, chop the tomato, crush the garlic and squeeze the lemon. Put all the ingredients into a bowl, season to taste and eat or stick it in the fridge until you are ready for it. A variety of herbs or spices can be added to change the taste to suit your pallet. Serve with crusty bread and cold, smoked mackerel or tuna fish.

Rating: Delicious and refreshing. The freshest, sweetest tomatoes will make all the difference to this salad.

Magickal benefits: Add herbs to compliment your magickal working. Basil can be used in rituals for protection and love and to bring prosperity. Black pepper is perfect for rituals to ask for courage.

Banana Pancakes

This is a fabulous dessert or snack when you need to spoil yourself.

Pancakes

Scotch pancakes should only take about ten minutes to make so why not make your own rather than buying them. You'll avoid added preservatives and they're simply so much nicer.

Ingredients

8 oz (250g) plain flour
1 tsp baking soda
2 tsps cream of tartar
$\frac{1}{2}$ tsp salt
1 oz (30g) sugar
1 large egg
$\frac{1}{2}$ pint (250 ml) milk

Method

Sieve together the flour, baking soda, cream of tartar and salt. Dissolve the sugar in the milk. Beat the egg and mix with the milk. Gradually beat together the liquid and the dry ingredients with a balloon whisk, taking care not to create any lumps. Beat until you have a smooth but relatively thick batter. Heat a girdle or thick-bottomed frying ban and smear with a thin coating of butter. Drop spoonfuls of the mixture onto the girdle, around four at a time. When the surfaces of the pancakes show some bubbling flip them over and brown the other side.

Bananas and Syrup

Ingredients

2 or 3 bananas
Half cup of golden syrup
2–3 oz (50–90g) butter
Fresh cream to accompany

Method

Put the butter and the syrup in a large, flat pan – a clean frying pan is fine. Allow the butter to melt with the syrup over a low heat stirring all the time. Drop the pancakes in to cover the base of the pan and then add chopped bananas. Keep turning the bananas and pancakes until they are all covered with the butter and syrup mixture and remove them before the bananas get too soft. Cover with cream or crème fresh.

Rating: Sumptuous and not for the faint hearted.

Magickal benefits: Who needs one?
However, bananas are high in potassium which is essential for healthy function of the nervous system and the muscles. But who's thinking about that when faced with a delicious plate of syrupy treats?

Chicken with Tarragon

The herby creamy chicken dish smells wonderful as it cooks, and tastes even better.

Ingredients

2 breasts of chicken
1 small onion
Plain flour
Fresh or dried tarragon (as much as you prefer. A generous seasoning might be 2 tsp, but tasting is recommended)
Knob of butter
Fresh cream

Method

Chop the onion very finely and gently fry in a little oil until it is transparent but not brown. When the onion is cooked you can remove it from the pan and set it to one side. Wash the chicken breasts in cold water then dip them into the flour so that they are coated on both sides.

Now add the butter to the pan and, when it is melted, gently place the chicken fillets into the melted butter and allow them to fry slowly, turning when the first side is cooked. Now add the glazed onion to the chicken, pour in the fresh cream and add the tarragon.

Serve with boiled potatoes or perfect rice and garnish with some parsley or coriander.

Chicken with Tarragon

Rating: Delicious and impressive

Magickal benefits: With this combination of herbs, this recipe assists in magickal spells for victory, communication or secrets. Tarragon helps to stimulate the appetite and was traditionally claimed to cure toothache.

Dandelion Salad

This is really easy to make and can be added to other salads. Do not gather the leaves from the side of the road because they may be polluted by traffic fumes, but rather look in a country field or a garden.

Ingredients

Gather a pot full of dandelion leaves
1 red onion
6 cherry tomatoes
Some fresh or dried basil
Salt and pepper to season

Method

Wash the dandelion leaves, halve and finely slice the red onion and halve the cherry tomatoes. Add all the ingredients to a salad bowl, drizzle with a little olive oil and season and serve on its own or as an accompaniment to other dishes.

Rating: Will really get your taste buds zinging!

Magickal benefits: While you are picking the leaves notice the sap appearing from the broken stems. This sap, from the root or the stem of the dandelion can be applied to warts to help them disappear. The leaves of dandelions are rich in iron, potassium and calcium and also contain beta carotene. When eaten, they are great for disease prevention

Dandelion Salad

because they have powerful antioxidant properties. With the combination of basil, this dish would be ideal to follow a ritual for protection, especially with regard to health.

Roast Pork with Rosemary

Nothing welcomes your family home quite like a roast dinner and this delicious roast is one of the most aromatic and welcoming

Ingredients

4 lb (1.8 kg) pork roast
2 cloves garlic, chopped
Rosemary, dried or sprigs of fresh
Olive oil

Method

Preheat your oven to 325°F (160°C). Place the roast in a pan, then rub the meat first with olive oil and then the chopped garlic and rosemary. Pierce the pork with a knife all over the fatty surface and stick in some pieces of garlic and rosemary.

Cook for approximately 35–40 minutes per pound of meat.

Rating: Delicious and warming, and what a wonderful smell!

Magickal benefits: Use this dish to assist spells for success. When eaten, rosemary is believed to be beneficial in nervous and digestive complaints and can relieve headaches and neuralgia and feverish symptoms from colds. Garlic is anti-viral and anti-bacterial so it can also help fight colds.

Sunflower Seed, Petals and Pasta Salad

Ingredients

12 oz (340g) of pasta
1 tbsp olive oil
1 clove of garlic, crushed
2 tbsps sunflower petals
1 tbsp sunflower seeds
1 dsp chopped chives
Sunflower, nasturtium or pansy
    petals for garnish

Method

Bring a large pan of water to boiling point. Add the pasta and cook until tender but firm – usually about eight to ten minutes will do depending on the type of pasta that you use. When the pasta is cooked, drain it in a colander.

Heat the oil in a large pan, add the garlic and toss in the pasta, stir well, remove from the heat and pour into a serving bowl. Mix the sunflower petals, sunflower seeds and chives into the pasta and garnish with some fresh nasturtiums or pansies. Serve immediately with a side salad.

This dish can be served cold. To use cold wait until the pasta has cooled before putting it in the fridge. When you are ready to use it add 1 tablespoon mayonnaise and blend in well. Garnish as before and serve.

Rating: Delicious and, garnished with flowers, looks beautiful.

Sunflower Seed, Petals and Pasta Salad

Magickal benefits: Can be used to assist any spell for prosperity or financial gain.

Sunflower seeds are a great source of vitamin E which is an antioxidant which protects the body against diseases. They are high in unsaturated fatty acids which are vital components of cell membranes.

Easy Lemon and Rosemary Biscuits

3 oz (85 g) butter or margarine
1 oz (30 g) sugar
4 oz (110 g) self-raising flour
6 oz (170 g) icing sugar
2 tsps water (approximately)
Juice from $\frac{1}{2}$ lemon, freshly squeezed
1 sprig fresh rosemary about 4 in (10 cm) long
golden sugar to sprinkle on top

Method

Strip the leaves from the stem of the rosemary and roughly chop them.

Beat the butter and sugar together to a cream. Sieve the flour and mix it gradually into the butter and sugar. Add the chopped rosemary and the lemon juice and blend together until the mixture forms a firm dough. Roll out thinly to about $\frac{1}{8}$ inch (3 mm) and cut into rounds using a pastry cutter. Lay your biscuits on a baking sheet and sprinkle them with golden sugar. Place them on a greased and floured baking tray and bake on the middle shelf of the oven for around 10 minutes 180°C (350°F/gas mark 4), or until golden, but not too brown.

Makes around a dozen biscuits depending on the size of your cutter. When ready allow to cool, and store in an airtight container. Mine have never lasted longer than the day that they are baked – they are eaten immediately.

Rating: Impressive, delicious and irresistible!

Magickal Benefits: Use with any spell for success.

Pumpkin Seed Cake

This is my favourite cake, in fact this is the favourite cake of anyone who comes to visit me. Consequently, I always make a large one and I have included the amounts in brackets so that once you have tried it out you can make the large batch too.

Ingredients

4 portions	(10 portions)
4 oz (110 g) butter or margarine	(10 oz, 280 g)
4 oz (110 g) golden sugar	(10 oz, 280 g)
2 eggs	(3 eggs)
4 oz (110 g) wholewheat flour, self-raising	(10 oz, 280 g)
1/4 oz (7 g) baking-powder	(5/8 oz, 17g)
1/2 cup pumpkin seeds	(1 1/4 cup)
Golden sugar to sprinkle	

Method

Cream the fat and sugar until soft and fluffy, then gradually add the beaten eggs. Gradually mix in the flour, and baking powder. Put the mix into your baking tin and sprinkle the top generously with pumpkin seeds and, lastly, a fine dusting of golden sugar to finish.

You can bake this cake in two small trays or one larger tray depending on your mood but you will have to adjust the baking time to suit. 12–15 min at 200°C (390°F) will do the small cake. I generally use a deep round tin and bake it as one cake.

Pumpkin Seed Cake

Rating: Delicious and different

Magickal benefits: A useful addition to prosperity spells.

Lavender Rice

Ingredients

4 oz (110 g) pudding rice
2 oz (55 g) sugar
1 pt (570 ml) milk,
1/2 oz butter
A large sprig of lavender, bruised
1 can evaporated milk

Method

Wash the rice, place in a deep casserole and add the sugar and the fresh milk mix together and add the butter. Lastly hold the lavender in your right hand a draw it through your left hand so that you bruise it. Lay the bruised lavender sprig on the top of you mixture. Bake at 180–200°C (370–395°F) until the milk starts simmering then reduce the heat and allow the pudding to cook slowly. Check after ½ hour and at this point add 1 can of evaporated milk and another knob of butter and bake for another ½ hour.

Rating   Delicious

Magickal benefits: A useful addition to love, courage and health spells. Lavender can boost the appetite and the aroma is soothing and relaxing.

Phases of the Moon

THESE are included to enable you to find the best time to carry out your magick and rituals. Please refer to the chapter on Cycles for the information on when are the most auspicous times to perform your magick.

The best times for magick are during waxing or full moons in your sign. Worst times are when the moon is passing between signs.

Aquarius	♒	Libra	♎
Pisces	♓	Scorpio	♏
Aries	♈	Sagittarius	♐
Taurus	♉	Capricorn	♑
Gemini	♊	Full moon	☺
Cancer	♋	Waning moon	☽
Leo	♌	New moon	●
Virgo	♍	Waxing moon	☾

2006

2006

	May			June			July			August		Day
1	♊		/			/			/			m
2	♋		/			/			1	♎		t
3	♋		/			/			2	♏ ☾		w
4	♋		1	♌		/			3	♏		t
5	♌ ☾		2	♌		/			4	♏		f
6	♌		3	♍		1	♍		5	♐		s
7	♍		4	♍ ☾		2	♍		6	♐		s
8	♍		5	♍		3	♎ ☾		7	♑		m
9	♍		6	♎		4	♎		8	♑		t
10	♎		7	♎		5	♎		9	♒ ☺		w
11	♎		8	♏		6	♏		10	♒		t
12	♏		9	♏		7	♏		11	♓		f
13	♏ ☺		10	♏		8	♐		12	♓		s
14	♐		11	♐ ☺		9	♐		13	♈		s
15	♐		12	♐		10	♑		14	♈		m
16	♐		13	♑		11	♑ ☺		15	♉		t
17	♑		14	♑		12	♒		16	♉ ☽		w
18	♑		15	♒		13	♒		17	♊		t
19	♒		16	♒		14	♓		18	♊		f
20	♒ ☽		17	♓		15	♓		19	♋		s
21	♓		18	♓ ☽		16	♓		20	♋		s
22	♓		19	♈		17	♈ ☽		21	♋		m
23	♈		20	♈		18	♈		22	♌		t
24	♈		21	♉		19	♉		23	♌ ●		w
25	♉		22	♉		20	♉		24	♍		t
26	♉ ●		23	♉		21	♊		25	♍		f
27	♊		24	♊		22	♊		26	♍		s
28	♊		25	♊ ●		23	♋		27	♎		s
29	♊		26	♋		24	♋		28	♎		m
30	♋		27	♋		25	♋ ●		29	♏		t
31	♋		28	♌		26	♌		30	♏		w
/			29	♌		27	♌		31	♏ ☾		t
/			30	♌		28	♍		/			f
/			/			29	♍		/			s
/			/			30	♍		/			s
/			/			31	♎		/			m
/			/			/			/			t
/			/			/			/			w
/			/			/			/			t
/			/			/			/			f
/			/			/			/			s
/			/			/			/			s

2006

	September			October			November			December		
m	/			/			/			/		
t	/			/			/			/		
w	/			/			1	♓		/		
t	/			/			2	♓		/		
f	1	♐		/			3	♈		1	♈	
s	2	♐		/			4	♈		2	♈	
s	3	♑		1	♑		5	♉	☺	3	♉	
m	4	♑		2	♑		6	♉		4	♉	
t	5	♒		3	♒		7	♊		5	♉	☺
w	6	♒		4	♒		8	♊		6	♊	
t	7	♓	☺	5	♓		9	♋		7	♊	
f	8	♓		6	♓		10	♋		8	♋	
s	9	♈		7	♈	☺	11	♋		9	♌	
s	10	♈		8	♈		12	♌	☽	10	♌	
m	11	♉		9	♉		13	♌		11	♍	
t	12	♉		10	♉		14	♍		12	♍	☽
w	13	♊		11	♊		15	♍		13	♍	
t	14	♊	☽	12	♊		16	♍		14	♎	
f	15	♊		13	♋		17	♎		15	♎	
s	16	♋		14	♋	☽	18	♎		16	♏	
s	17	♋		15	♌		19	♏		17	♏	
m	18	♌		16	♌		20	♏	●	18	♏	
t	19	♌		17	♌		21	♏		19	♐	
w	20	♌		18	♍		22	♐		20	♐	●
t	21	♍		19	♍		23	♐		21	♑	
f	22	♍	●	20	♎		24	♑		22	♑	
s	23	♎		21	♎		25	♑		23	♒	
s	24	♎		22	♎	●	26	♒		24	♒	
m	25	♎		23	♏		27	♒		25	♒	
t	26	♏		24	♏		28	♓	☾	26	♓	☾
w	27	♏		25	♐		29	♓		27	♓	
t	28	♐		26	♐		30	♓		28	♈	
f	29	♐		27	♐		/			29	♈	
s	30	♑	☾	28	♑		/			30	♉	
s	/			29	♑	☾	/			31	♉	
m	/			30	♒		/			/		
t	/			31	♒		/			/		
w	/			/			/			/		
t	/			/			/			/		
f	/			/			/			/		
s	/			/			/			/		
s	/			/			/			/		

347

2007

January			February			March			April			
1	♊		/			/			/			m
2	♊		/			/			/			t
3	♋	😊	/			/			/			w
4	♋		1	♋		1	♌		/			t
5	♌		2	♌	😊	2	♌		/			f
6	♌		3	♌		3	♍		/			s
7	♌		4	♍		4	♍	😊	1	♍		s
8	♍		5	♍		5	♍		2	♎	😊	m
9	♍		6	♍		6	♎		3	♎		t
10	♎		7	♎		7	♎		4	♎		w
11	♎	🌓	8	♎		8	♏		5	♏		t
12	♎		9	♏		9	♏		6	♏		f
13	♏		10	♏	🌓	10	♏		7	♐		s
14	♏		11	♏		11	♐		8	♐		s
15	♐		12	♐		12	♐	🌓	9	♐		m
16	♐		13	♐		13	♑		10	♑	🌓	t
17	♐		14	♑		14	♑		11	♑		w
18	♑		15	♑		15	♑		12	♒		t
19	♑	🌕	16	♒		16	♒		13	♒		f
20	♒		17	♒	🌕	17	♒		14	♓		s
21	♒		18	♓		18	♓		15	♓		s
22	♓		19	♓		19	♓	🌕	16	♈		m
23	♓		20	♈		20	♈		17	♈	🌕	t
24	♈		21	♈		21	♈		18	♉		w
25	♈		22	♉		22	♉		19	♉		t
26	♉	🌗	23	♉		23	♉		20	♊		f
27	♉		24	♊	🌗	24	♊		21	♊		s
28	♊		25	♊		25	♊	🌗	22	♋		s
29	♊		26	♊		26	♋		23	♋		m
30	♋		27	♋		27	♋		24	♋	🌗	t
31	♋		28	♋		28	♌		25	♌		w
/			/			29	♌		26	♌		t
/			/			30	♌		27	♍		f
/			/			31	♍		28	♍		s
/			/			/			29	♎		s
/			/			/			30	♎		m
/			/			/			/			t
/			/			/			/			w
/			/			/			/			t
/			/			/			/			f
/			/			/			/			s
/			/			/			/			s

2007

	May			June			2007 July			August		
m	/			/			/			/		
t	1	♎		/			/			/		
w	2	♏	☺	/			/			1	♓	
t	3	♏		/			/			2	♓	
f	4	♐		1	♐	☺	/			3	♈	
s	5	♐		2	♐		/			4	♈	
s	6	♐		3	♑		1	♑		5	♈	☽
m	7	♑		4	♑		2	♑		6	♉	
t	8	♑		5	♒		3	♒		7	♉	
w	9	♒		6	♒		4	♒		8	♊	
t	10	♒	☽	7	♓		5	♓		9	♊	
f	11	♒		8	♓	☽	6	♓		10	♋	
s	12	♓		9	♈		7	♈	☽	11	♋	
s	13	♓		10	♈		8	♈		12	♌	
m	14	♈		11	♈		9	♉		13	♌	●
t	15	♈		12	♉		10	♉		14	♍	
w	16	♉	●	13	♉		11	♊		15	♍	
t	17	♉		14	♊		12	♊		16	♍	
f	18	♊		15	♊	●	13	♋		17	♎	
s	19	♊		16	♋		14	♋	●	18	♎	
s	20	♋		17	♋		15	♋		19	♏	
m	21	♋		18	♌		16	♌		20	♏	
t	22	♌		19	♌		17	♌		21	♏	☾
w	23	♌	☾	20	♌		18	♍		22	♐	
t	24	♍		21	♍		19	♍		23	♐	
f	25	♍		22	♍	☾	20	♎		24	♑	
s	26	♍		23	♎		21	♎		25	♑	
s	27	♎		24	♎		22	♎	☾	26	♒	
m	28	♎		25	♎		23	♏		27	♒	
t	29	♏		26	♏		24	♏		28	♒	☺
w	30	♏		27	♏		25	♐		29	♓	
t	31	♏		28	♐		26	♐		30	♓	
f	/			29	♐		27	♐		31	♈	
s	/			30	♑	☺	28	♑		/		
s	/			/			29	♑		/		
m	/			/			30	♒	☺	/		
t	/			/			31	♒		/		
w	/			/			/			/		
t	/			/			/			/		
f	/			/			/			/		
s	/			/			/			/		
s	/			/			/			/		

2007

September			October		**2007**	November			December			
/			1	♊		/			/			m
/			2	♊		/			/			t
/			3	♋	☽	/			/			w
/			4	♋		1	♋	☽	/			t
/			5	♌		2	♌		/			f
1	♈		6	♌		3	♌		1	♍	☽	s
2	♉		7	♌		4	♍		2	♍		s
3	♉		8	♍		5	♍		3	♍		m
4	♊	☽	9	♍		6	♍		4	♎		t
5	♊		10	♎		7	♎		5	♎		w
6	♋		11	♎	●	8	♎		6	♏		t
7	♋		12	♎		9	♏		7	♏		f
8	♌		13	♏		10	♏	●	8	♏		s
9	♌		14	♏		11	♏		9	♐	●	s
10	♌		15	♐		12	♐		10	♐		m
11	♍	●	16	♐		13	♐		11	♑		t
12	♍		17	♐		14	♑		12	♑		w
13	♎		18	♑		15	♑		13	♑		t
14	♎		19	♑	◐	16	♑		14	♒		f
15	♎		20	♒		17	♒	◐	15	♒		s
16	♏		21	♒		18	♒		16	♓		s
17	♏		22	♒		19	♓		17	♓	◐	m
18	♐		23	♓		20	♓		18	♈		t
19	♐	◐	24	♓		21	♈		19	♈		w
20	♐		25	♈		22	♈		20	♉		t
21	♑		26	♈	☺	23	♉		21	♉		f
22	♑		27	♉		24	♉	☺	22	♊		s
23	♒		28	♉		25	♊		23	♊		s
24	♒		29	♊		26	♊		24	♋	☺	m
25	♓		30	♊		27	♋		25	♋		t
26	♓		31	♋		28	♋		26	♋		w
27	♈	☺	/			29	♌		27	♌		t
28	♈		/			30	♌		28	♌		f
29	♉		/			/			29	♍		s
30	♉		/			/			30	♍		s
/			/			/			31	♎	☽	m
/			/			/			/			t
/			/			/			/			w
/			/			/			/			t
/			/			/			/			f
/			/			/			/			s
/			/			/			/			s

2008

	January			February			March			April		
m	/			/			/			/		
t	1	♎		/			/			1	♒	
w	2	♎		/			/			2	♒	
t	3	♏		/			/			3	♓	
f	4	♏		1	♐		/			4	♓	
s	5	♐		2	♐		1	♐		5	♓	
s	6	♐		3	♐		2	♑		6	♈	🌕
m	7	♐		4	♑		3	♑		7	♈	
t	8	♑	🌕	5	♑		4	♑		8	♉	
w	9	♑		6	♒		5	♒		9	♉	
t	10	♒		7	♒	🌕	6	♒		10	♊	
f	11	♒		8	♒		7	♓	🌕	11	♊	
s	12	♓		9	♓		8	♓		12	♋	🌗
s	13	♓		10	♓		9	♈		13	♋	
m	14	♓		11	♈		10	♈		14	♌	
t	15	♈	🌗	12	♈		11	♉		15	♌	
w	16	♈		13	♉		12	♉		16	♍	
t	17	♉		14	♉	🌗	13	♊		17	♍	
f	18	♉		15	♊		14	♊	🌗	18	♎	
s	19	♊		16	♊		15	♋		19	♎	
s	20	♊		17	♋		16	♋		20	♎	🌑
m	21	♋		18	♋		17	♋		21	♏	
t	22	♋	🌑	19	♌		18	♌		22	♏	
w	23	♌		20	♌		19	♌		23	♐	
t	24	♌		21	♌	🌑	20	♍		24	♐	
f	25	♍		22	♍		21	♍	🌑	25	♐	
s	26	♍		23	♍		22	♎		26	♑	
s	27	♎		24	♎		23	♎		27	♑	
m	28	♎		25	♎		24	♎		28	♒	🌓
t	29	♎		26	♏		25	♏		29	♒	
w	30	♏	🌓	27	♏		26	♏		30	♒	
t	31	♏		28	♏		27	♐		/		
f	/			29	♐	🌓	28	♐		/		
s	/			/			29	♐	🌓	/		
s	/			/			30	♑		/		
m	/			/			31	♑		/		
t	/			/			/			/		
w	/			/			/			/		
t	/			/			/			/		
f	/			/			/			/		
s	/			/			/			/		
s	/			/			/			/		

2008

May			June			July			August			
/			/			/			/			m
/			/			1	♊		/			t
/			/			2	♊		/			w
1	♓		/			3	♋	●	/			t
2	♓		/			4	♋		1	♌	●	f
3	♈		/			5	♌		2	♌		s
4	♈		1	♉		6	♌		3	♍		s
5	♉	●	2	♉		7	♍		4	♍		m
6	♉		3	♊	●	8	♍		5	♍		t
7	♊		4	♊		9	♎		6	♎		w
8	♊		5	♋		10	♎	☾	7	♎		t
9	♋		6	♋		11	♎		8	♏	☾	f
10	♋		7	♌		12	♏		9	♏		s
11	♌		8	♌		13	♏		10	♐		s
12	♌	☾	9	♌		14	♐		11	♐		m
13	♍		10	♍	☾	15	♐		12	♐		t
14	♍		11	♍		16	♐		13	♑		w
15	♍		12	♎		17	♑		14	♑		t
16	♎		13	♎		18	♑	☺	15	♒		f
17	♎		14	♏		19	♒		16	♒	☺	s
18	♏		15	♏		20	♒		17	♒		s
19	♏		16	♏		21	♒		18	♓		m
20	♏	☺	17	♐		22	♓		19	♓		t
21	♐		18	♐	☺	23	♓		20	♈		w
22	♐		19	♑		24	♈		21	♈		t
23	♑		20	♑		25	♈	◐	22	♉		f
24	♑		21	♑		26	♈		23	♉		s
25	♑		22	♒		27	♉		24	♊	◐	s
26	♒		23	♒		28	♊		25	♊		m
27	♒		24	♓		29	♊		26	♊		t
28	♓	◐	25	♓		30	♋		27	♋		w
29	♓		26	♓	◐	31	♋		28	♋		t
30	♈		27	♈		/			29	♌		f
31	♈		28	♈		/			30	♌	●	s
/			29	♉		/			31	♍		s
/			30	♉		/			/			m
/			/			/			/			t
/			/			/			/			w
/			/			/			/			t
/			/			/			/			f
/			/			/			/			s
/			/			/			/			s

2008

Day	September		October		November		December	
m	1	♍	/		/		1	♑
t	2	♎	/		/		2	♑
w	3	♎	1	♎	/		3	♒
t	4	♏	2	♏	/		4	♒
f	5	♏	3	♏	/		5	♓ ☾
s	6	♏	4	♐	1	♐	6	♓
s	7	♐ ☾	5	♐	2	♐	7	♓
m	8	♐	6	♐	3	♑	8	♈
t	9	♑	7	♑ ☾	4	♑	9	♈
w	10	♑	8	♑	5	♑	10	♉
t	11	♑	9	♒	6	♒ ☾	11	♉
f	12	♒	10	♒	7	♒	12	♊ ☺
s	13	♒	11	♒	8	♓	13	♊
s	14	♓	12	♓	9	♓	14	♋
m	15	♓ ☺	13	♓	10	♈	15	♋
t	16	♈	14	♈ ☺	11	♈	16	♌
w	17	♈	15	♈	12	♉	17	♌
t	18	♈	16	♉	13	♉ ☺	18	♍
f	19	♉	17	♉	14	♊	19	♍ ☽
s	20	♉	18	♊	15	♊	20	♎
s	21	♊	19	♊	16	♋	21	♎
m	22	♊ ☽	20	♋	17	♋	22	♏
t	23	♋	21	♋ ☽	18	♌	23	♏
w	24	♋	22	♌	19	♌ ☽	24	♏
t	25	♌	23	♌	20	♌	25	♐
f	26	♌	24	♍	21	♍	26	♐
s	27	♍	25	♍	22	♍	27	♑ ●
s	28	♍	26	♍	23	♎	28	♑
m	29	♎ ●	27	♎	24	♎	29	♑
t	30	♎	28	♎	25	♏	30	♒
w	/		29	♏ ●	26	♏ ●	31	♒
t	/		30	♏	27	♐	/	
f	/		31	♐	28	♐	/	
s	/		/		29	♐	/	
s	/		/		30	♑	/	
m	/		/		/		/	
t	/		/		/		/	
w	/		/		/		/	
t	/		/		/		/	
f	/		/		/		/	
s	/		/		/		/	
s	/		/		/		/	

2009

January			February			March			April			
/			/			/			/			m
/			/			/			/			t
/			/			/			1	♊		w
1	♒		/			/			2	♋	☾	t
2	♓		/			/			3	♋		f
3	♓		/			/			4	♌		s
4	♈	☾	1	♈		1	♈		5	♌		s
5	♈		2	♉		2	♉		6	♍		m
6	♉		3	♉	☾	3	♉		7	♍		t
7	♉		4	♉		4	♊	☾	8	♍		w
8	♊		5	♊		5	♊		9	♎	☺	t
9	♊		6	♊		6	♋		10	♎		f
10	♋		7	♋		7	♋		11	♏		s
11	♋	☺	8	♋		8	♌		12	♏		s
12	♌		9	♌	☺	9	♌		13	♐		m
13	♌		10	♌		10	♍		14	♐		t
14	♍		11	♍		11	♍	☺	15	♐		w
15	♍		12	♍		12	♎		16	♑		t
16	♎		13	♎		13	♎		17	♑	☽	f
17	♎		14	♎		14	♎		18	♒		s
18	♎	☽	15	♏		15	♏		19	♒		s
19	♏		16	♏	☽	16	♏		20	♒		m
20	♏		17	♏		17	♐		21	♓		t
21	♐		18	♐		18	♐	☽	22	♓		w
22	♐		19	♐		19	♑		23	♈		t
23	♐		20	♑		20	♑		24	♈		f
24	♑		21	♑		21	♑		25	♉	●	s
25	♑		22	♑		22	♒		26	♉		s
26	♒	●	23	♒		23	♒		27	♊		m
27	♒		24	♒		24	♓		28	♊		t
28	♒		25	♓	●	25	♓		29	♋		w
29	♓		26	♓		26	♓	●	30	♋		t
30	♓		27	♈		27	♈		/			f
31	♈		28	♈		28	♈		/			s
/			/			29	♉		/			s
/			/			30	♉		/			m
/			/			31	♊		/			t
/			/			/			/			w
/			/			/			/			t
/			/			/			/			f
/			/			/			/			s
/			/			/			/			s

	May			June			July			August		
m	/			1	♍		/			/		
t	/			2	♎		/			/		
w	/			3	♎		1	♎		/		
t	/			4	♏		2	♏		/		
f	1	♋	☾	5	♏		3	♏		/		
s	2	♌		6	♏		4	♐		1	♐	
s	3	♌		7	♐	○	5	♐		2	♐	
m	4	♍		8	♐		6	♐		3	♑	
t	5	♍		9	♑		7	♑	○	4	♑	
w	6	♎		10	♑		8	♑		5	♒	
t	7	♎		11	♑		9	♒		6	♒	○
f	8	♏		12	♒		10	♒		7	♒	
s	9	♏	○	13	♒		11	♒		8	♓	
s	10	♏		14	♓		12	♓		9	♓	
m	11	♐		15	♓	☽	13	♓		10	♈	
t	12	♐		16	♓		14	♈		11	♈	
w	13	♑		17	♈		15	♈	☽	12	♈	
t	14	♑		18	♈		16	♉		13	♉	☽
f	15	♑		19	♉		17	♉		14	♉	
s	16	♒		20	♉		18	♉		15	♊	
s	17	♒	☽	21	♊		19	♊		16	♊	
m	18	♓		22	♊	●	20	♊		17	♋	
t	19	♓		23	♋		21	♋		18	♋	
w	20	♈		24	♋		22	♋	●	19	♌	
t	21	♈		25	♌		23	♌		20	♌	●
f	22	♈		26	♌		24	♌		21	♍	
s	23	♉		27	♍		25	♍		22	♍	
s	24	♉	●	28	♍		26	♍		23	♎	
m	25	♊		29	♎	☾	27	♎		24	♎	
t	26	♊		30	♎		28	♎	☾	25	♏	
w	27	♋		/			29	♏		26	♏	
t	28	♋		/			30	♏		27	♏	☾
f	29	♌		/			31	♐		28	♐	
s	30	♌		/			/			29	♐	
s	31	♍	☾	/			/			30	♑	
m	/			/			/			31	♑	
t	/			/			/			/		
w	/			/			/			/		
t	/			/			/			/		
f	/			/			/			/		
s	/			/			/			/		
s	/			/			/			/		

2009

September		October		November		December		Day
/		/		/		/		m
1	♑	/		/		1	♉	t
2	♒	/		/		2	♊ ☺	w
3	♒	1	♓	/		3	♊	t
4	♓ ☺	2	♓	/		4	♋	f
5	♓	3	♓	/		5	♋	s
6	♓	4	♈ ☺	1	♈	6	♌	s
7	♈	5	♈	2	♈ ☺	7	♌	m
8	♈	6	♉	3	♉	8	♍	t
9	♉	7	♉	4	♉	9	♍ ☾	w
10	♉	8	♊	5	♊	10	♎	t
11	♊	9	♊	6	♊	11	♎	f
12	♊ ☾	10	♊	7	♋	12	♎	s
13	♋	11	♋ ☾	8	♋	13	♏	s
14	♋	12	♋	9	♌ ☾	14	♏	m
15	♌	13	♌	10	♌	15	♐	t
16	♌	14	♌	11	♍	16	♐ ●	w
17	♍	15	♍	12	♍	17	♑	t
18	♍ ●	16	♍	13	♎	18	♑	f
19	♍	17	♎	14	♎	19	♑	s
20	♎	18	♎ ●	15	♏	20	♒	s
21	♎	19	♏	16	♏ ●	21	♒	m
22	♏	20	♏	17	♏	22	♓	t
23	♏	21	♐	18	♐	23	♓	w
24	♐	22	♐	19	♐	24	♓ ☽	t
25	♐	23	♐	20	♑	25	♈	f
26	♑ ☽	24	♑	21	♑	26	♈	s
27	♑	25	♑	22	♑	27	♉	s
28	♑	26	♒ ☽	23	♒	28	♉	m
29	♒	27	♒	24	♒ ☽	29	♉	t
30	♒	28	♒	25	♓	30	♊	w
/		29	♓	26	♓	31	♊ ☺	t
/		30	♓	27	♓	/		f
/		31	♈	28	♈	/		s
/		/		29	♈	/		s
/		/		30	♉	/		m
/		/		/		/		t
/		/		/		/		w
/		/		/		/		t
/		/		/		/		f
/		/		/		/		s
/		/		/		/		s

PSYCHIC
POWERS

Introduction

THE chances are that if you have been drawn to pick up this book you have had experiences that may have lead you to believe that you might be – even just the tiniest bit – psychic. Well, the good news is that you are right. We are all psychic.

I am sure you will have had the experience of standing in a crowded room and feeling as though someone is staring at you. You try to remain casual, despite a slight creepy feeling, as you turn and look around, and there across the room looking right at you is an old friend, grinning from ear to ear. Instantly, you forget your initial apprehension and you probably spend the next ten minutes laughing about your mutual experience. I say mutual because when your friend relates his or her side of the story they will probably tell you that they have been watching you for ages – willing you to turn around.

Coincidence or psychic experience?

You are thinking of someone you haven't seen for ages and 'ping!' an email arrives from them or the phone rings. 'I was just thinking about you!' you say.

Psychic: the *Collins English Dictionary* defines this as 'outside the possibilities defined by natural laws as mental telepathy' or 'sensitive to forces not recognised by natural laws' and 'a person who is sensitive to parapsychological forces or influences'.

Yet how can having psychic powers be outside natural laws when it is the most natural thing in the world? We cannot explain it and so in scientific terms it becomes unnatural – how typical of our times, when we expect everything to be explained by science.

My interpretation of a psychic is someone who is sensitive to the vibrations around them, seen or unseen. You are unable to touch your psychic instincts, or explain them in scientific terms but to deny them or say that they are outside natural laws is like denying animal instincts; the wolf's need to howl at the moon, the bird's need to migrate, the adult salmon's need to return to the river where it was conceived.

You know that you have instincts, but the sad thing is that most people have forgotten how to use them. Have you ever been confined to bed after an illness or an operation and found that the first time you try to walk again your legs are like jelly? It's almost as though you have forgotten how to walk.

It's the same with your psychic ability. If you don't use it, you begin to forget how. All you have to do now is practise every day, at every opportunity, and soon, just like walking again after an illness, you regain full strength.

I often hear people asking me whether I am psychic or clairvoyant. My initial response is usually to ask them if they know the difference and more often than not they don't. Clairvoyance, from the French, means to see clearly, to see things beyond the limits of what we imagine our five senses can perceive. A clairvoyant believes they can foretell the future through divination. A psychic is sensitive to the energies around them. They are both (mostly unused) talents that can be retrieved through practice and meditation.

The collective name for any form of seeing into the future is 'divination' and there are many ways to do this which are listed in this book. But, before you can even begin, you must be able to tune in to your higher self. In the following chapters are exercises to optimise your sensitivity to the energies around you and achieve this link with your higher self.

This may demand new skills that are presently unfamiliar to you. Perhaps you will have heard of some of the terms that you are about to read about before, but were unaware of what they meant.

All will become clear.

Chakras

Learning About Your Chakras

The simplest way to explain chakras is to describe them as energy power points within your body. We have twenty-one minor chakras and seven major chakras within our bodies. In this book we will be focusing on the latter. Each chakra has its own specific location, traditional name, common name, colour and function, as shown in the illustration. This will be a fairly brief description to give you a working base but should you wish to expand on this subject, there are many specialist books on chakras.

The Source of Infinity Above

The chakra which connects you to the source of infinity above is situated approximately twenty-four inches above your head, more specifically, at the end of your fingertips when you have your arm stretched high above you. The colour of this chakra is brilliant white. Its function is to make the connection between you and the energy from infinity.

The Chakras

The Source of Infinity
Above
Brilliant white
Makes the connection
between you and the
energy from infinity

The Crown Chakra
Violet
Awakening this chakra
enhances spirituality

The Third Eye
Dark blue
Awakening this chakra
enhances telepathy and
clairvoyance.

The Throat Chakra
Blue
Awakening this chakra
enhances clairaudience

The Heart Chakra
Green or pink
Awakening this chakra
enhances your
sensitivity and
awareness

The Solar Plexus
Chakra
Bright yellow
Awakening this
chakra enhances
fulfilment

The Sacral Chakra
Deep red
Awakening this
chakra enhances
psychic abilities

The Base Chakra
Very dark red
Awakening this
chakra enhances the
ability to ground
yourself

The Source of Infinity
Below
Rich brown
Connects you to the
source of infinity in the
core centre of the earth

The Crown Chakra

Most people think of the crown chakra as the first chakra. It is situated at the top of your head.
The traditional name is *Sahasrara*.
The colour is violet.
The associated flower is the lotus.
The associated crystal is clear quartz crystal (double pointed where possible).
Awakening this chakra enhances spirituality.

The Third Eye Chakra

The third eye is situated in the middle of the forehead between the eyebrows.
The traditional name is *Ajna*.
The colour is very dark blue.
The associated flower is the orchid.
The associated crystal is lapis
Awakening this chakra enhances telepathy and clairvoyance.

Throat Chakra

The throat chakra is situated in the throat and governs the mouth, ears and nose.
The traditional name is *Vishuddha*.
The colour is blue.
The associated flower is the cornflower.
The associated crystal is turquoise.
Awakening this chakra enhances clairaudience (the ability to hear sounds beyond the range of normal hearing).

The Heart Chakra

The heart chakra is situated in the heart and
the centre of unconditional love.
The traditional name is *Anahata*.
The colour is green or pink.
The associated flower is the rose.
The associated crystal is rose quartz.
Awakening this chakra enhances your
sensitivity and awareness to all things.

The Solar Plexus Chakra

The solar plexus chakra is situated in your
upper abdomen, just beneath your rib cage.
The traditional name is *Manipura*.
The colour is bright yellow.
The associated flower is the sunflower.
The associated crystal is sunstone or citrine.
Awakening this chakra enhances fulfilment.

The Sacral Chakra

The sacral chakra is positioned on the
abdomen, just below your navel and just
above the pubic bone.
The traditional name is *Swadisthana*.
The colour is deep red.
The associated flower is the poppy.
The associated crystal is carnelian or moonstone.
Awakening this chakra enhances psychic abilities.

The Base Chakra

The base chakra is positioned at the base of the spine.
The traditional name is *Muladhara*.
The colour is very dark red.
The associated plant is the roots of the lotus or a tree.
The associated crystal is obsidian.
Awakening this chakra enhances the ability to ground yourself.

The Source of Infinity Below

This chakra connects you to the source of infinity in the core centre of the earth and is situated approximately twenty-four inches below your feet.
The colour is rich brown.
The associated plant is the roots of your favourite tree.
The associated crystal is clear quartz.

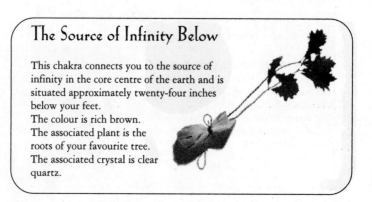

When performing any kind of spiritual work it is important that you are connected to the source of infinity above and below.

Once you are familiar with the location and function of each of the major chakra points you can begin to practise opening your chakras. I can almost hear you asking 'Why would I want to do this?' That's like saying: 'I have a nice car but I keep it in the garage because I don't drive'.

Your chakras are the unseen power centres that stimulate or suppress your energy. Closed or asleep they suppress your energy, while opened and awake they stimulate it.

Memorising the Chakras

At this point it would be useful to make your own chakra cards. Take nine pieces of card and draw, depending on your artistic ability, either a circle or a flower. You could draw the flower that is associated with the chakra. With coloured pencils, paint or felt tips colour each circle or flower with the colour which relates to each chakra. Underneath add the details about the charkas, the traditional names and their popular names.

Take the chakra cards and, if you have them, the appropriate crystals and lay them out in a straight line. This will help you imagine or visualise what being connected looks like.

Gather the cards, mix them, and then turn them over and again lay them in the correct order. Do this several times until you get the sequence correct. Do not tire yourself out or you will become disheartened. The traditional names can be difficult to pronounce so, as you work with each card, try to focus on the common name, the colour and the function. For example, for the crown chakra, the colour is violet and the flower is the lotus. Practise in this way until you feel as though you know all the chakras, their functions and their colours, then you will be ready to move on to the next exercise.

Learning How to Relax

BEING able to relax is crucial to becoming receptive to the energies around you. The first lesson in learning how to relax is discovering how to make yourself unavailable to telephone calls or visits from friends and family. You only need thirty minutes in the day or evening when you can switch off the phone and tell your loved ones not to disturb you, unless of course it is an emergency. You can practise in your bath or on your bed, your favourite chair or even the floor if you prefer it.

Once the phone has been switched off, make yourself warm and comfortable and begin to breathe slowly and deeply. Close your eyes and listen to the sound of each breath as it fills your lungs and then listen to the sound each breath makes as you breathe out.

Try to visualise each breath in as being brilliant white and healing. Don't panic if you think you can't visualise – you can imagine instead. There is a difference. Imagining happens in your crown chakra, whilst visualising happens in your third eye, but I will explain more of this in the following pages.

As you breathe out visualise that you are breathing out all the negative energy from your body. Maintain this steady flow of watching positive healing energy filling your body and negative energy leaving your body.

Visualisation

Gradually you will be filled with a sense of calm and peace but after a short while your logical side will try to take over and the distractions will begin.

At this point all manner of things can pop in and out of your mind, which is frustrating. It's called 'monkey brain' and the cure is simple. Go back to visualising positive energy flowing into your body and when a distracting thought comes in send it to the back of your head and again focus on your breathing. Each time a distracting thought occurs send it to the back of your brain.

Practise this relaxation technique as often as you can and soon you will be ready for the next step.

Visualisation Exercise

Make yourself comfortable. Close your eyes and begin to breathe in positive energy as before. When you feel relaxed and your breathing is slow and steady, focus all your attention on your third eye.

Remember your third eye is the space between your eyebrows in the middle of your forehead. Imagine that inwardly you are looking at that space. Sometimes the image of an eye will appear. Don't worry, this is normal. Many people tell me that they can see the eye but nothing else.

The secret here is, when you see your third eye look right through it. At first you may only see a black or dark space but gradually images may begin to appear. Do not try to force this, just remain relaxed and focused and then when the images do come all you have to do is observe them. As you become more comfortable and familiar with this technique you may hear or have the impression of hearing sounds, words, and even music. Sometimes you may want to focus on a particular theme and 'monkey brain' continually distracts you. The following exercises will help you to maintain your focus.

Focus Exercise One

Aim: An exercise to establish an image that will help focus your mind and prevent thoughts wandering to the everyday.

Make yourself comfortable. Close your eyes and begin to breathe in positive energy as before. When you feel relaxed and your breathing is slow and steady, focus all your attention on your third eye.

Visualise an apple pip before you. The skin of the apple pip is dark brown and shiny. In your mind's eye, turn the seed around so that you can look at it from all angles. The moment that you begin to feel distracted focus again on the apple pip and begin to see a tiny little green shoot appearing at the top of it. The shoot begins to grow, and there before your eyes it has produced two tiny leaves. It grows taller, gaining in strength until it is a young tree. As the leaves begin to mature you can see buds forming which burst into bloom. As the apple blossom begins to fade the fruit begins to grow. There before you is an apple. It is red and juicy and ripe for picking. In your mind's eye you pick the apple and begin to eat the fruit. Be aware of the sweetness of the fruit and the feeling of the flesh and juice in your mouth. Soon you are down to the core and all you are left with is the apple pip.

Spend a few moments focusing again on the apple pip and then gradually come back into yourself. Stretch your legs and arms, take a deep breath of positive energy and open your eyes.

Focus Exercise Two

Aim: An exercise practising the abilities you developed, and the image that you focused on, in exercise one. You are learning to focus on that image every time a distraction pops into your head.

Make yourself comfortable. Close your eyes and begin to breathe in positive energy as before. When you feel relaxed and your breathing is slow and steady, focus all your attention on your third eye.

See again before you the apple pip but this time do not allow it to grow. You may look at it from many angles but always try to stay with the apple pip as it is. Any time that a distracting thought comes into your mind discard it and return to the picture of the apple pip. Practise this exercise until you can stay with the apple pip for at least ten minutes. When you have finished, gradually come back into yourself. Stretch your legs and arms, take a deep breath of positive energy and open your eyes.

Focus Exercise Three

Aim: Trying to lengthen the time which can be spent focusing the mind and to leave the mind open to new images.

Make yourself comfortable, close your eyes and begin to breathe in positive energy as before. When you feel relaxed and your breathing is slow and steady, focus all your attention on your third eye. Again, see before you the apple pip. This time remove the apple pip from the picture and focus on the space that the pip has left. Each time that a distracting thought occurs send it to the back of your mind and again focus on the space that the apple pip occupied. Try to maintain your focus on this for at least ten minutes. Gradually come back into yourself, stretch your legs and arms, take a deep breath of positive energy and open your eyes.

Practise this exercise every day until you can maintain your focus on the empty space, and soon you will be ready for the next exercise.

Focus Exercise Four

Aim: To create the state of mind in yourself in which psychic images come to the fore.

Make yourself comfortable, close your eyes and begin to breathe in positive energy as before. When you feel relaxed and your breathing is slow and steady, focus all your attention on your third eye. Look into the same space that the apple pip occupied and this time allow images to flow freely. Do not allow thoughts to distract you but maintain your attention on the space. Do not become disheartened if nothing happens for a while. Everyone is different and will make progress at a different rate. Gradually, with daily practice, images will begin to appear and all you have to do is observe. These images may mean nothing at all and it can almost feel as though you are watching a video. Sometimes unpleasant images appear. Discard these immediately and return to the last pleasing image. You are always in control here and it is important to remember this. Do this exercise for ten to fifteen minutes and when you have finished stretch your legs and arms, take a deep breath of positive energy and open your eyes.

Opening Your Chakras

Chakras take in and give out energy. Opening your chakras leaves you more receptive to the energies around you. You must also read the exercise on closing your chakras which immediately follows.

This next part is best done lying down on your bed, sofa or even the floor. I prefer the floor because I can surround the area on which I am going to be lying with crystals. Disconnect the telephone and prepare your surroundings so that you can be completely comfortable.

Lie down in the space that you have prepared and begin to breathe slowly and deeply. With each inward breath visualise positive energy filling your body and the space that you are lying in. Visualise a pure, brilliant white light about a foot above your head and allow this light to flow down from infinity above you into the top of your head.

As this pure light from above touches you, visualise that it is touching a lotus bud. Allow the colour to change from white to violet and see the lotus being blessed from above and awakening. Petal by petal the lotus blossom begins to open until this flower covers the entire top of your head. In the centre of the lotus is a swirling ball of energy. This is the core centre of your intelligence and your spirituality. Blessed by the light, the flower opens, so too does your spirituality.

The light from above travels further down and rests upon your third eye in the middle of your forehead between your eyebrows. Touched by the light and the love from above, the colour begins to change into a very dark blue. You begin to see an orchid. Visualise it as just a bud, asleep and waiting to be awakened. As it is touched by the light, the orchid begins to bloom and open. In the centre of the orchid is a swirling ball of energy. This is the core centre of your ability to create and see your future before you. When the orchid opens, it awakens your third eye chakra and stimulates telepathy and clairvoyance.

The light from above travels further down and rests upon your heart. As this pure light from above touches your heart, visualise the colour beginning to change to the colour pink and a rose bud waiting to be awakened. As it is touched by the light, the rose bud begins to bloom and open into the most beautiful rose that you have ever seen. In the centre of the rose is a swirling ball of energy. This is the core centre of your ability to feel. As the rose opens, it awakens your heart chakra and stimulates your sensitivity and love, bringing awareness to all things, increasing your psychic power and your ability to instinctively know and understand.

Further down, the light from above travels and enters the middle of your body. As this pure light from above touches your centre, visualise the colour beginning to change to yellow and then into the bud of a giant sunflower. As it is touched by the light, the sunflower begins to bloom and open. In the centre of the sunflower is a swirling ball of energy. This is the core centre of your power. As the sunflower opens, it awakens your solar plexus chakra and stimulates your strength and determination, helping you to achieve fulfilment.

The light from above travels further down and enters the

Opening Your Chakras

lower part of your body just above your pubic bone. As this pure light from above touches this area, visualise the colour beginning to change to red and then into the bud of a poppy. As the poppy is touched by the light, it begins to bloom and open. In the centre of the poppy is a swirling ball of energy. This is the core centre of your psychic power. As the poppy opens, it awakens your ability to respond to psychic stimulus.

Further down, the light from above travels and enters the base of your spine. As this pure light from above touches your base, visualise the colour beginning to change to very dark red and the roots of a giant tree. As the light touches the roots they begin to come to life. In the centre of these roots lies a swirling ball of energy. This is the core centre of your ability to ground yourself and remain connected to the earth below. Visualise these roots travelling down through your hips, your thighs, your legs and through your feet to the source of infinity below. As the roots touch infinity below they begin to hold on and draw nourishment and healing up into your body.

Visualise your body as being filled with all the colours in the rainbow and as these colours swirl around your body they will heal and re-energise both your physical and spiritual life.

Relax and enjoy the experience and fill your heart, mind and spirit with peace, love and joy. See in your mind's eye each of your chakras as open and active.

Everyone has a guardian angel, sent by the great spirit to accompany us on our journey through life – good times and bad times. Visualise your guardian angel approaching you carrying a purple cloak. This cloak will protect you from negative energy. Allow your guardian angel to wrap the cloak of protection around you. Once this is done it is time for you to come back into the here and now.

Take a deep breath, stretch your arms and legs, and slowly, in your own time, open your eyes. Do not jump up and start hurrying around. Take things slowly and easily. Make yourself a cup of tea and relax. Some people feel light headed after this type of exercise. If you experience this eat something that is made from ingredients grown in the earth, like a potato scone or a packet of crisps, rather than something which comes from the branches above the earth, like an apple, or something made from wheat like bread or crackers.

Practise this exercise every morning or evening and gradually you will find that it takes less and less time to open your chakras. Soon opening your chakras will be like switching on a light. When you can do this – and only then – you will be ready to move on to other exercises.

Closing Your Chakras

Closing your chakras is as important as opening them because they pick up the energy that is around you. Perhaps you have been meditating in the morning before you go to work. Feeling good inside and out, you go to work and when you get there the atmosphere is hostile because of some event. There are angry faces and voices everywhere you go, and people full of moans and groans. This drains your energy and makes you feel angry or miserable too. Drawing a purple cloak of protection around you at the end of a meditation will help to ward off these negative energies, keeping your energy field pure and unbroken. Closing down your chakras will do this too but you must remember to open them again when the energy around you is better.

To close your chakras, find a comfortable place to sit, switch on your light from infinity above you and as it touches your crown chakra see the flower closing, petal by petal, until it once again becomes a bud. Repeat this process until you come to your heart chakra. Allow this chakra to remain open. Keeping your heart chakra opened will allow you to maintain pure loving thoughts regarding any negative situation or person you might encounter.

Move down through the remaining chakras closing each one until you come to your base chakra. As you reach this chakra visualise your roots drawing back up into a tight ball at the base of your spine. Closing your base chakra will help to prevent you from becoming depressed by a negative situation.

After a bad day go and sit or lie down in your favourite place and perform your chakra opening exercise once more, and visualise peace and harmony flowing through all your chakras.

Meditation

Crystal Meditation

You will need at least eight crystals for this exercise and they can be of any size or colour. If you are just beginning to collect crystals the most common and easy to obtain are clear quartz, amethyst, rose quartz and citrine, although the Crystal List in this book will help you make your selection for specific purposes.

Prepare an area where you can lie down and have your chosen crystals to hand. Have a glass of water or fresh fruit juice and a small snack nearby. When everything is ready, place one crystal just above where your head will be when you are lying down. Place another just below your feet. Position one crystal where you will be able to reach it by your left side and another by your right side. Holding the remaining crystals in your hand, lie down and place a crystal on your forehead just above and between your eyebrows. Position another on your throat. Place one crystal on your heart and another on your solar plexus. Pick up the crystals that are by your hands and hold them throughout the following meditation.

Make yourself comfortable, close your eyes, and begin to breath in positive energy. When you feel relaxed and your breathing is slow and steady, focus all your attention on the crystal that is in the position above your head. See this crystal

Crystal Meditation

filling with bright, positive, sparkling energy and as it fills and overflows allow that energy to move down through the top of your head to meet with the crystal that is situated between your eyebrows. As before, see it filling with bright, positive energy and as it begins to overflow allow it to trickle down through your chest to the crystal that is over your heart. This crystal will also begin to fill and overflow with bright, sparkling energy and as it does so allow it to trickle down to the crystal on your solar plexus. Allow this crystal to fill and expand with energy and as it overflows it will move down through your body to connect with the crystal at your feet and across to the crystals in each hand. Now see your entire being vibrate with pure, sparkling energy and allow this energy to expand outwards to fill your surroundings. When you have reached this state it is time to ask your guardian angel to step forward.

Close your eyes and visualise your guardian angel forming before you. Imagine a smiling, loving, being surrounding you with protective light. When you see your guardian angel ask for his or her protection or advice or whatever it is that you wish to know, for example:

'Guardian Angel (use his or her name if you know it), friend and protector, with your love I know that I am not alone in this world. With love and respect I humbly ask that you come forward. I ask for your help as I seek answers and ask you to protect and guide me. Please surround me with your light. Thank you for your constant presence and unquestioning love.'

Spend some time in quiet meditation with your guardian

angel and, when you are ready, give thanks and gradually begin to come back to yourself. Visualise all the sparkling energy being locked into your body.

Visualise a protective cloak being placed round your shoulders and see roots emerging from the base of your spine and travelling down through your body into the ground beneath you. Say these words: 'I am now ready to come back to myself feeling refreshed, revitalised and confident.' Gradually curl and relax your toes and muscles, and when you are ready, open your eyes. Gradually sit up, take a sip of water and enjoy your prepared snack. Do not hurry your movements. Instead, take your time and, when you are ready to stand, do so slowly.

Music Meditation

Choose your favourite piece of music – something that really moves or stimulates you. I find that shamanic chanting, pan pipes, native American and Japanese music or wolf and dolphin sounds can take me into quite deep and interesting places. Listen to your chosen piece of music and become familiar with it.

When you are comfortable with all the variations and subtleties of it and are happy with your choice, prepare an area to lie down on and have a glass of water or fresh fruit juice and a small snack nearby.

When you have everything ready, sit or lie down and make yourself comfortable, switch on your music and begin to breathe in a slow, steady fashion. As you breathe in visualise bright light energy flowing into your body and as you breathe out breathe away negative energy. Feel the music and allow it to take you wherever you want to go. Drift free with the sounds and vibrations. When the music has ended, gradually begin to come back to yourself. Visualise all the sparkling energy being locked into your body.

Visualise a protective cloak being placed round your shoulders and see roots emerging from the base of your spine and travelling down through your body into the ground beneath you. Say these words: 'I am now ready to come back to myself feeling refreshed, revitalised and confident.' Gradually curl and relax your toes and muscles and, when you are ready, open your eyes. Gradually sit up. Take a sip of water and enjoy your prepared snack. Do not hurry your movements. Instead take your time and, when you are ready to stand, do so slowly.

Candle Meditation

Your main priority when working with candle meditations should be safety. Make sure that there is nothing nearby that can be set alight and that the candle is secure in a holder. Candles can be purchased in many colours so choose one appropriate to your desires.

White signifies purity, cleansing and knowledge.
Red signifies passion, excitement and action.
Pink signifies love and romance.
Orange signifies strength, power and courage.
Yellow signifies energy, vitality and motivation.
Green signifies healing, growth and fertility.

Candle Meditation

Blue signifies tranquillity and peace.
Purple signifies protection, meditation and spirituality.
Turquoise signifies communication, protection and travel.
Black signifies grounding and dispelling negative energies.

Candle Meditation One

Choose the colour of candle that you wish to work with and secure it into a holder, remembering to keep it away from any flammable objects or surfaces. Prepare an area where you can sit quietly and comfortably. Do not have any music playing. Have a glass of water or fresh fruit juice and a small snack nearby. When you have everything ready, light your candle, make yourself comfortable and relax.

Fix your focus on the flame of the candle and begin to breathe in a slow, steady fashion. As you breathe in visualise bright light energy flowing into your body and as you breathe out expel negative energy. Keep your eyes focused on the candle and gradually your vision will begin to distort. Do not try to refocus. You may feel as though your eyes are very heavy but maintain this fixed stare at the flame of the candle. If you are naturally gifted or if you have been practising enough, pictures will gradually begin to form in the flame.

Follow the movement and colours of the flame and try to stay with this meditation for at least ten minutes. When you are ready to stop and come back to yourself you can begin to visualise sparkling energy being locked into your body.

Visualise a protective cloak being placed round your shoulders and see roots emerging from the base of your spine and travelling down through your body into the ground beneath you. Say these words: 'I am now ready to come back to myself feeling refreshed, revitalised and confident.' Gradually curl and relax your toes and muscles and, when you are ready, open your eyes. Gradually sit up, take a sip of water and enjoy your prepared snack. Do not hurry your movements. Instead, take your time and when you are ready to stand do so slowly.

Always remember to do this after any meditation and if you feel lightheaded remember to eat something. Afterwards you may want to make a note of the time and date, and write down anything you saw or felt that you want to remember. This will also give you something to refer back to later if you realise that you been given advance notice of something.

Candle Meditation Two

Choose the colour of candle that you wish to work with and secure it into a holder, remembering to keep it away from any flammable objects or surfaces. Prepare an area where you can sit quietly and comfortably. This time you can play some music and, as before, have a glass of water or fresh fruit juice and a small snack nearby. When you have everything ready, switch on your music, light your candle, make yourself comfortable and relax. Fix your focus on the flame of the candle and begin to breathe in a slow steady fashion.

As you breathe in visualise bright light energy flowing into your body and as you breathe out expel negative energy. Keep your eyes focused on the candle and gradually your vision will begin to distort. Do not try to refocus. You may feel as though your eyes are very heavy but maintain this fixed stare at the flame of the candle. You may begin to realise that the flame of the candle moves in time with the music and the flame may grow and diminish with the beat. The more upbeat the tempo the more active the flame will become. As you watch focus your mind on the candle and try to communicate with the flame.

See the flame stretching and then in your mind tell the candle flame to grow smaller. Pictures may form and all you have to do is watch and try to remember everything that you see. Follow the movement and colours of the flame and try to stay with this meditation for at least ten minutes. As you become more experienced with meditation you can increase this time but do so gradually. When you are ready to stop and come back to yourself you can begin to visualise sparkling energy being locked into your body.

Visualise a protective cloak being placed round your shoulders and see roots emerging from the base of your spine and travelling down through your body into the ground beneath you. Say these words: 'I am now ready to come back to myself feeling refreshed, revitalised and confident.' Gradually curl and relax your toes and muscles and, when you are ready, open your eyes. Gradually sit up. Take a sip of water and enjoy your prepared snack. Do not hurry your movements. Instead take your time and when you are ready to stand do so slowly. Afterwards make a note of the time and date, and write down anything you saw or felt that you want to remember.

Third Eye Meditation
Exercise One

Prepare your meditation area and for this first third eye meditation work in silence. Have a glass of water or fresh fruit juice and a small snack nearby. When you have everything ready, make yourself comfortable and relax. Breathe in a slow steady fashion. As you breathe in visualise bright light energy flowing into your body and as you breathe out expel negative energy. Bring light energy down through all your chakras and fill your entire being with sparkling light. When you are completely and totally relaxed focus all your attention on your third eye which is in the space just above and between your eyebrows. Do not be alarmed if you suddenly see an eye. It is yours. This is your third eye and all you have to do now is stare straight into it and through it. At first you might see nothing at all except an empty space. This is not unusual. Be patient and practise this as often as you are comfortable with and gradually pictures may begin to form. When you are ready to stop and come back to yourself you can begin to visualise sparkling energy being locked into your body. Visualise a protective cloak being placed round your shoulders and see roots emerging from the base of your spine and travelling down through your body into the ground beneath you. Say these words: 'I am now ready to come back to myself feeling refreshed, revitalised and confident.' Gradually curl and relax your toes and muscles and, when you are ready, open your eyes. Gradually sit up and take a sip of water and enjoy your

Third Eye Meditation

prepared snack. Remember not to hurry your movements and, when you are ready, slowly get up. Afterwards make a note of the time and date and write down anything that you saw or felt that you want to remember.

Exercise Two

Prepare your meditation area, choose some ambient music, have a glass of water or fresh fruit juice and a small snack nearby. When you have everything ready, make yourself comfortable and relax. Breathe in a slow, steady fashion. As you breathe in visualise bright light energy flowing into your body and as you breathe out expel negative energy. Bring light energy down through all your chakras and fill your entire being with sparkling light. When you are totally relaxed focus all your attention on your third eye in the space just above and between your eyebrows. Look deep into your third eye, and be patient. Gradually pictures may begin to form. As before, when you are ready to stop and come back to yourself you can begin to visualise sparkling energy being locked into your body. Visualise a protective cloak being placed round your shoulders and see roots emerging from the base of your spine and travelling down through your body into the ground beneath you. Say these words: 'I am now ready to come back to myself feeling refreshed, revitalised and confident.' Gradually curl and relax your toes and muscles and, when you are ready, open your eyes. Gradually sit up, take a sip of water and enjoy your prepared snack. Remember not to hurry your movements and, when you are ready, slowly get up. Afterwards make a note of the time and date and write down anything that you saw or felt that you want to remember.

Exercises in Divination

I N the following list you may find several exercises that you are already familiar with and some that you feel drawn to. Remember to trust your instincts. We are all different and some of us are good at one thing while others are good at something else.

Once you have become familiar with practising various meditation techniques you will begin to realise that you can very quickly attain a meditative state. This is the frame of mind and being that is required to begin to see into the future by any chosen method, whether it be playing cards, Tarot cards, dice or anything else.

As with any new skill, practice is the key to improvement. Do your meditaion exercises as often as possible,and try as many of these divination exercises as you can.

Aeromancy
Cloud Divination

Aeromancy simply means telling the future based on the formation of the clouds in the sky. I am sure there have been times in your life when you have seen faces or recognisable shapes in the formations of the clouds and not paid any particular attention except perhaps to say to a friend 'Look at that.' Wouldn't it be wonderful if you could actually 'read' the clouds?

Aeromancy Divination Exercise

Place a comfortable chair by a window where you can see the sky or, better still, on a fine day sit in the garden, your local park or somewhere in the countryside.

Begin to breathe slowly and deeply and visualise sparkling light moving through all your chakras. When you are completely relaxed look at the various formations of the clouds and choose the cloud pattern that you want to work with. Once you have selected one, stare at these clouds and become aware of the patterns and shapes that they show you.

Each time you see a shape that can be identified stop and make a note of it. Later you can look up the interpretations section in this book and make notes on what you think you are being told. Each time you make an entry into your notebook include the time and the date. After a few weeks you can look back over your notes to see if your interpretations are accurate.

Ailuromancy
Cat Divination

Ailuromancy is all about cats. We are all familiar with the legendary 'lucky black cat' and most cat owners know that these creatures can be very sensitive. One of the most characteristic things about cats is probably their independence.

When my daughter Tori was young we went to an animal rescue centre to give a home to a cat. We called him Hassan. He was very handsome with his shiny black coat. Later, when he grew fat and we realised that he was having kittens, he became Hassani and then Ani for short. One day Tori said to me: 'This cat has got to go.'

When I looked over at Tori she was stroking and loving Ani while the cat completely ignored her.

'We have had this cat for eighteen months and she has never shown me any sign of affection,' said Tori.

That's what cats are like. They are capable of loving you and purring all over you but only when it suits them. This is one of the reasons that the cat represents independence and freedom.

In ancient Egypt the cat was worshipped. The goddess Basset is portrayed as a woman with a cat's head, sometimes with a litter of kittens. For this reason she is known as the protector of pregnant women. In spite of this, many mothers and grandmothers re-home their cats when a baby is due fearing that the cat might suffocate their baby.

Most witches love cats and consider them to be their 'familiar' (spirit guide) although in some cultures they are considered to be unlucky. There are several sayings associated with cats. For instance some say that a black cat crossing your path or coming to visit your home will bring you luck. A cat following you is believed to indicate that money will come to you before the week is out. Be wary of a stranger in the home that your cat hides from. A stranger in your home to whom your cat is attracted is safe. If your cat is staring out of the window, a letter, call or visitor should arrive.

Ailuromancy Divination Exercise

For the next few weeks pay close attention to your cat and its behaviour. Rather than just thinking of your cat as your pet, think of it as your guide. When your cat is in its resting place, unplug the telephone, light a candle and place the candle between you and your cat.

Sit in your most comfortable chair opposite your cat and begin to relax. Think of the cat sitting on your lap and see yourself stroking it. In your mind tell your cat how comfortable it would be to sit on your lap.

Visualise your cat stretching, getting up and coming over to you. Do not speak or move – just concentrate. Practise this exercise for about five to ten minutes every day.

Gradually your cat will begin to realise that you are communicating with it and it will come to you. Sometimes you may need to visualise tempting pictures for your cat to come. Its favourite food, perhaps a can of tuna fish, something that you know your cat cannot resist.

When your cat finally gets the message give it a reward and make a fuss of it. Once you have mastered this art of communicating silently with your cat, you can begin to work on a more serious level, especially problem solving or decision-making.

Alectryomancy
Divination Using a Bird and Bird Seeds

Birds could be said to symbolise our own 'flights of fancy'. Who wouldn't love to be able to fly? The saying 'free as a bird' reflects the desire of humans to be able to do this. In many cultures the bird can symbolise thoughts and dreams, even the human soul. Fortune telling by birds could be used in instances where you need to ask questions about hopes, dreams, aspirations and wishes.

Letters of the alphabet, or possible outcomes, are written on pieces of paper and placed on the floor. Birdseeds are then scattered over the pieces of paper and the bird is allowed to peck at the seeds. Whenever the bird pecks at a seed on a piece of paper the letter is noted and soon the answers are found. Be respectful to the bird and thank it.

Alectryomancy Divination Exercise

Traditionally a hen would be used for this exercise but unless you live near a farm, the chickens you are most likely to have easy access to will be in the freezer section of Asda, and this is not suitable! However, if you know someone who has a pet bird you could try this form of divination with their pet if they, and the bird, will allow you.

Prepare an area of the floor and lay out pieces of paper on which are written letters of the alphabet, and one slip of paper with the word 'yes', one slip of paper with the word 'no' and one slip of paper with the word 'maybe'.

You could alternatively write possible outcomes and then place all your papers in a circle on the floor ready to receive your prophetic bird. Scatter some birdseed over the papers. Before you introduce the bird to the exercise spend a few moments focusing on the area and visualising positive energy filling the space. Ask your question and then set the bird down in the space and take note of which letters or answers are uncovered or pecked at in the order that they are 'chosen'.

If you know a nice place by a pond or loch where wild birds come to feed you could do exactly the same exercise. Don't choose a windy day though or you may lose all your pieces of paper and be fined for littering the area!

Aleuromancy
Fortune cookies

When my husband and I got married we got my granddaughter Ashie to give all the guests fortune cookies instead of favours and everyone opened their cookies right away to read their fortunes. Traditionally these biscuits were used to hide secret messages and were distributed by the patriotic revolutionary Chu Yuan-Chang in disguise as a Taoist priest.

During the American gold rush and the railway boom the Chinese '69ers were building the great American railway lines through the Sierra Nevada to California. They put happy messages inside biscuits to exchange at the moon festival, instead of cakes, and so the tradition of fortune cookies began. The Chinese settled in San Francisco and a cottage industry in fortune cookies emerged.

Aleuromancy Divination Exercise

Before you begin this exercise why not make your own fortune cookies? You can vary the messages that you put inside and do not forget to include yes and no answers. You could even include a full set of rune symbols (see entry for runes), drawing one symbol per piece of paper and using one per biscuit. Before you begin to make your cookies, write your messages on small, thin rectangular strips of paper and have them close to hand. Each message must be folded into the baked biscuit while they are still hot otherwise the cookies will crumble and break.

You will need the following ingredients:

1 egg white

Aleuromancy

$^1/_4$ cup/1 oz (28g) of caster sugar
$^1/_4$ cup/ 1 oz/ (28g) of flour
1 tbsp water
$^1/_4$ cup/ 1 oz/ (28g) of melted butter
$^1/_4$ tsp salt
$^1/_8$ tsp vanilla extract
Makes around 6 cookies.

Prepare some paper 'fortunes', around 5 cm long (2 inches), to place inside your cookies. Preheat the oven to 400°F/ 200°C/gas mark 6. Grease and lightly flour two flat baking trays. Put the egg white and sugar in a small bowl and mix till foamy but not stiff. Mix in the flour with a little water if necessary and add the melted butter, vanilla and salt and mix well. At this point it would be best to let the batter rest for around an hour.

After the batter has rested, place 1 tbsp of the mixture on the baking tray for each cookie; they should be around 6 cm (3 inches) in diameter. Using the back of a spoon, swirl the drops around until the cookies are spread very thin. Only bake one or two at a time because you need to work very quickly, but prepare your next tray while the others are cooking. Now bake for five minutes, or until lightly browned on the edges. Remove the cookies from the oven and quickly, while they are still hot, remove from the tray with a spatula and place upside down on a wooden surface. Put a fortune in the middle of the cookie and fold each cookie in half, across the width of the fortune and seal the edges as best, and as quickly, asyou can, trying to make sure that the sides

of the cookie puff outwards. Then in the opposite direction pinch the two corners towards each other (but not touching) across the fold to make that familiar crescent shape.

You could place the cookie over the edge of a glass or a cup to help you with this as you guide each pointed corner downwards. Allow the biscuits to cool in small drinking glasses or egg cup trays so that they keep their shape. Keep them in an airtight container.

Alternatively, if this is too fiddly for you (and believe me it is fiddly!) fortune cookies are fairly cheap to buy, especially if you get them from a specialist Chinese supermarket. But, I like the idea of having your own personal messages inside, so it's worth a try.

Each morning or last thing at night before you get ready for bed sit quietly and meditate on the day's events. Focus your mind and ask one question, then put your hand into your fortune cookie jar and choose one cookie. Break it open and read the answer to your question. Make notes in your diary of your questions and the answers you are given and later you can look back and see how accurate you were.

Apantomancy
Chance Meetings With Animals

Many years ago when my children were very small, an interesting incident occurred while we were driving along the main dual carriageway into Edinburgh. The traffic was heavy and moving slowly and about 50 yards ahead of us we noticed that a flock of sparrows were feeding on some discarded food. Suddenly a sparrow hawk flew past us about six inches above the pavement and swooped straight into the feeding sparrows. We were all yelling at each other excitedly, 'Look at that, look at that!' As we drew alongside we were able to see that the sparrow hawk had successfully pinned a sparrow beneath his talons. He shrouded his prey with his wings and looked defiantly at the passing cars.

This would be described as Apantomancy, a chance meeting with animals. I pondered on this event for a long time afterwards and wondered what message was being given to me by chancing upon a bird of prey in the middle of a busy city. I wondered if maybe the message was not for me but was meant for someone else travelling along the same road, witnessing the same sight. Strangely, however, it was on my return from this trip that I discovered I was pregnant with my long-awaited third child Tori. On this occasion the hawk did indeed foretell of a message that brings enlightenment.

Apantomancy Divination Exercise

It is not possible to engineer a divination exercise for this subject but you should pay attention from now on to all chance encounters with creatures in the animal kingdom and always make a note of the circumstances. You may not always understand at the time what the event means but referring to your notes later will help you to learn and be more aware as your experience grows.

Arithmomancy
Numerology (ALSO SEE SEPARATE ENTRY)

This is my favourite form of divination and I use it all the time. To me arithmomancy, or numerology, is my first language and every day I am aware of the significance of the numbers that are associated with that day or those numbers that I come across during the course of my work or leisure.

When working with numerology you need only to be concerned with the numbers one to nine, unless of course you plan to make a lifetime study of the subject.

* One is the number of leadership, new beginnings, new ideas and inspiration. The number one will show exciting new changes ahead.
* Two is the number of tact and diplomacy, balance and harmony. Be prepared for some surprises if the number two is significant.
* Three is the number of pregnancy and nursing or nurturing. Socialising, having good times with friends and joining clubs, societies or organisations will be relevant.
* Four is the number of security, assets and the home. Major changes around the home such as repairs, renovations and renewals can be expected, or visits from older males. Four is a very dependable number.
* Five is a number signifying keys that will unlock the answers to your questions or the door to your new home. It is the number that shows the problem areas in your life or any conflict that will be experienced. It is also linked to uniforms of any description.

- Six is the number of tenderness, compassion and difficult choices that have to be made, of crossroads being reached and the eternal triangle. Whereas five highlights the problem, six is the number that provides the solution.
- Seven is the number of control, and questioning comes in here. Control cannot be obtained without full knowledge of all facts surrounding you. With inner questioning, you can then resume control in your life.
- Eight is the number of strength, determination and stubbornness. This number will show that you or someone close to you will have to be very stubborn to achieve cherished goals.
- Nine is the number of completion, seeing the light at the end of the tunnel, or finding your way after stumbling around in the dark. It signifies difficult tasks being completed.

Arithmomancy Divination Exercise

Write a question on a piece of paper and write the numbers one to nine on separate sheets of paper. Mix the numbered pieces of paper and place them face down in a circle on the floor or on a table and put your question face up in the middle. Place both hands with palms facing downwards over the papers and focus all your attention on the question that you have written. Relax and concentrate. When you are ready, choose at random three numbered pieces of paper. Turn them over and look at the numbers.

Think about how you feel about the numbers that you have chosen or what, if anything, these numbers remind

Arithmomancy

you of. Spend a few minutes doing this and then add all the numbers together until you achieve a single number. That will be the answer to your question.

For example, imagine your question had been, 'Will my finances improve?' and your choice of numbers was two, four and eight. If you were born on one of these dates then you would consider your choice to be favourable since most people consider their birth number to be their lucky number. (To calculate your birth number see page 98.) Then you would look at each number independently.

Two is the number of tact and diplomacy, balance and harmony. Be prepared for some surprises if the number two is significant.

This could be an indication that you must balance your accounts and avoid unnecessary expenditure.

Four is the number of security, assets and the home. Major changes around the home such as repairs, renovations, and renewals can be expected or visits from older males. Four is a very dependable number.

I would be inclined to take this as an indication that you are on the right track and that you should concentrate on developing your assets rather than frivolous spending. There may also be some domestic expenses ahead that you will have to be prepared for, hence the advice given by the two should be heeded.

Eight is the number of strength, determination and stubbornness. This number will show that you or someone close to you will have to be very stubborn to achieve cherished goals.

Arithmomancy

This is self-explanatory and is clearly telling you that you must persevere with a strict budget to generate the improvements that you desire.

Now the fun begins: add the numbers two, four, and eight together and we have the total fourteen. Fourteen is made up of one and four.

One is the number of leadership, new beginnings, new ideas and inspiration. The number one will show exciting new changes ahead.

Four is the number of security, assets and the home. Major changes around the home such as repairs, renovations and renewals can be expected or visits from older males. Four is a very dependable number.

Add these two numbers together and we have the number five.

Five is the number representing keys, which will unlock the answers to your questions or the door to your new home. Five is the number that shows the problem areas in your life or any conflict that will be experienced. It is also linked with uniforms of any description.

I would interpret this answer as being linked to property or expenses associated with property. However, the one and the four show me that you will soon find a new form of financial security which will come to you through changes in or around your present home, provided that you are sensible and stick to a reasonable budget.

Astragyromancy
Divination Using Dice

For this form of divination you can use as many or as few dice as you like and then refer to the interpretations on the numerology list, but, generally speaking, two, three or four dice are best.

Astragyromancy Divination Exercise

Write a question on a piece of paper and place your written question face up in the middle of your table. Place both hands, palms facing downwards, over the question and focus all your attention on the question. Once again, relax and concentrate. When you are ready throw your dice. Remember to pay attention to any numbers that are particularly significant to you. Think about how you feel about the numbers that you have thrown and what, if anything, these numbers remind you of. Spend a few minutes doing this and then add all the numbers together until you achieve a single number. That will be the answer to your question.

Bibliomancy
Divination Using Books

For this form of divination you would think of a question or problem and then choose a favourite book, the Bible or a dictionary. Then, using a variety of methods, you randomly select a passage or word in the hope that this produces an answer or a clue to an answer.

If you would like to try this form of divination there are many inspirational books, such as the *Little Book of Fortune, Little Book of Calm* and *Words of Wisdom,* and books about guardian angels on the market. Alternatively, you can use a favourite book of mine by one of my favourite authors, Richard Bach. He says in his book *Illusions*:

'You are never given a wish without also being given the power to make it true. You may have to work for it, however.'

'There is no such thing as a problem without a gift for you in its hands. You seek problems because you need their gifts.'

'What the caterpillar calls the end of the world, the Master calls a butterfly.'

In another of his books entitled *Jonathan Livingston Seagull,* the character of the same name is one of a flock of seagulls who cares less about scrounging for food, and more about mastering the art of flying, than the other gulls. Jonathan Livingston Seagull loves to experience the thrill and exhilaration of flying faster and more dangerously than any gull has flown before.

More often than not he crashes, but he always gets up, gives himself a good shake and begins again. The other birds are furious with him and don't understand why he does this. The elders have a meeting and declare him an outcast. In this little book Jonathan Livingston Seagull says: 'When you come to the edge of all the light you have known, and are about to step out into darkness, faith is knowing one of two things will happen, there will be something to stand on, or you will be taught to fly.'

If this has whetted your appetite for more then perhaps Bibliomancy is for you.

Bibliomancy Divination Exercise One

First choose the book that you are going to work with. Make it one that holds a certain significance for you. Then make yourself comfortable in a chair or under a tree, somewhere that you will not be disturbed.

Follow your own pattern of breathing and relax, allowing yourself to drift deeply into your question or problem. Keep your chosen book in your hands whilst doing this and after some time, when you feel as though you are ready, randomly open your book and begin to read.

You should find your answer or something that helps you to find your answer on the pages that face you now. If the answer confuses you or you need more information - ask another question reatgarding this and open the book again, but content yourself with only one more question.

Bibliomancy Divination Exercise Two

Choose the book that you are going to be working with but this time you will need a pencil too. Follow the above relaxation exercise but this time when you open your book keep your eyes closed and use the pencil to mark the part that has your answer. Don't use a pen or you will not be able to rub out the mark that you have made.

Botanomancy
Divination Using Burning Branches and Leaves

This aspect of divination is entirely dependent on whether you have a garden and if you are permitted to burn garden refuse in your area. If this is permitted, the next time that you are having a clear out in the garden and you make a bonfire to clear away all the dead branches you will be able to read the signs in the sparks and the smoke created by the fire. Even the smell that is given can serve to remind you of things or trigger an inner knowledge.

Botanomancy Divination Exercise

For this exercise it is important to depend on your intuition and instincts. Before you begin, select the pieces of tree branches that are going to be used for answering your questions. Remember that the branches or twigs have at some time come from a living plant and proper respect and reverence should be shown. Also you will be using the element of fire and respect should be used here too. A verse to use could be:

Fire engulfing plant and tree,
Grant answers in your flames for me.
To these branches here alight
I ask my questions here tonight.

Alternatively, it would be a nice personal touch if you wrote your own verse.

Set the branches alight and sit in front of the flames, allowing your thoughts to drift over your current problems or questions. Use a notepad to jot down anything that you see or feel and always make sure that your fire is safe. You should never leave a fire unattended. Ideally you should allow the fire to go out of its own accord, but if you cannot, before the fire is extinguished thank the elements for assisting you and then smother the flames.

Capnomancy
Divination Using Smoke

This is similar to Botanomancy, but with Capnomancy you can use smoke from any burning source. A bonfire or a hearth fire will do nicely and all you have to do is sit in front of your chosen fire.

Capnomancy Divination Exercise

Be comfortable and relaxed and, as before, allow your gaze to blur whilst in your mind focus on the issues concerning you. It is also fine to just let your mind drift. As images come try to remember them so that you can make a note of them when you are done.

Cartomancy
Divination Using Playing Cards

In a deck of playing cards there are fifty-two cards made up of four suits – Wands, Cups, Diamonds and Swords. Each suit has cards numbered one to ten and then there are three Royal cards, the Jack, Queen and King. Most people are unaware that ordinary playing cards actually origninated from the set of seventy-eight Tarot cards. When it became dangerous to be found with Tarot cards, due to the threat of imprisonment and/or death, the scholars of the Tarot concealed the four Knights of the Tarot and the twenty-two Major Arcana, or Trump cards, leaving fifty-two cards of four suits. These suits were then identified as the ordinary playing cards, which we know today. Spades in Tarot are known as Wands, Hearts are referred to as Cups, Diamonds are known as Pentacles, and Clubs are known as Swords. It should be noted at this point that some people prefer to relate Clubs to Wands and Spades to Swords.

This equivalence shows how it is possible to read ordinary playing cards. However, the reading cannot be truly accurate because the Major cards, which show the changes caused by destiny, are missing and only the effects can be shown. Therefore only part of the story can be told.

Cartomancy Divination Exercise
to Answer One Question

Find a quiet place to sit with a work surface to put your cards on. Make sure that you will not be disturbed and make yourself comfortable. Have your cards and a notepad handy and put the date and time on the top of your page. Next write your question and sit quietly thinking of this question. While you are doing so hold your playing cards in both hands. Spread the cards face down in front of you and choose one card. You can then look to the following interpretations and write down in your notepad the card and the interpretation given. Also write down any feelings that you have pertaining to this.

When you have finished you should thank the higher energies for helping you. Later, when the problem or situation has reached a conclusion, refer back to your notes and write down the outcome as it developed and any circumstances surrounding the outcome or the lead up to it.

Cartomancy Divination Exercise for General Guidance

Find a quiet place to sit with a work surface to put your cards on. Make sure that you will not be disturbed and make yourself comfortable. Have your cards and a notepad handy and put the date and time on the top of your page. Next write 'General Guidance' on the page and then sit quietly thinking of your life as it is and how you would like it to be or of any issues that concern you. While you are doing so hold your playing cards face down in both hands. Count out five cards and put these five cards to the bottom of the deck and the sixth card to one side. Count out five cards and as before put these five cards to the bottom of the deck and the sixth card on top of your first 'sixth card'. Continue to do this until you have six cards in your pile. Now turn over your pile of six cards.

The first card relates to your life up till now.

The second card relates to your present circumstances.

The third card relates to your immediate future.

The fourth card relates to your future circumstances.

The fifth card relates to your objective.

The sixth card relates to the influences that will be present.

You can then look to the following interpretations and write down in your notepad the card and the interpretation given. Also write down any feelings that you have pertaining to this.

When you have finished thank the higher energies for helping you. Later, when the problem or situation has reached a conclusion, refer back to your notes and write down the outcome as it developed and any circumstances surrounding the outcome or the lead up to it.

Short Interpretations of Ordinary Playing Cards

Spades (Wands in the Tarot deck)

The suit of Spades, which is associated with the element of Air, tells you about things that you have on your mind and refers to the season of spring.

Ace of Spades – this will be a fertile period in your life.

Two of Spades – you will make a short journey.

Three of Spades – you will plan for your future.

Four of Spades – you will be more content than you have been in recent times.

Five of Spades – quarrels and confusion will upset you.

Six of Spades – you will hear news that will be to your advantage.

Seven of Spades – stick to your principles.

Eight of Spades – you will make several journeys in the near future.

Nine of Spades – you will feel worn out and wonder if you can cope.

Ten of Spades – you will reach the end of your tether.

Jack of Spades – the sign of Sagittarius will be significant and you will have an unexpected visitor.

Queen of Spades – the sign of Leo will be significant and you will hear some gossip.

King of Spades – the sign of Aries will be significant and you will receive an offer of work.

Hearts (Cups in the Tarot deck)

The suit of Hearts, which is associated with the element of water, tells us about things that we have in our hearts and our feelings, and refers to the season of summer.

Ace of Hearts – you will be loved and cherished.

Two of Hearts – you will receive a proposal or a romantic offer.

Three of Hearts – you will celebrate with friends.

Four of Hearts – someone is thinking of you romantically.

Five of Hearts – you will be filled with sadness or regret.

Six of Hearts – you will receive an apology or have a reunion.

Seven of Hearts – you will choose between two loves.

Eight of Hearts – you will have a change of heart.

Nine of Hearts – your wishes will be granted.

Ten of Hearts – your heart will be filled with joy.

Jack of Hearts – the sign of Pisces will be significant and you will hear of a pregnancy or birth.

Queen of Hearts – the sign of Scorpio will be significant and someone with fair hair will bring good news.

King of Hearts – the sign of Cancer will be significant and an older person will be helpful.

Diamonds (Pentacles or Coins in the Tarot deck)

The suit of Diamonds, which is associated with the element of fire, tells us about our finances and anything to do with how we spend or earn our money, and refers to the season of autumn.

Ace of Diamonds – you will be given the chance to start again.

Two of Diamonds – you will buy new shoes. You will struggle financially.

Three of Diamonds – contracts will be signed and weddings and christenings will be significant.

Four of Diamonds – financial security will come to you.

Five of Diamonds – you will lose money.

Six of Diamonds – you will receive or win money.

Seven of Diamonds – you will find something that you are looking for.

Eight of Diamonds – you will learn something new and work with your hands.

Nine of Diamonds – you will experience a new-found abundance.

Cartomancy

Ten of Diamonds – you will study a new subject and have a
family reunion.

Jack of Diamonds – the sign of Capricorn will be significant
and money will arrive.

Queen of Diamonds – the sign of Aquarius will be significant
and an older woman will be helpful.

King of Diamonds – the sign of Gemini will be significant
and you will discuss or arrange mortgages, investments or
insurances.

Clubs (Swords in the Tarot deck)

The suit of Clubs, which is associated with the element of
earth, tells us about the things that we can do or are doing,
and refers to the season of winter.

Ace of Clubs – you will feel empowered and be able to achieve
things as opposed to merely wishing for them.

Two of Clubs – be patient and do and say nothing.

Three of Clubs – you will shed tears.

Four of Clubs –do not make changes or become involved
with another's problems.

Five of Clubs – gossip and jealousy will upset you.

Six of Clubs – you will move to a new home.

Seven of Clubs – beware of theft and people who cannot be
trusted.

Eight of Clubs – you will feel trapped in your present
situation.

Nine of Clubs – you will be let down at the last minute.

Ten of Clubs – you will crumble under pressure and feel

unable to cope, but things will improve.

Jack of Clubs – the sign of Taurus will be significant and papers will be signed.

Queen of Clubs – the sign of Virgo will be significant and you will experience or witness anger and resentment.

King of Clubs – the sign of Libra will be significant and legal or medical matters will require attention.

Catoptromancy
Crystal Gazing in the Moonlight

This form of divination requires a full moon, a mirror and some warm clothes, especially if it is a chilly night, and, of course, a safe place to work.

Catoptromancy Divination Exercise

Once you have gathered together all the things that you need, place your mirror on the ground or on a suitable surface where it will capture the rays or the reflection of the moon. Make yourself comfortable and sit or stand in front of your mirror and gaze at the reflection of the moon in the mirror. Allow your focus to drift and blur whilst concentrating on any issue that you have on your mind. With practice images may come to you and when you are done note your thoughts or anything of importance that you have felt or seen. Later, when you are at home, you can go over your notes and you can also refer back to them at a later date.

Ceroscopy
Divination Using Wax in Water

This method of divination is messy but interesting. You will need a bowl of water, a lighted candle, your notebook, a pen and a solid surface to work on. Before you attempt to answer a question you should practise dropping the melted wax into the bowl of water and analysing the shapes that form.

Ceroscopy Divination Exercise

Make yourself comfortable and ensure that you will not be disturbed. Prepare all the things that you need – notepad and pen, candle and matches, and, of course, your bowl of water. Focus your attention and allow your mind to drift into a higher state. Recite the following verse:

> *Candle burn and water flow*
> *Show me shapes, that I may know.*

When you are ready take the candle in your right hand, tilt it to one side and allow drops of melted wax to fall into your bowl of water. Try to identify the shapes that form and note them in your notepad. When working with methods of divination that require both hands it is sometimes easier to record your notes on a tape recorder. Later you can copy your impressions into your notepad. When you feel comfortable with this method of divination you can progress to answering single questions.

Cleidomancy
Divination Using a Key

This method of divination can be carried out using a key, a needle or a piece of jewellery and is often referred to as dowsing. You can make your own dowser or pendulum by tying a piece of string to a key, or using a needle suspended from a piece of thread or a ring suspended from a chain. Once you have made your pendulum you can begin to practise using it. Hold your pendulum. Think 'yes' and observe the movement of the object that you are using. It may spin gently in a circular movement or it may swing gently from side to side. Think 'no' and observe the movement or lack of movement. Once you are familiar with this you can try the following exercises.

Cleidomancy Divination Exercise to Find Something That is Lost

Close your eyes and imagine a white light above your head. Allow your thoughts to focus on the lost object and try to think back to the last time that you saw or held the missing item. Hold the pendulum in your right hand, draping the cotton or chain over your index finger so that the ring, key or crystal is suspended about six inches below your hand. Stand in the middle of your room and mentally draw a line down the centre of the floor. Hold the pendulum at arm's length to your right and mentally ask if the item is on this side of the line. Observe the movement. Room by room, then section by section, you can gradually narrow down the location of the missing object. You can also write on pieces of paper various locations or questions, then fold them up, lay them in a line and mentally ask for the answer while holding your pendulum over each one. Keep trying, trust your instincts and this should work for you.

Cleidomancy Divination Exercise One, to Answer a Question

Before you begin, gather together everything that you need – a pen and a piece of paper and your pendulum. Write your question on the piece of paper and then hold your pendulum in your hand. Close your eyes and imagine a white light above your head and allow your thoughts to focus on your question. Now place the pendulum over the question that is written on your piece of paper and watch to see if there is any movement.

Cleidomancy Divination Exercise Two to Answer a Question

For this exercise write the words 'yes' and 'no' on two separate pieces of paper and lay them face down on your work surface. Shuffle the pieces of paper around so that you do not know which one says what. When you are ready, think of your question and then dowse over each piece of paper to find the answer.

Coffee Gazing
Divination Using Coffee Grounds

For me, this is where it all began because when I was small I used to watch my mum fortune telling for neighbours. She insists that it was using cups of coffee but my memory tells me tea. No matter. Either way, coffee gazing is very accurate but only with practice and only if you are totally prepared to trust your instincts. This is a really nice relaxed social method of divining.

Divination Exercise

Make yourself a pot of freshly ground coffee. Do not use a coffee filter. A percolator is fine as long as when the coffee is poured and drank some grains and dust are still left in the cup. It is best to use a shallow, white, fluted cup rather than a mug. If you are reading for someone other than yourself make sure that your guest does not talk about personal issues or discuss the reason why they wish to have a reading.

After the coffee is finished take the guest's cup and look into it. If there are no grains at the bottom of the cup then another cup will be required. If this happens again it could be that you are not meant to read for that person or that they are meant to solve their problem themselves. If there is too much liquid remaining in the cup, slowly pour the excess into a saucer but do not discard it as this too can be read.

Excess liquid is often an indication of tears but these can be tears of joy as well as sadness and the reading will give you a clue as to which. Undissolved sugar gathered in the cup indicates sweetness, compliments and pleasant times ahead. The symbols that are at the top of the cup are those that are closest in time and those near the bottom are further away in time. Sometimes grounds in the shape of numbers and signs of the Zodiac that are next to symbols will guide you. Study the interpretations at the end of this book and, where you can, memorise them and use them to interpret the shapes you see in the grounds. But do not forget that your intuition will be the most accurate method that you can use.

Crystallomancy
Divination using Crystals

This is a simple form of divination and to use this method it is important to have a good selection of crystals. My interpretations for crystal divination use the more popular, easy to obtain crystals, and even if you only use this form of divination occasionally you will get a great deal of pleasure from the beautiful crystals in your collection.

Preparation and Dedication of Crystals

Make sure that you keep your crystals clean and uncontaminated by negative energies. A simple method for cleaning crystals is to rinse them in spring or even tap water but every now and then I use a mixture of one tablespoonful of cider vinegar water, one tablespoonful of coarse salt and a few pints of warm water. Mix them all together but do not put the crystals into the mixture until the temperature is hand hot. If the water is any hotter than this you could crack some crystals. Leave the crystals to soak for twenty minutes and then rinse in clean running water.

Once you have done this, if you have the time, put them on a windowsill as the moon is rising (waxing) and leave them there until the moon is full. While your crystals are being 'charged' you can busy yourself preparing a mat to work with when you are divining them.

It is best to use a silk cloth. I have one that I use when I am working with my Tarot cards. I bought a plain black napkin and a fabric pen and I drew my favourite spread on my mat. I drew patterns and symbols on it that I wanted to remember. By the time I had finished my project, a week later, I had succeeded in remembering the meanings of the symbols. In addition, I had a cloth that was personalised and that I was very proud of. You can do the same and design it in any way that you choose. Do not worry if you are not good at drawing because you can always buy New Age magazines or books where you will find zodiac symbols that you can trace and then copy onto your mat.

When your mat is ready and your crystals are fully charged the next step is to dedicate your crystals to your purpose. To do so, prepare a work surface and make it as pretty or as simple as you like. Place a candle in a candle holder on your work surface. You could dedicate a green taper candle to the process of finding answers by anointing it with three drops of essential oil of marjoram mixed with 10 ml of almond oil. [After the divination is over let the candle burn down naturally or extinguish with a snuffer but not by blowing out.]

Spread your cloth. Light your candle and spread your charged crystals on the mat. Place both hands, palms down, above the crystals and visualise bright golden white light spreading through your hands from above and covering your crystals and your mat. Say your chosen verse from the list below or use words of your own and spend some time sharing the good energy with your crystals. The same method can be used to cleanse and dedicate a single crystal. When your crystal or crystals are charged and dedicated put them in a small pouch and keep them in the pouch until you are ready to use them.

Verses for Crystal Dedications

Dedication for divination:

> Crystals, pure and filled with light,
> Your purpose true upon this night,
> Let your power shine for me
> In the secrets that you free.

Dedication for recalling dreams:

> A dream I had, but can't recall
> I ask this crystal, which knows all,
> To share with me my sleeping thoughts
> An answer from my dreams is sought.

Dedication for healing:

> Little crystal, power pure
> Bring good health to ***** for sure.
> Your healing power is what I ask
> To help me in my healing task.

Dedication for improved finances:

> Little crystal gleaming bright
> Boost my money, hear my plight
> Better off I wish to be
> So I can be worry free.

Crystallomancy

Dedication for love

> Mutual love, that is good and kind,
> Passionate, faithful and of like mind,
> With crystal power I seek a mate
> I put my trust in you and fate.

Divination Exercise Using Crystals

Now that you are ready to begin, gather all your things ready for use:

> Crystals, in their pouch
> Divining mat
> Candle and holder
> Matches
> A small bowl in which to put spent
> matches
> A bottle containing 3 drops of
> essential oil of marjoram and
> 10 ml of almond oil (with which
> to anoint your candle if you wish)
> A bowl of water and a flannel to
> wipe your hands on

Prepare yourself mentally for the task you are about to perform and make sure that your hands are clean. Prepare your work surface with the items listed, make yourself comfortable and, if you are doing this for someone other than yourself, make sure that they are relaxed and comfortable too.

Hold the pouch of crystals in both hands and spend a few quiet moments thinking of your questions and sharing positive energy.

If you are divining for yourself put your left hand into the pouch and draw out one handful of crystals and allow the cystals to fall onto the mat.

If you are divining for someone else pass the pouch of crystals to the person that you are reading for and ask them to hold them, spending a few moments thinking of their questions and sharing positive energy with the crystals. Have the subject put their left hand into the pouch and draw out one handful of crystals and allow them to fall onto the divining mat.

Be aware of the predominance of certain colours
The colours will give you clues and the colour chart will help you to understand what you are being told.

- **White** is for purity, cleansing and knowledge.
- **Red** is for passion, excitement and action.
- **Pink** is for love and romance.
- **Orange** is for strength, power and courage.
- **Yellow** is for energy, vitality and motivation.
- **Green** is for healing, growth and fertility.
- **Blue** is for tranquillity and peace.
- **Purple** is for protection, meditation and spirituality
- **Turquoise** is for communication, protection and travel.
- **Black** is for grounding and dispelling negative energies.

The numbers formed

Look at the grouping, as you may find that some crystals have separated from the rest and they may be lying in groups of, for example, three or seven. This too may give you greater insight.

- One is the number of leadership, new beginnings, new ideas, and inspiration. One will show exciting new changes ahead.
- Two is the number of tact and diplomacy, balance and harmony. Be prepared for some surprises if the number two is significant.
- Three is the number of pregnancy and nursing or nurturing. Socialising, having good times with friends and joining clubs, societies or organisations will be relevant.
- Four is the number of security, assets and the home. Major changes around the home such as repairs, renovations, and renewals can be expected or visits from older males. Four is a very dependable number.
- Five is the number representing keys that will unlock the answers to your questions or the door to your new home. Five is the number which shows the problem areas in your life, or any conflict that will be experienced. Also linked with the number five are uniforms of any description.
- Six is the number of tenderness, compassion, difficult choices which have to be made, cross roads being reached, and the eternal triangle. However, where five shows the problems, six is the number that provides the solution.
- Seven is the number of control, and questioning comes in

here. Control cannot be obtained without full knowledge of all facts surrounding you. With inner questioning, one can then resume control in one's life.

- Eight is the number of strength, determination and stubbornness. This number will show that you or someone close to you will have to be very stubborn to achieve cherished goals.
- Nine is the number of completion or seeing the light at the end of the tunnel, finding your way after stumbling around in the dark. It represents the completion of difficult tasks.

Once you have examined these things you can then begin to look at the meanings in each separate crystal.

Sample divination

In this reading seven crystals fell.

1 Agate – Difficult obstacles will be overcome.

2 Bloodstone – Legal and business matters will be dealt with and the outcome will be in your favour.

3 Malachite – You will overcome an obstacle that you thought was insurmountable.

4 Labradorite – Be persistent in all your efforts and you will be rewarded.

5 Hematite – You will be offered a helping hand from an unexpected source.

6 Jasper – You will be touched by a sharing experience with someone.

7 Tourmaline Green – You will become more active and your prosperity will increase.

There were seven crystals and so the reading for seven is relevant:

'Seven is the number of control. Control cannot be obtained without full knowledge of all facts surrounding you. With inner questioning, one can then resume control in one's life.'

The crystals fell in two groups:

'Two is the number of tact and diplomacy, balance and harmony. Be prepared for some surprises if the number two is significant.'

There were two crystals in one group: one Malachite and one Agate. Both these crystals indicate that obstacles will be overcome and the significance of the number two indicates that information that you do not have will be revealed and this is what will make the difference.

Five crystals were in the other group: Bloodstone, Labradorite, Hematite, Jasper and Green Tourmaline.

• Bloodstone indicates that legal and business matters will be dealt with and the outcome will be in your favour.
• Labradorite indicates that you should be persistent in all your efforts and you will be rewarded.
• Hematite indicates that you will be offered a helping hand from an unexpected source.
• Jasper indicates that you will be touched by a sharing experience with someone.
• Tourmaline Green indicates that you will become more active and your prosperity will increase.

'Five is the number representing keys that will unlock the answers to your questions or the door to your new home. Five is the number which shows the problem areas in your life, or any conflict that will be experienced. Also linked with the number five are uniforms of any description.'

I would consider this to be a reading with a good outcome especially as far as business and legal matters are concerned.

Crystal interpretations for divination:

You can use the following interpretations as a guide when divining with crystals:

Agates – Difficult obstacles will be overcome.

Agate Blue Lace – You will receive a letter or telephone call.

Agate Moss – An emotional problem will be solved and you will feel more content with your life.

Amber – You will be blessed with good fortune.

Amethyst – A decision will be made.

Aquamarine – Although you may not think so, you will be strong and cope with a difficult situation and all will be well.

Aventurine – You will be given additional responsibilities and financial increase.

Bloodstone – Legal and business matters will be dealt with and the outcome will be in your favour.

Calcite – Old friends will reappear and misunderstandings will be settled.

Carnelian – You will be involved in a passionate affair and the arts will be important.

Crystallomancy

Celestite – Do not despair, calm will return and your pain will be eased.

Citrine – You will receive an unexpected windfall.

Fluorite – You will be protected from an abusive or aggressive situation or person.

Hematite – You will be offered a helping hand from an unexpected source.

Jade – You will be more organised and this will reflect on other areas of your life and help you to attract what you want.

Jasper – You will be touched by a sharing experience with someone.

Labradorite – Be persistent in all your efforts and you will be rewarded.

Lapis Lazuli – You will enjoy sharing quality time with friends or family members.

Malachite – You will overcome an obstacle that you thought was insurmountable.

Moldavite – An unexpected situation may catch you out but you will deal with whatever comes and do what must be done.

Moonstone – You will hear news of a pregnancy or birth.

Obsidian Black – You will be reluctant to commit to something or to someone's request and you are right to feel this way.

Pearl – Peace will be restored and ther will be a happy outcome to a fretful situation.

Peacock Ore – You will re-evaluate your plans or have a change of heart.

Crystallomancy

Peridot – You will feel stronger and filled with renewed energy.

Pyrite – You will move to a new location.

Quartz – You will instinctively know what to do next and when to do it.

Rose Quartz – Romance is in the air and you will have a new found happiness.

Ruby – You will be successful in all your endeavours.

Rutilated Quartz – Someone may try to meddle in your affairs but you will politely let them know that their advice or attention is neither required nor helpful.

Sapphire – Partnerships may require some additional attention to improve.

Smoky Quartz – You may have to study a new subject or look more closely at a problem to find the correct solution.

Sodalite – You will receive news that will give a deeper understanding of a person or situation that you are confused about.

Tiger-eye – New subjects will be studied and you will be hopeful about a future opening.

Tourmaline – You may feel as though you are stuck in the middle but soon you will make the correct decision and be able to decide where you stand.

Tourmaline Black – An unexpected development will remove you or yours from a difficult situation.

Tourmaline Pink – A new friend will be made or a new romance will begin.

Tourmaline Red – You will be determined to succeed and succeed you shall.

Tourmaline Green – You will become more active and your prosperity will increase.

Turquoise – You will be surprised by conflict among friends or in the workplace. Do not allow yourself to become involved in this.

Cyclomancy
Divination Using a Wheel

I can recall playing with this form of divination as a child and remember getting a coloured card wheel in a 'lucky bag' or perhaps a Christmas cracker. The wheel was divided up into sections like a pie and each section was a different colour and had a different number printed on it.

There was a wooden spindle through the centre and when you twisted it, the wheel spun and finally settled on one part of the edge. The part of the edge that touched the floor indicated the number and colour that related to your question.

Cyclomancy Divination Exercise

You could make your own Cyclomancy fortune telling wheel by cutting a piece of card to the size of a dinner plate. Using a pen, divide the wheel into twelve sections in the form of a pie chart. Colour each section to correspond with the twelve signs of the zodiac and decorate each section with zodiac symbols.

Aries	♈	red
Taurus	♉	red, orange, blue
Gemini	♊	orange, silver, grey
Cancer	♋	silver, white, yellow, orange
Leo	♌	yellow, gold, orange
Virgo	♍	grey, yellow, green
Libra	♎	green, light blue
Scorpio	♏	green, blue, dark red

Cyclomancy

Sagittarius	♐	blue, purple
Capricorn	♑	deep blue, dark green
Aquarius	♒	indigo, pale blue, green
Pisces	♓	violet

Number each section from zero to eleven and then pierce the centre of the wheel with a skewer.

Relax and focus on your wheel and your own thoughts and ask your question in the usual fashion. Spin the wheel and see where it stops. Use the number and colour interpretations listed in this book to help you find your answers. For the number ten read good luck, winning and changes connected to transport or home. For the number eleven, read legal and medical matters and power. The significance of the rest the numbers has been covered under the heading of Arithmomancy.

Dactylomancy
Divination Using a Ring

This method of divination is similar to dowsing, except that a ring is used. The ring is dangled on a piece of cord over words or numbers.

Dactylomancy Divination Exercise

You can try the above method of divining by suspending a ring on a cord or chain and you can obtain your answers just by thinking of the question or by writing things on pieces of paper and then suspending the ring over each piece of paper until the ring spins. Always remember to treat any form of divination (fortune telling) seriously. If you approach it flippantly then it will not work. In any case, you should respect the powers that

Geomancy
Divination Using Random Drawings

Sometimes people refer to this form of divination as ghost writing, spirit writing or automatic writing. (The poet WB Yeats and his wife Georgina were both interested in occult practices – Yeats was a Member of the Order of the Golden Dawn – and they both participated in automatic writing.)

Some people find it really easy to perform and even write books using this method whilst others find it almost impossible to do. The object of the exercise is to allow yourself to drift into a subliminal state while holding a pen and paper and then you wait until your hand begins to spontaneously write.

Geomancy Divination Exercise

First prepare yourself mentally for the task you are about to perform. Make sure your surroundings are neat and tidy and that you will not be disturbed. Have a work surface ready with pen and paper, and perhaps some incense and a candle. Make yourself comfortable and relax.

Place the pen or pencil in your hand over the blank paper and allow yourself to drift into a higher state of awareness. Some people give themselves a fright when they actually start to write things but don't be put off. Just allow the pen or pencil to move and gradually become comfortable with this method. If words are produced, their meaning may be obvious to you or they may need some interpretation. Similarly, if symbols or random drawings are produced that don't initially seem to hold significance for you, you may have to consult the lists of symbols at the end of this book.

After some practice you may find that this is a successful method of divination for you.

Graphology
Divination Using Handwriting

There is a complete science devoted to the study of handwriting. Everything is taken into consideration – the size, style, angle and the shape of the letters, and much more and so there is no space here to do study of the subject justice. I have a simpler method though, using intuition rather than a scientific or psychological approach, that you might like to try.

Graphology Divination Exercise

Ask a friend to bring you a selection of letters or even just the envelopes and begin by practising on these. Hold the letters and scan the handwriting, though not the content, of the letters, allowing your impressions and feelings to guide you rather than attempting a scientific approach. Talk to your friend and describe what you feel when you hold the letters, and the impression you get of the writer's feelings and intentions, and ask your friend to make notes. When you have finished ask your friend whether your conclusions were accurate.

Again, with practice you can perfect this form of divination. If you find you have a particular talent and intuition for 'reading' letters in this way, why not study one of the many books on graphology that are available and expand on your ability.

Gyromancy
Divination by Walking in a Circle

This is simply a much bigger version of Cyclomancy, divination using a wheel. Fans of *Big Brother* in the UK (with long memories) may remember the game that Kate and Tim played in Big Brother 3 when they ran around a brush handle and, in a severe state of dizziness, then were sent running across the room. They had consumed quite a bit of alcohol, and funny though it was, I don't recommend that for this exercise, you'll be dizzy enough. The object of the exercise is to randomly select letters to form words that will give a message or answer a question.

Gyromancy Divination Exercise

Gather together a brush handle, a pack of A4 paper, a marker pen … and a very good friend who will not think that you have lost your senses! You will need fourteen pieces of A4 paper, each halved in two. Print a letter of the alphabet on each piece of paper and on the last two the words 'yes' and 'no'. Place the papers randomly in a circle on the floor face up. And now the fun begins. Stand in the middle of the circle of papers with your right hand on the top of the brush handle and begin to walk quickly round in a tight circle. When you become dizzy you will begin to stagger about and as you touch a piece of paper your friend should make a note of the letter. With any luck you might just have your question answered – though you'll probably be lauging so much you won't care whether you do or not!

Numerology
Divination Using Numbers

This form of divination has ancient origins, but is also a modern way of interpreting names and dates in terms of vital numbers, all of which are indicative of individual traits. I have been asked in the past to look at why certain individuals have success in their lives while others appear to have nothing but problems. On analysing their numbers I have discovered that those who are successful have positive numbers while those who are beset by problems have negative ones. Numerology is a more in-depth look at arithmomancy and uses all the numbers that are involved in the search.

Have you ever wondered just what makes you tick? Some people will say they are typical of their astrological star sign while others will say that they are nothing like theirs. Why is that so? There is a link between where and when you were born which forms part of your character and decides how you will act in, or react to, given situations in your life, but there is so much more than just the astrological influence at work.

Did you know that the numbers in your date of birth play a very large part in forming your character? In fact, these numbers will motivate and mould you, and their influence will be with you for the rest of your life.

There are also numbers in your name. Alan, for example, is a one and this is the number of leadership. Anyone whose name adds up to one should never be afraid to follow his or her dreams. They will also have moments of pure genius but it is up to them whether or not they pursue these insights. Unlike your birth number, your name number is not constant. It can change if, for example, you have a nickname. If Alan is sometimes called Al he then becomes a four, and the influences of this number are different. As a four he will be more concerned with stability and security, and will not be easily unsettled in a crisis. He is so dependable as a four that often friends or family will go to him for advice or support.

It is important also to look at surnames because these too influence our lives. When a woman takes a man's name in marriage she drops her surname and its number and adopts his surname and his number.

Sometimes this complements the numbers and attributes that she already has, although on other occasions it can create conflict or negative influences. So, if you've just got married and feel out of kilter, don't immediately jump to the conclusion that all is not well, it might just be your numbers.

There is a solution though – just by changing how you spell your name you can make a difference. For example, Anne adds up to eight whereas Ann adds up to two. It's only when we know and understand the meaning of numbers and how they influence our lives that we can begin to use them to our advantage.

Two of my clients are celebrities who were out of work and not achieving their potential. They felt that they were not being recognised for their talents. After an initial consultation I was able to discover that they each had influences in their names that were not significant to success in their chosen fields. With a few changes to the spelling of their names they have both gone on to have successful careers.

Most people will have a lucky number, or a number that has some special significance to them. So if you are going to try the next exercise, jot down on a piece of paper the number or numbers that you feel are important to you.

Numerology Divination Exercise – Character Analysis

Before you begin you must find the numbers that are significant to you. Start off by using the number and letter chart below to find the numbers that are relevant in your date of birth and your name.

Birth Number

This is the number that motivates your life. This is obtained by adding the numbers in your date of birth.

For example, Dave Reynolds' date of birth is
22.12.1949
$(2 + 2 + 1 + 2 + 1 + 9 + 4 + 9) = 30$
$(3 + 0) = 3$

Birth number $= 3$

Your birth number is the number that motivates and moulds you throughout your life and, unlike your name number, no changes can be made here.

Name Number

The next step is to find your name numbers. Use the following chart to change the letters of your name to their numerical value. Most people consider this their lucky number.

1	2	3	4	5	6	7	8	9
A	B	C	D	E	F	G	H	I
J	K	L	M	N	O	P	Q	R
S	T	U	V	W	X	Y	Z	

First Name Number

Write your first name and its associated numbers, and add the numbers together as you did for your birth number.

For example:

D   A   V   E
4   1   4   5 = 14
1 + 4
First name number = 5

Here the major influence in the first name Dave is five. Include any other name that you have if it is used in your daily life. For example, your first names may be Sarah and Jane, and you are addressed as Sarah Jane.

My other first name is Elizabeth but it is a name that is never used so I do not consider it when working with numerology.

Your first name displays the character that you show to

your friends, those people who address you by no other name than your first name.

Now find the vowels in your first name, enter them in the grid below and add them together until you again have a single digit.

Vowel Number

For example:

D   A   V   E

     1   5 = 6

The vowels in your first name will show your inner personality. This is the side of your character or nature that you keep to yourself.

Consonant Number

Now find the consonants in your first name, enter them below and add them together until you again have a single digit.

For example:

D   A   V   E

4   4   = 8

The consonants in your first name will show the side of your nature that you allow others to see, your outer personality.

Surname Number

Now repeat this exercise with your surname:

R	E	Y	N	O	L	D	S
9	5	7	5	6	3	4	1

$9 + 5 + 7 + 5 + 6 + 3 + 4 + 1 = 40$

$4 + 0 = 4$

Whole Name Number

Now add together your first name number and your surname number only.

Dave Reynolds' first name number is 5 and his surname number is 4, therefore his whole name number is 9.

The whole name number displays the character that you show to associates or in situations where you are required to sign your name.

Destiny Number

The next step is to find your destiny number. Your destiny number is a combination of your name and birth numbers and, as with your name number, changes can occur here through marriage, divorce or choice.

For example:
Birth number: 3
Whole name number: 9

Add the two together until you have a single digit:

$3 + 9 = 12$

$1 + 2 = 3$

Dave Reynolds' destiny number is 3.

Prediction Number

This will show the general indications for any month of any year and must be recalculated each year as your numbers will change from year to year. To discover your monthly number you must first take your destiny number and then add the value of the month and year in question. Each month has its own value and the following table will help you with your calculations.

Jan	= 1	Feb	= 2	Mar	= 3
Apr	= 4	May	= 5	June	= 6
July	= 7	Aug	= 8	Sep	= 9
Oct	= 1	Nov	= 2	Dec	= 3

Example:

To calculate the month of October 2008 for Dave Reynolds the following formula is used:

His destiny number = 3
October = 1
2008 (2 + 0 + 0 + 8) = 10 = 1 + 0 = 1
This new total is the prediction number =
3 + 1 + 1 = 5

You can expand on this by adding the entire date, For example, to use the date 25/10/2008 the numbers that you would add together would be:

For the day = 2 + 5 = 7
For the month = 1 + 0 = 1

For the year 2008 = (2 + 0 + 0 + 8) = 10 = 1+ 0 = 1
Total = 7 + 1 + 1 = 9
Then Dave would add his destiny number, three, to the number nine.
9 + 3 = 12 = 1+ 2 = 3

To recap:

Dave's first name number	5
Dave's inner personality	6
Dave's outer personality	8
Dave's full name	9
Dave's birth number	3
Dave's destiny number	3

Missing numbers

Pay close attention to the numbers that do not appear in your profile since you can learn a lot about your character here too. If you choose, you can add these numbers into your name by adding an initial (number) in between your first name and surnames.

Definition of Name Numbers

One: This is the first number and people who have the number one as their name number tend to be leaders. They like to be first at everything – first in the queue, first to know something and, of course, first to do things. These people are, or appear to be, generally impulsive and often have moments of sheer brilliance. They are more likely to be leaders than followers, they are generally very popular socially and professionally.

They have the courage of their convictions and are not afraid to speak their minds. Negative aspects, however, may make them appear to be pushy, forceful, eccentric, egotistical, domineering and sometimes paranoid or self-conscious. If you have this number as your name number, recognise your positive traits and work with them, and do your best to avoid the negative aspects of this influence.

Two: This is the number of balance and harmony, truth and beauty. People who have this name number are generally very deep, and friends and family members may feel as though they never really know what they are thinking. This person will mostly be respected and admired because they make good friends or companions and are helpful in difficult situations without becoming too involved. They are good judges of character and when they have made up their mind about something they are difficult to shift. They prefer to follow rather than lead but they are very capable of leading without any difficulty. Negative aspects that these individuals have are being secretive and picky, as well as sometimes narrow-minded and biased.

Three: People whose name corresponds to this number tend to be friendly and outgoing yet sympathetic and charitable. They will be self-sacrificing and would do without to help another. Very often these individuals trust their instincts. Although they are ambitious, they value their security and are unlikely to make rash decisions. They will have good friends and make entertaining and interesting company.

Capable of overcoming obstacles, they will achieve their ambitions. A negative trait is beingover-indulgent and excessive on the social scene.

Four: This is a very dependable name number and people whose name corresponds to four can be relied upon in a crisis and make true and loyal friends. They value and respect their homes, and property matters will concern them to the extent that a second home will be desired and probably obtained. They like to be active and involved in a variety of things and will have many interesting experiences. On the negative side, they can fall to pieces if they have a crisis of their own to deal with and become despondent if others think that they can cope instead of offering a helping hand. They can also be a little boring, valuing their security to the extreme.

Five: People whose name corresponds to this number are likely to be extremely curious and will often answer a question with another question. For example, if you say: 'Why did that happen?' they are likely to say: ' Why do you ask?' They change their friends as often as they change their shoes and absolutely must have variety in their life to survive. On the negative side, they can be ruthless and nosey and, at worst, enjoy spreading gossip.

Six: People whose name corresponds to this number will always find it hard to make decisions or choices. Although when asked a favour they will say 'yes', they will often avoid carrying out the favour, believing it is easier to say 'yes' and let someone down rather than say 'no' in the first place. They are, however, among the kindest and most charitable people. On the negative side they cannot be depended upon and are often infuriating when it comes to decision-making.

Seven: This is the number that is associated with control, and people whose name corresponds to this figure will want to do things their own way in spite of any advice or guidance that they may be offered. On the surface they may appear to be reckless and have a tendency to make rash decisions, when in fact they have probably thought long and hard before making their choice and simply have not discussed this with anyone. They tend to be studious and intellectual, and often have an amazing collection of books on a variety of spiritual and unusual subjects. On the negative side, they can be domineering and forceful, and expect to have everything their own way.

Eight: This is the number of strength and determination, and people whose number corresponds to the number eight will have strong personalities. They are very honest, balanced and hard working, and will persevere with a problem or task when others have long since given up. They appear to be placid and even-tempered but when pushed they have a tendency to erupt like a volcano.

Nine: This is the number of completion and blesses the bearer with the ability to complete tasks that others cannot cope with. Friendly and charming, individuals whose number corresponds to nine often appear rather eccentric, and are changeable like the weather. They have vivid imaginations and are capable of making up stories that will entertain and amuse, but you only discover this when you really get to know them as initially they can appear refined and stand-offish.

Eleven and twenty-two are power numbers that hold special significance and so should be analysed without being reduced like the others.

Eleven: Anyone who corresponds to this name number will be a strong, powerful individual who will possess the courage to take on any challenge and also the persistence to see it through to the end. They thirst for adventure and quickly become bored with the more mundane aspects of life. On the negative side, they are restless and intolerant of others who are not as smart as they are.

Twenty-Two: People whose name corresponds to this number will always feel as though they are on the edge of something great – but they usually do not have the courage to take the next step. They tend to act younger than their years and sometimes blame others or outside circumstances for their lack of success. People with this name number have to work very, very hard to achieve.

Definition of Birth and Destiny Numbers

One: You will lead rather than follow and reach the top of any career that you choose. You will make your own choices and if someone else has already done something you will know that you can too. If no one has achieved a particular thing then you will decide that you can be the first. The sign of Capricorn will be prominent in your life.

Two: Although your life will be interesting and successful you could do better if you chose to. Law, medicine and journalism may interest you. With the ability to listen to both sides of an argument and find a happy medium you would make an excellent arbitrator. The sign of Aquarius will be prominent in your life.

Three: You will have many friends and be liked and admired by them all. The caring professions will attract you because you will enjoy looking after the needs of others less fortunate than yourself. Children, family, pets and horticulture will be significant and important to you. The signs of Pisces and Scorpio will be prominent in your life.

Four: Your life will be successful because of the effort you put into it and nothing will hold you back or stand in your way. Property and all things connected to property will attract you, and friends will come to recognise your reliability to do what you say and say what you mean. The sign of Aries will be prominent in your life.

Numerology

Five: You will have a varied and interesting life because you will do everything in your power to make it so. Engineering, investigative journalism, the police force, the military and education will be of some interest or significance. The sign of Taurus will be prominent in your life.

Six: Do not be afraid to take a few chances or make changes in your life, otherwise when you are older you will find yourself saying 'I remember the chances I missed,' or 'I wish I could do it all over again,' and 'I would do this or that.' If you take the odd chance you can be successful. The sign of Gemini will be prominent in your life.

Seven: Success, success, success. You are off to a good start and from there you will make things happen. However, you will have to work hard for it though. Sometimes you may feel frustrated at other's inadequacies but you will shine and outshine those who compete with you. The sign of Cancer will be prominent in your life.

Eight: You will be hard-working, eager to succeed and diligent in your efforts. Financially, you may not be very good at looking after your money. 'Save' is the key word that you should remember and then you can help to overcome or even avoid this negative tendency. The sign of Leo will be prominent in your life.

Nine: You will enjoy a variety of experiences and, although this will make you an interesting individual, you may find that you come across as a 'know it all'. Only a nine could cram so much into one life and this is because you find it hard to stick to one thing. On the positive side you will find that this variety of experiences gives you the ability to be able to turn your hand to almost anything and you will be a great help in an emergency because of your ability to know what to do next. Well, you will have seen it all before! The sign of Virgo will be prominent in your life.

Eleven: If you are involved in group activities you will be the one to take control because yours is a power number. The only time that this may not be true is when another person in the same group also has the number eleven in their profile. Then the power struggle will begin and others will watch in amazement. You will make your mind up about situations or people very quickly and if you do not like what you see or hear you will turn and walk away without a backward glance. You will be successful in your life because you will grab opportunities and make the most of them. If they do not suit you later, you will drop them. The sign of Libra will be prominent in your life.

Twenty-Two: You will be responsible for creating your own problems and will most certainly be your own worst enemy. Knowing this, you can change it and be observant of your attitude and actions. You can be easily led or manipulated and should be more cautious of the company that you keep and the people that you trust. Success can be yours but only if you can learn from your mistakes and overcome a tendency to act immaturely and not face up to your responsibilities. The sign of Sagittarius will be prominent in your life.

Prediction Numbers

When you are trying to find out what a particular day will hold for you, calculate the date and your destiny number together as you have been shown in the previous pages. Keep adding up the numbers until you have a single digit and then look at the list below to see if you are forecast a good or not-so-good day.

One: New business and career opportunities will come during this time and you will form new friendships. This is an important and lucky time and you can do or achieve almost anything that your heart desires.

Two: Patience will be required as things will not happen as quickly as you would like. There is likely to be a house move in the near future and overseas travel will be important. Old friends will return and a few surprises will catch you out.

Three: Accomplishment, recognition and the realisation of ambitions are forecast. Marriage or new business partnerships are highlighted. Make the most of this vibration as everything is possible. News of a pregnancy or a birth will be significant.

Four: Concentrate on the home, property and business

matters and do not burn the candle at both ends. Your focus should be on your finances, your security and your stability. People who are older than you will be important.

Five: Change, change, change. Contracts and documents will be important. Complete transformations are possible. This is a good time to take chances, but only if you are aware of all the facts and figures.

Six: Renewing old friendships and settling differences is possible now. A happy home life and success in relationships is in store. Your soulmate will be very significant at this time.

Seven: In business this is a prosperous time, but care should be exercised when making large purchases. You are warned not to work too hard. Expect the unexpected.

Eight: You will now begin to see the results of efforts that you have made in the past, even though it feels as though it has been a long time coming. This is a good time to invest in property.

Nine: Completion of projects is forecast here and the need to take a little time to yourself. Avoid impulsive actions and think carefully before embarking on new directions.

Eleven: At this time you will be able to realise your ambitions and overcome any obstacles that have been standing in your way. Expect good news concerning legal medical or business matters.

Twenty-Two: Stay close to home, do not make any changes and be careful whom you trust. Reschedule any important meetings to a day that corresponds to a better number. Youngsters may cause you problems too.

Further Clues
   1 Beginnings
   2 Surprises
   3 Pregnancy
   4 Property
   5 Keys
   6 Lovers
   7 Arrivals
   8 Persistence
   9 Reunions
   10 Luck
   11 Justice
   12 Change
   13 Peace
   14 Caution
   15 Fear
   16 Despair
   17 Fame
   18 Betrayal
   19 Brightness
   20 Interviews

Numerology

21 Endings	50 Bliss
22 Caution	51 Taurus
23 Sagittarius	52 The unexpected
24 Abuse	53 Virgo
25 Leo	54 Libra
26 Aries	55 Division
27 Impregnation	56 Tolerance
28 Temporariness	57 Grief
29 Permanence	58 Caution
30 Contentment	59 Conflict
31 Confusion	60 Movement
32 News	61 Theft
33 Accomplishment	62 Prison
34 Travel	63 Disappointment
35 Burdens	64 Exhaustion
36 Despair	65 Capricorn
37 Pisces	66 Chance
38 Romance	67 Aquarius
39 Scorpio	68 Gemini
40 Cancer	69 Opportunity
41 Love	70 Struggle
42 Marriage	71 Celebration
43 Celebration	72 Security
44 Depression	73 Poverty
45 Sadness	74 Windfall
46 Reunion	75 Find
47 Choices	76 Receptions
48 Re-evaluation	77 Abundance
49 Accomplishment	78 Study

Numerology

79 Nostalgia
80 Perseverance
81 Conclusions
82 Surprises
83 Success
84 Change
85 Endings
86 Decisions
87 Fear
88 Crisis
89 Accomplishment
90 Answers
91 Excitement
92 Triumph
93 Transformation
94 Loss
95 Self-control
96 Dread
97 Disaster
98 Reputation
99 Misery
100 Inevitability

Psychometry
Divination Using Touch

Some time ago I was having a coffee and a chat with a biker friend of mine. Del hadn't a clue about tarot, divination, runes or any of the subjects that I love. If you had asked him about his higher self he would have looked at you with an expression of panic and confusion. Anyway, we were sitting having a chat and he asked me if I could tell him anything about himself. Here we go again, I thought, but I began by looking at his name and date of birth and the number that made up his profile. He was so amazed that he asked me if I would read his tarot cards. I did that too and again he was stunned by all the things that I knew about him.

By this time I was getting pretty fed up and tired answering all his questions but he was on a roll. 'Tell me more, tell me more,' he said.

'Right, this is the last thing that I am going to do for you; get me something that you have had for a long time.'

He jumped up from his chair and dashed about looking for something for me to hold. Forgetting that Del knew nothing about divination, I thought to myself, 'Why doesn't he just give me his ring or his watch?'

'Here, try these,' he said, coming back into the room with his slippers. I laughed so much the tears were running down my face. Of course, he didn't know what I was laughing at and I was laughing too much to tell him. But it worked. I actually did read his slippers. That is what psychometry is all about, reading what you feel using the power of touch.

Psychometry Divination Exercise

Invite a few of your friends around one evening for a practice session on psychometry and tell them to bring pieces of jewellery (not slippers!). Have them put these items into a dish. Put a piece of your jewellery into the dish too. When everyone is comfortable and relaxed take turns choosing a piece of jewellery from the dish and begin to discern what you see and feel. No one should guide you in any way and you might find that you instinctively know who the piece belongs to. Say everything that you see or feel and ask someone to take notes. When you are finished, someone else can take a turn. If this is practised regularly you can achieve some amazing results.

Runes
Divination Using an Ancient Wisdom

Everyone, all over the world, from every kind of walk of life, is familiar with the use of symbols or signs in their communication. We have them on our roads telling us to slow down, speed up or stop. Supermarkets, oil companies, political parties, the Church and the medical profession, to name just a few, all use symbols to identify their organisations and the elements within them.

Some symbols are modern, designed by graphic designers and artists in marketing companies, but some are drawn from history and tradition. Here we are going to look at some symbols that come from ancient Nordic culture: the Runes.

Of all the esoteric disciplines that are used today, for me, the runes have proved themselves time and again to be among the most accurate of them all.

The Scottish National Party uses a runic symbol called Othel or Othillo, which can be interpreted to stand for home, family and integrity. When we cross our fingers to make a wish, we are making another symbol called *Gefu*, which represents harmony and togetherness.

I was fascinated when I first became acquainted with runes and I wondered how they could help me in my life. I put them in an onyx box and kept them beside my bed. Each night before I went to sleep I would draw one rune, asking as I did so, 'What have I experienced today?' It was not long before I realised how accurate they were. Later, I would draw one in the morning, asking what the day would have in store for me. I managed to take advantage of opportunities that were shown to me and to avoid some pitfalls too.

When you are using the runes for guidance, it is very important to think of one question only. Also runes cannot answer an 'either-way' question. You can ask 'What will be the result if I do this?' but you cannot ask, 'Is it better to do this or that?' When you have prepared a single question in your mind, draw a rune from the box or bag where you keep them. You can draw again for other questions, but no more than three times in any day.

There are twenty-five runic symbols and each one represents a letter of the Germanic alphabet. Each rune tells a historical story to help us to understand or deal with issues in our lives. Some runes, no matter which way they fall, look exactly the same.

An x, for example, looks the same both ways while others in the upside down position give a more negative interpretation. I have listed the runes below in alphabetical order with a brief description so that you can easily refer to them. If you would like to know more see my *Book of the Runes*.

Ansur or *Ansuz* for communication

Beork or *Berkana* for rebirth, new beginnings and fertility

Dagaz or *Daeg* for hope and promise

Eoh for reliability and travel

Eolh for friendship and protection

Runes

Fehu for wealth, property, power and status

Gefu or *Geofu* for partnerships, marriages and engagements

Hagall or *Hagalaz* for projects or situations

Ing or *Inguz* for fertility

Runes

 Isa or Is represents a standstill

 Jara or *Ger* represents rewards for
your efforts

 Ken or *Kano* for openings and
invitations

Lagu for water related topics and
the feminine element

Mann or *Mannaz* for true sharing friendship

Neid or *Nauthiz* for restrictions or problem areas

Othel or *Othillo* for the home, family and integrity

Peorth or *Perth* for secrets and hidden information

Runes

Rado or *Rad* for travel and transport

Sigel for victory.

Thorn or *Thurizas* for cautious action

Tir or *Teiwaz* for winning

Runes

 *Uruz* for overcoming challenges

Wunjo or *Wynn* for joy

the
blank
rune

Wyrd for the inevitable

 Yr for continuous effort

Tarot
Divination Using Tarot Cards
(See also CARTOMANCY)

Prepare yourself and your cards and either ask your question or ask for guidance. Then, when you feel ready, draw one card from the pack. You can either choose the top card or you can fan your cards in front of you and choose the card that feels right to you.

If you don't understand what you are being told or if you draw a court card that relates to the astrological sign of someone you know, you can draw an additional card.

The Three-Card Spread

Prepare yourself as before and this time draw three cards. You can ask to be given guidance for past, present, and future or for a particular issue. You are in control here and you will be given any guidance that is available, providing you ask in the first place. As with the earlier spread you can draw an additional card or cards if necessary.

Tarot Interpretations
The Major Arcana

0 The Fool

The Fool in a reading shows that you are coming to the end of a cycle and that a new one of some importance is about to begin. The fool can be looked upon as the bridge to be crossed.

1 The Magician

This is an exciting card. Having completed a cycle of life's experiences, you are about to begin another. You are being given the chance to do it all again and this time you can do it without mistakes, providing you remember those made in the past and the lessons that have been learned from them.

2 The High Priestess

The High Priestess is known as The Keeper of Secrets and The Mistress of Destiny. She contains all the wisdom and knowledge of times gone by and times to come. Patience will be required during this waiting time. Papers, certificates and documents will be important. There will be surprises, renewals and reunions. Higher education is also indicated.

3 The Empress

The Empress is an indication of pregnancy, and can also show someone who is involved in a caring profession, such as maternity care, childcare, care of the elderly, social work or teaching.

4 The Emperor

The Emperor shows major changes around the structure of your life. This can mean a change of job, a change of residence or someone moving into the home. Security and stability are shown by the appearance of this card.

5 The High Priest

Keys, promotion, advancement and opportunities are

associated with this card. Buildings of historical or architectural importance and uniforms can be significant.

6 The Lovers
Your soulmate is with you or will appear. Choices will have to be made here, and which direction, which job, which partner can be some of the questions asked.

7 The Chariot
Since the chariot is a mode of transport, this card can be telling you about changes around your vehicle. Driving lessons and tests can be significant here. This is also a card which speaks of new directions being pursued and of unexpected arrivals.

8 Strength
The key words are strength, determination, and persistence. You are being told to hang in there. Although you may feel things are not going your way, you will soon reach a conclusion or find a solution.

9 The Hermit
Someone or something will enter your life bringing solutions to problems, an end to loneliness and light at the end of the tunnel. This card can also indicate a child being born.

10 The Wheel
This card indicates gatherings and getting together with friends. Since the wheel links to movement and travel, you

can be looking at changes regarding your vehicle. New tyres, tax discs and driving tests can be significant here.

11 Justice
Any official, legal or medical matters will be resolved with a good result. Something that went wrong in the past will be righted on your behalf.

12 The Hanged Man
Suspended animation or being stuck in a rut is exactly how you will be feeling when The Hanged Man appears in a reading. This will change overnight and a very active period will begin.

13 Death
A period of turbulence and sadness is coming to an end and will be replaced by security and stability.

14 Temperance
Go with the flow for the time being and try to exercise moderation in everything that you do. There are indications within this card that you or someone close to you has a dependency problem.

15 The Devil
Fear is the key here. You may be afraid to make changes in your life or experience panic attacks. Opportunities will be missed if this fear is not overcome.

16 The Tower

The Tower can be your worst nightmare. It can range from losing your purse to losing everything that you have. It can be over in a second or it can go on for a long time. Some people call it a run of bad luck. This card denotes misfortune, but before you panic, look to the other cards that accompany it in a spread to make your interpretation.

17 The Star

This is a beautiful card because it speaks of hopes being fulfilled and dreams being realised. Brightness and recognition are indicated as well as opportunities and chances that will be presented to you.

18 The Moon

Depression, anxiety, feeling stabbed in the back and not knowing who to trust are shown with this card.

19 The Sun

This is such a happy card after the previous one. It bestows brightness, joy, vitality and many other positive qualities. This card is especially potent when it appears after or covering a difficult one.

20 Judgement

When Judgement comes into a spread, it is referring to some kind of confrontation. You will either instigate this or be the recipient of it. If your conscience is clear then you have nothing to worry about.

21 The World

The World card indicates that a cycle is being completed and you are being advised that you are going to be given a chance to start again. The World is an indication that everything is achievable and distance is no object. Patience will be required.

The Minor Arcana
The Suit of Wands

Wands are connected to Air and so remember that when you see them in a spread you are mainly looking at thoughts and ideas. That is to say, how you think or will think.

Wands are symbolic of artistic or creative projects, such as writing, drawing or painting, but they can also show mundane, ordinary chores or tasks.

The Ace of Wands

This card brings excitement, enthusiasm and motivation, symbolising a new lease of life.

The Two of Wands

This card brings surprising changes. It symbolises temporary conditions such as planning a short break.

The Three of Wands

This card denotes the making of plans and looking forward to the future.

The Four of Wands
This card indicates peace of mind and contentment in and around the area that this card occupies. Refer to the cards surrounding this one too.

The Five of Wands
This card indicates conflict and confusion, too many obstacles or problems in your way.

The Six of Wands
This card indicates that you will get a good result regarding something. You will hear good news, or feel a sense of victory.

The Seven of Wands
This card indicates that you should stick to your principles and not back down.

The Eight of Wands
This card indicates that packing and unpacking suitcases will be important.

The Nine Wands
This card indicates that problems and responsibilities will overwhelm you.

The Ten of Wands
You will feel as though you have reached the end of your tether. You have, as this is the end of the present period of difficulties.

The Knight of Wands
This card indicates emotional, verbal or physical abuse. Road rage or minor road accidents might also be represented. If this appears with the tower in the same house or a connected house, the situation will be major and care should be used when explaining this.

NEVER leave a querent (person addressing the cards with a question) with fear.

The Page of Wands, Sagittarius
This card indicates that you will recieve long-distance letters, telephone calls, invitations and visitors.

The Queen of Wands, Leo
This card means that you will hear a piece of news or information to your advantage.

The King of Wands, Aries
This card suggests that a job offer or business opportunity will be given.

The Suit of Cups

The first thing to remember when you are looking at Cups is that they are linked to water which is connected to our emotions. When Cups appear in a reading they are referring to how you feel or will feel about things. Bear in mind the significance of the number of the card as this will help your interpretation.

The Ace of Cups
This card symbolises perfect truth, love and harmony.

The Two of Cups
This card indicates proposals, promises or contracts.

The Three of Cups
This card denotes celebrations, gatherings and heartfelt joy.

The Four of Cups
This card indicates that someone is thinking of making you an offer.

The Five of Cups
This card expresses that the querent is looking back with sadness and regret, wishing things could be as they were.

The Six of Cups
This card symbolises apologies and memories from the past returning.

The Seven of Cups
This card warns that you should choose carefully and not sell yourself short.

The Eight of Cups
This card symbolises the re-evaluation of your life and the making of changes.

The Nine of Cups
This card indicates that, whatever they are, your wishes will be granted.

The Ten of Cups
This card indicates that things will turn out much better than you expect.

The Knight of Cups
This card indicates that friendship, romance, and love that are linked to your past, are about to come back into your life.

The Page of Cups, Pisces
This card indicates that a small gift will be offered and you will hear of a pregnancy.

The Queen of Cups, Scorpio
This card indicates that contentment and happiness is promised.

The King of Cups, Cancer
This card symbolises a generous offer, a kindred spirit or someone or something that will be supportive.

The Suit of Swords

Swords are all about actions and words. Although some of the sword cards bring good influences, most bring problems and have to be handled carefully.

Look to the other cards in the spread for guidance.

The Ace of Swords
This card symbolises decisive action, clean breaks, fresh starts and purpose and direction.

The Two of Swords
This card indictes the need to tolerate situations that cannot be influenced.

The Three of Swords
This card symbolises grief and heartache.

The Four of Swords
This is a warning: do not get involved in other people's problems or you will be blamed for causing them.

The Five of Swords
Conflict, accusations, arguments and hassle. You are caught in the middle of other people's problems and are being blamed.

The Six of Swords
With the appearance of this card, a house or job move is indicated.

The Seven of Swords
This card indicates that a thief is around, be careful of personal security.

The Eight of Swords
This card could indicate that you feel trapped or restricted. Its symbolism may be more literal – you may hear of someone who has been given a jail sentence.

The Nine of Swords
This card indicates that you feel as though you just can't take any more, but another problem will be revealed.

The Ten of Swords
This card indicates that you feel as though you've reached the end of your tether. This is the last straw but a fresh start will come soon.

The Knight of Swords
This card symbolises a sudden change in circumstances will sweep you off your feet.

The Page of Swords, Taurus
This card could indicate an official demand for money, or official documents that require further action.

The Queen of Swords, Virgo
This card symbolises anger, resentment and bitterness – either being felt, expressed or heard of.

The King of Swords, Libra
This card indicates the involvement of a lawyer, doctor, dentist or professional person acting on your or another

person's behalf.

The Suit of Pentacles

Pentacles are about money, security, work, assets and opportunities.

The Ace of Pentacles
This card indicates a chance to start again, a golden opportunity.

The Two of Pentacles
This is a card of mixed metaphors: you are walking a tightrope, trying to make ends meet and spreading yourself too thin. In short, your time, money and patience are being stretched.

The Three of Pentacles
This card symbolises the signing of contracts and/or the receiving of a sum of money.

The Four of Pentacles
This card symbolises financial security and stability.

The Five of Pentacles
This card symbolises deprivation, loss of security and fear of the future.

The Six of Pentacles
This card symbolises a windfall, unexpected financial gains.

The Seven of Pentacles
This card indicates that financial help will come from an unexpected source.

The Eight of Pentacles
This card denotes working for yourself or being responsible for how much you can earn through commissions or bonuses. It could indicate that you will soon be earning more money or learning new manual skills.

The Nine of Pentacles
This card symbolises abundance and security.

The Ten of Pentacles
This card indicates the achievement of new academic skills because of, or leading to, new opportunities.

The Knight of Pentacles
This card symbolises an offer which at first does not look very important, although it will develop into something more significant.

The Page of Pentacles, Capricorn
This card indicates that you will receive a valuable gift, money or a cheque.

The Queen of Pentacles, Aquarius
This card symbolises achieving or receiving financial security.

The King of Pentacles, Gemini
This card indicates that bank managers, accountants,
financial advisers or influencial people will be supportive.

Tasseography
Divination using tea leaves (see coffee gazing)

Zodiac
Divining the future through the positions of the planets

The twelve signs of the Zodiac are traditionally subdivided into a number of groups.

Triplicities or Elements

Fire

Aries, Leo and Sagittarius are the fire triplicity. Subjects of this element are represented by a keenness and enthusiasm in all their ventures – a fire for life – but also a potential for a certain impatience and selfishness.

Earth

Taurus, Virgo and Capricorn are the earth triplicity. This element is summed up by the phrase 'down to earth'. Earth signs are practical and reliable but can be considered dull by the more lively signs.

Air

Gemini, Libra and Aquarius form the air triplicity. They are full of ideas and exciting ventures, but as the symbolism suggests, these might be 'up in the air' as their practical or cautious side is sometimes lacking.

Water

Cancer, Scorpio and Pisces form the water triplicity which is characterised by emotion, intuition and a desire to be protective of others. They have the potential to let their strong emotions overrule their common sense sometimes.

Quadruplicities or Qualities

Cardinal signs

Aries, Libra, Cancer and Capricorn are of cardinla quadruplicity. This means that peolple with this sign dominant in their chart are outgoing and tend to lead.

Fixed signs

Taurus, Scorpio, Leo and Aquarius are of fixed quadruplicity. These signs show a desire to remain stable, maintain normality, and show a resistance to change.

Mutable signs

Gemini, Sagittarius, Virgo and Pisces all have the ability to accept and welcome change. They adapt to fit environments.

Positive and Negative, Masculine and Feminine

Positive, Masculine

Aries, Gemini, Leo, Libra, Sagittarius and Aquarius have more of a tendency towards the qualities of being self-expressive and extrovert.

Negative, Feminine

Taurus, Cancer, Virgo, Scorpio, Capricorn and Pisces have more of tendency towards the qualities of being receptive and introvert.

Polarity

On a circular representation of the signs the following signs are opposite each other. However, this does not mean they are complete opposites. In fact they have very compatible qualities and complement each other.

Aries and Libra   Cancer and Capricorn
Taurus and Scorpio   Leo and Aquarius
Gemini and Sagittarius   Virgo and Pisces

Planets

Each sign has a ruling planet, each planet has a sign in which it works well (exaltation), a sign in which it is debilitated (detrimental), and a sign in which it is weak (fall). These are shown below:

Planet		Ruling	Exalted	Detrimental	Fall
Sun	☉	Leo	Aries	Aquarius	Libra
Moon	☽	Cancer	Taurus	Capricorn	Scorpio
Mercury	☿	Gemini and Virgo	Virgo	Sagittarius	Pisces
Venus	♀	Taurus and Libra	Pisces	Aries	Virgo
Mars	♂	Aries	Capricorn	Libra	Cancer
Jupiter	♃	Sagittarius	Cancer	Gemini	Capricorn
Saturn	♄	Capricorn	Libra	Cancer	Aries
Uranus	♅ ♁	Aquarius	Scorpio	Leo	Taurus
Neptune	♆	Pisces	Leo	Virgo	Aquarius
Pluto	♇ ♀	Scorpio	Virgo	Taurus	Pisces

The Sun Signs

Aries ♈
The First Sign of the Zodiac: 21 March–20 April

Born under the Fire sign of Aries, a cardinal sign that is ruled by Mars, your fortunate gemstones are amethyst, diamond, bloodstone and opal. The colour red and the numbers six and seven are important to you and your best day of the week is Tuesday. Your best choices of occupation are in the fields of security, law and the military, and you can be very successful in running your own business. Your most fortunate location to live or work in is a large city. You are most compatible with the signs Aries, Gemini, Libra, Leo, Sagittarius and Aquarius, but you do not favour the signs of Taurus, Cancer, Scorpio, Capricorn, Virgo and Pisces.

You have a dynamic personality and can be very intense, and you need plenty of fresh air, sunshine and good food to support your drive. Your sign governs the head and face and these are the areas where you will be most susceptible to ailments. Look after your eyes, teeth and gums, and avoid head colds and throat infections. One of the advantages that you have is that when stricken, you recover well. In affairs of the heart you can be extremely sensitive but can be prone to jealousy and this is something that you should avoid.

Your earning capacity is good however you are inclined to be a generous spender and you prefer to have the very best rather than what you can afford.

As a friend you are very loyal but, when crossed, you can be unforgiving and tend to hold a grudge. You should try to be more patient with yourself and others.

The Aries child will require careful handling and does not like to be pushed or forced into doing anything. He or she can be led and encouraged but will react stubbornly if driven. Aries children are adventurous and have no fear whatsoever.

The Aries woman is the traditional good woman behind the successful man. She is witty and charming and likes to look smart and attractive. Regardless of how successful her husband is, she will want to do something for herself and is very capable of doing so.

The Aries man tends to be distinguished in his appearance and always has somewhere to go and someone to see. He is always busy and is capable of being in charge of several things at one time. He likes his partner to be smart, good looking and considerate of his needs. He has a healthy appetite in all aspects of his life and needs to feel fulfilled.

Things to avoid are restlessness, anger and a tendency to act impulsively.

Famous People who share your sign are actors Marlon Brando, Charlie Chaplin and Sir Alec Guinness and Soviet premier Nikita Khrushchev.

Taurus ♉
The Second Sign of The Zodiac: 21 April–20 May

Born under the Earth sign of Taurus, a fixed sign that is ruled by Venus, your fortunate gemstones are amethyst, diamond sapphire and moss agate. Friday is your best day of the week and the colours red/orange and blue, and the numbers one and nine will be fortunate to you. Your most fortunate location to live or work is anywhere that is quiet, and your best choice of occupation is in the fields of the arts, drama and music, cosmetics and the land. You are most compatible with the signs Taurus, Cancer, Scorpio, Capricorn, Virgo and Pisces but you do not favour the signs of Aries, Gemini, Libra, Leo, Sagittarius and Aquarius.

You have an easy-going personality until you are crossed and then you become obstinate and headstrong. Your sign governs the ears, neck and throat, and any sensitivity will be present in those areas. Typical of the bull, you may have a tendency to indulge in all things pleasurable so you should exercise some control over what you eat and drink. If you are sensible with your diet, you will avoid many common ailments.

In affairs of the heart, you have to feel as though you are adored and if your loved one does not pay you enough attention, a dark cloud descends over you.

Your success will come through dedicated application and you have the patience and persistence to forge ahead when others would fall by the wayside.

The Taurus child is generally very even-tempered and good-natured but they are quick to anger and can be very stubborn. They will, however, recognise their mistakes and learn from them. They are capable children and, although they mix well with others, they enjoy their own company.

The Taurus woman is affectionate and friendly. She makes a loyal partner and a devoted mother. She can be very determined and will be driven to achieve success or to assist her partner in achieving his. She needs material security in her life and will do all she can to develop it.

The Taurus man is dependable and very reliable. He generally exudes a sex appeal that makes him attract many female friends. He is supportive of his wife and family, and always puts them first. When single he will play the field with a healthy appetite but once he has chosen his partner he will be content and seldom strays. He has a great appreciation of beauty and likes to see this in his partner.

Things to avoid are jealousy, rage and a stubborn attitude.

Famous people who share your sign are artist Salvador Dali, singer Bing Crosby, dramatist William Shakespeare and Queen Elizabeth II.

Gemini ♊
The Third Sign of The Zodiac: 21 May–21 June

Born under the Air sign of Gemini, a mutable sign that is ruled by Mercury, your fortunate gemstones are emerald, tourmaline and lapis lazuli. The colours orange, silver and grey, and the numbers three and four will be lucky for you, and your best day of the week is Wednesday. The most fortunate location to live or work is anywhere that is high above sea level, and your best choice of occupations are in the fields of aviation, law, medicine, writing, printing, the media and travel. You are most compatible with the signs Aries, Gemini, Libra, Leo, Sagittarius and Aquarius, but you do not favour the signs of Taurus, Cancer, Scorpio, Capricorn, Virgo and Pisces.

You have a magnetic and attractive personality and will have many admirers. You enjoy the respect of others but can occasionally take people by surprise because of your short temper.

Your sign governs the hands, arms, chest and lungs and you should do your best to avoid coughs and colds. You can be inclined to overwork your mind and body and this can play havoc with your health too. In affairs of the heart, you are more likely to be stimulated by the mind of your lover rather than how he or she looks.

Your earning capacity will vary from time to time and you would be well advised to keep something by for rainy days. As a friend, you are interesting and you will have many acquaintances and a very active social life.

The Gemini child is curious and will keep you occupied

answering questions about everything. They are very versatile and can handle almost anything, appearing to be little geniuses. The only thing that they find difficult is finishing what they have started and this is a skill which they have to be taught at an early age.

The Gemini woman is capable of running a home and a family with the same ease as someone who is running a business. She is meticulous in her approach to every job, large or small, and demands just reward for every effort that is made. If it comes to a battle of wits, she will win.

The Gemini man likes change and variety, and enjoys being many things to many people. He can work for an employer and run a small business on the side. He is usually very attractive and interesting to be with.

Things to avoid are restlessness and a tendency to be overconfident.

Famous people who share your sign are actress Marilyn Monroe, actress/singer Judy Garland, actor Errol Flynn and comedian/actor Bob Hope.

Cancer ♋
The Fourth Sign of The Zodiac: 22 June–22 July

Born under the water sign of Cancer, which is a Cardinal sign, your fortunate gemstones are pearl, moonstone aquamarine and sapphire. Your ruling planet is the Moon and the colours silver, white, yellow and orange are fortunate to you. Your best day of the week is Friday, and the numbers eight and three will be lucky for you. Your most fortunate location to live or work is close to water, and your best choice of occupations are in the fields of law, medicine, teaching, Engineering, catering, and the arts. You are most compatible with the signs of Taurus, Cancer, Leo, Scorpio, Capricorn and Pisces but you do not favour the signs of Aries, Gemini, Virgo Libra Sagittarius and Aquarius.

You have a quiet reserved personality and prefer a few loyal friends rather than many. Your sign governs the chest and stomach, and although you will have a strong constitution, you should maintain a healthy diet which will help you to guard against stomach disorders. You have a sensitive nervous system and should avoid worry, stress and depression. In affairs of the heart you are very affectionate and regard love as a serious matter. You will be totally devoted to your partner and easily roused to jealousy.

The Cancer child is receptive, imaginative and versatile. They can be timid and retiring, and are generally more comfortable in the home around family rather than mixing with newcomers and outsiders.

The Cancer woman can be quite difficult to get through to because of her crusty shell but she is the most motherly of all the signs. She is patient and devoted to the people she cares for and is very protective. She should guard against moodiness and depression, and overcome fear of achieving success.

The Cancer man is devoted to home and family but if too many demands are made on him he can turn into a nasty, old crab. He likes to spend a lot of time in and around the home and he likes it to be neat and tidy. His biggest fears are failure and poverty but he is likely to be successful. The Cancer man is very sensitive and easily hurt but he would never admit to this. If he is hurt in any way he will show his crusty exterior and this is almost impossible to penetrate.

Things to avoid are jealousy, spite, fear and gambling.

Famous people who share your sign are Roman Emperor Julius Caesar, actor James Cagney and jazz musician Louis Armstrong.

Leo ♌
The Fifth Sign of The Zodiac: 23 July–23 August

Born under the fire sign of Leo, which is a fixed sign, your fortunate gemstones are ruby, emerald and black onyx. Your ruling planet is the Sun and the colours yellow, gold and orange will be fortunate to you. Your best day of the week is Sunday and the numbers five and nine will be lucky for you. The most fortunate location to live or work is anywhere where there is lots of space around you, and your best choice of occupation is in the fields of politics, insurance, public utilities and production. You are most compatible with the signs Aries, Gemini, Libra, Leo, Sagittarius and Aquarius, but you do not favour the signs of Taurus, Cancer, Scorpio, Capricorn, Virgo and Pisces.

Although you are courteous and considerate you can be forceful and commanding and have the ability to influence others. Your sign governs the heart and bestows you with a generosity second to none. You have amazing recuperative abilities and can bounce back quickly when sickness befalls you. In affairs of the heart you can be very intense and are inclined to let your heart rule your head. Your earning capacity can be improved by cultivating a conservative attitude and overcoming a tendency to be free with your money. As a friend, you are entertaining and amusing and prefer to be at home with companions rather than socialising in the bright lights.

The Leo child is wilful, preferring to lead rather than follow, but their pleasant nature tends to attract followers making it unnecessary for them to exert their dominance. They prefer to be outside, playing in wide-open spaces rather than being confined inside. When their tummies are full they are happy and content but they will be grumpy and fretful if they are hungry.

The Leo woman is passionate, attractive, and more often than not beautiful. Whatever she does, she puts her heart and soul into it. As a wife, she is a devoted partner but if her partner allows it, she will rule him to the limits of his endurance.

The Leo man is a very proud man and he likes his home and his family to reflect this. He is generous and kind but does not tolerate disloyalty or disobedience under any circumstances. He is the ruler of his pride of lions and demands to be treated as such. He is not easily fooled by anyone and does not suffer fools gladly.

Things to avoid are egotistical and impulsive behaviour.

Famous people who share your sign are political leader Napoleon Bonaparte, film producer/director Alfred Hitchcock and writer Sir Walter Scott.

Virgo ♍
The Sixth Sign of The Zodiac:
23 August –22 September.

Born under the Earth sign of Virgo, which is a mutable sign, your fortunate gemstones are diamond, jasper and sardonyx. Your ruling planet is Mercury and the colours grey, yellow and green, and the numbers eight and four will be lucky for you. Your best day of the week is Wednesday and the most fortunate location to live or work is a small city. Your best choice of occupation is in the fields of science, statistics, medicine, investments, publishing, promotions, property and anything to do with the land. You are most compatible with the signs Taurus, Cancer, Scorpio, Capricorn, Virgo and Pisces but you do not favour the signs of Aries, Gemini, Libra, Leo, Sagittarius and Aquarius.

As a friend you are you are trustworthy and diplomatic since you have a very good memory making you capable of examining all the facts and seeing both sides of any situation. You do not like being confined or restricted to small spaces and need freedom of movement to function to your fullest potential. Your sign governs the digestive organs and the intestine so you should look after your diet and get plenty of fresh air and sunlight. In affairs of the heart, you tend to be afraid to show your true feelings and suffer deeply if rejected. During your life, you will be presented with many opportunities to improve your finances and your success or failure will be depend on your dedication rather than good fortune. You are in control of your own destiny.

The Virgo child is intellectual and is best occupied with things that enable him or her to use their analytical capacities.

They do not handle stress or worries well and will manifest them as illness. They can be very talented musically and if this is recognised early this ability can be nurtured through to success.

The Virgo woman can appear cold, insensitive and very reserved. In astrology, she represents the virgin and, for the most part, this is the image she portrays. Given the opportunity, however, she can show an entirely different nature if one finds herself in the right circumstances with people who she can truly trust. Her attitude to everything is business-like and she likes everything to be in its proper place.

The Virgo man has a picture in his head of what he wants and how he wants things to be. He will spend his life searching for these things and will accept them even if they do not make him happy. He is precise, organised and not prone to showing any emotion, but he can be a very good friend and a loyal worker.

Things to avoid are stress, worry and a tendency to over-react.

Famous people who share your sign are conqueror Alexander the Great, writer HG Wells and actress Sophia Loren.

Libra ♎
The Seventh Sign of The Zodiac:
23 September–22 October

Born under the Air sign of Libra, which is a Cardinal sign, your fortunate gemstones are opal, pink jasper, and chrysolite. Your ruling planet is Venus. The colours green and light blue, and the numbers six and nine will be lucky for you. Your best day of the week is Friday and the most fortunate location to live or work is anywhere where there is lots of social activity. Your best choice of occupation is in the fields of law, import and export, the armed forces, music and art. You are most compatible with the signs Aries, Gemini, Libra, Leo, Sagittarius and Aquarius, but you do not favour the signs of Taurus, Cancer, Scorpio, Capricorn, Virgo and Pisces.

Many of the most beautiful women and handsomest men are born under your sign. You are charming, often graceful, generous and loyal but with a word or a look can cut to the bone. You love the company of others but then, without much warning, you need your own space and have no difficulty in creating it.

Your sign governs the loins, kidneys and back and they reflect the most vulnerable areas in your body. Care should be taken to avoid depression, fatigue and moodiness. In affairs of the heart, you can be affectionate, tender and romantic but you do not always display your feelings. You are very selective when making friends and can take instant likes or dislikes to people but once you have accepted someone, you will be very loyal. Financially, you can flirt between one extreme and the other, being a big spender one minute and behaving like a miser the next.

The Libra child must have his or her mind occupied at all times. When they are paying attention, they will do so one hundred percent, but if they are not interested, they will daydream and not hear a word you say. Libra children have strong artistic abilities and, when possible, this should be encouraged.

The Libra woman is often exotic in her appearance and attracts many friends and admirers, although she tends to be loyal to her partner. She likes to be surrounded by beautiful things and wants everything in her life to blend and balance.

The Libra man likes the excitement of the chase and, given the opportunity, he will sweep you off your feet like a knight in shining armour. He can be so charming and attentive that he could talk the birds out of the trees but, be warned, he can turn cold at the drop of a hat. When choosing his life partner the Libra man should do so carefully.

Things to avoid are excess and stress of any kind.

Famous people who share your sign are comedian/actor Groucho Marx, actress Brigitte Bardot and politician Eleanor Roosevelt.

Scorpio ♏
The Eighth Sign of the Zodiac:
23 October–22 November

Born under the water sign of Scorpio, which is a fixed sign, your fortunate gemstones are malachite, topaz and beryl. Some say that your ruling planet is Mars while others argue that it is Pluto. If you think before you act, Pluto is strong, but if you are more concerned with action rather than thinking about it, then Mars is your ruler. The colours green, blue and dark red, and the numbers three and five will be fortunate to you and your best day of the week is Tuesday. The most fortunate location for you to live or work is anywhere near water and you are capable of doing well in any choice of occupation but will excel in chemistry, medicine and surgery. You are most compatible with the signs Taurus, Cancer, Scorpio, Capricorn, Virgo and Pisces, but you do not favour the signs of Aries, Gemini, Libra, Leo, Sagittarius and Aquarius.

All the signs in the zodiac are easily recognisable by their traits with the exception of Scorpio. Taureans, for instance, particularly men, generally have thick necks and shoulders. Leos tend to have masses of hair, like the lion, or very short hair, which they fuss over constantly. But those who are born under the sign of Scorpio are not so easy to identify in terms of looks. Their particular trait is located in how they sound because they tend to talk a language of their own. Sometimes they like to sound poetic or mysterious. Your sign governs the reproductive areas of the body, making you the most sensuous, sexy and flirtatious sign in the zodiac. You have a magnetic, passionate personality and under normal circumstances you are considerate and loyal but you can have a very sharp and unexpected sting when roused to anger.

The Scorpio child likes to hide in small spaces just like a scorpion, and when these children are good they are very, very, good but when they are bad they can become little horrors. They like to have their own way and more often than not are determined to have the last word.

The Scorpio woman is not recognised for her tact or diplomacy. If she has something to say, she speaks her mind regardless of the consequences. She has a strong sexual appetite and makes a passionate partner.

The Scorpio man likes to rule the roost and can be very Victorian in his attitude towards his partner and children. He can be suspicious and jealous, guarding his possessions to the extreme. But if he can overcome this, he makes a loyal, loving and attentive partner.

Things to avoid are a sharp temper, restlessness and unreasonable jealousy.

Famous people who share your sign are artist Pablo Picasso, president Theodore Roosevelt and writer Robert Louis Stevenson.

Sagittarius ♐
The Ninth Sign of The Zodiac:
23 November–21 December.

Born under the Fire sign of Sagittarius, which is a mutable sign, your fortunate gemstones are turquoise, moonstone, and chrysolite. Your ruling planet is Jupiter, and the colours blue and purple, and the number nine will be fortunate to you. Your best day of the week is Thursday and the most fortunate location to live or work is the great outdoors. Your best choices of occupations are in the fields of travel, law, medicine, aviation, education, mechanics and writing. You are most compatible with the signs Aries, Gemini, Libra, Leo, Sagittarius and Aquarius but you do not favour the signs of Taurus, Cancer, Scorpio, Capricorn, Virgo and Pisces.

You are proud, independent and impulsive and dislike any kind of restriction, preferring to be a free spirit. You love adventure and travel, and given the opportunity will explore the universe. Your sign governs the thighs, and anything that involves movement, such as walking, running or dancing, will be important in your life. This influence will cause you to be restless in your nature and if you cannot fulfil your desire for travel, you will express it in other ways. You may move home many times or perhaps this will be reflected in your career. You should consider employment travelling as a salesperson or in the areas of seamanship, travel and tourism.

You have a nice personality and a good sense of humour and enjoy the respect and admiration of your friends. In affairs of the heart, you tend to be unsure of yourself one minute and overconfident the next. Choose your partner well because he or she will have to be able to put up with your restless nature.

The Sagittarius child is courageous and daring, and has a fiery, unpredictable temperament. These children are more likely to get into dangerous or difficult situations than other children are. They love animals and being outside, exploring.

The Sagittarius woman enjoys all types of outdoor activities and can be found participating in the more masculine sports such as hunting, fishing and riding. She loves activity of all kinds and has a real get-up-and-go attitude. She can bring out the best in her partner with very little effort. In the home, she is neat and tidy and she cares for her children well.

The Sagittarius man is interesting to know but difficult to pin down. He is an astute businessman and will be motivated by financial rewards rather than vocation. He tends not to be domesticated, preferring to leave that side of things to his partner or someone else. He is focused in his attitude and if something or someone no longer suits his purpose, he turns his back on them immediately.

Things to avoid are impulsive, thoughtless attitudes and a tendency to being bad tempered.

Famous people who share your sign are political leaders Sir Winston Churchill and Charles De Gaulle, and cartoonist and film producer, Walt Disney.

Capricorn ♑
The Tenth Sign of The Zodiac:
22 December–19 January

Born under the Earth sign of Capricorn, which is a Cardinal sign, your fortunate gemstones are onyx, ruby and garnet. Your ruling planet is Saturn, and the colours deep blue and dark green, in addition to the numbers seven and three will be fortunate to you. Your best day of the week is Saturday and the most fortunate location for you to live or work is a secluded, quiet place. Your best choice of occupation is in the fields of property, education, investigative journalism, writing and the land. You are most compatible with the signs Taurus, Cancer, Scorpio, Capricorn, Virgo and Pisces but you do not favour the signs of Aries, Gemini, Libra, Leo, Sagittarius and Aquarius.

You are trustworthy, dependable and loyal as a friend and will stand up for others who are unable to do so for themselves. Your sign governs the knees and, in order to maintain a healthy disposition, you should take regular, gentle exercise such as yoga rather than a hard workout. You will find success comes to you later in and, like the mountain goat, you will have some tough mountains to climb but you will get there in the end. You are persistent and stubborn and are not afraid of hard or repetitive work but, above all, you must feel fulfilled in what you do.

Given the choice of material success or job satisfaction you would probably choose the latter. In affairs of the heart, you are inclined to be reserved and reluctant to show your true feelings in case your love is rejected, but when your love is returned you lavish your partner with attention, tenderness and passion.

The Capricorn child is initially shy and reserved but as they get to know their peers, they become stronger and more confident. Friends they make in their early formative years tend to remember them in later years.

The Capricorn woman is strong in her principles and in her attitude, and it would be folly for anyone to try to dominate her. If she is dominated, it is only because she is allowing it. She is totally loyal and will do whatever is within her power to protect, encourage or direct her partner and children. She is businesslike in her approach to all matters whether this concerns family, home or romance. This can make her appear unfeeling at times but beneath this exterior lies a smouldering volcano.

The Capricorn man is the king and he expects all in his kingdom to obey him. Stick to this rule and you will be rewarded with support, love and encouragement. Break this rule and you will regret it. He can be miserly in his attitude and likes to maintain a tight rein on the bank balance, but, if he sees fit, can be very generous.

Things to avoid are pride, obstinacy and a selfish attitude.

Famous people who share your sign are martyr Joan of Arc, physicist Sir Isaac Newton and writer Rudyard Kipling.

Aquarius ♒
The Eleventh Sign of The Zodiac:
21 January–19 February

Born under the Water sign of Aquarius, which is a fixed sign, your fortunate gemstones are sapphire, jade, ruby and garnet. Your ruling planet is Uranus, and the colours indigo, pale blue and green, and the numbers eight and four will be fortunate to you. Your best day of the week is Wednesday and the most fortunate location for you to live or work is a large city, a place where there is a lot of activity. Your best choice of occupation is in the fields of aviation, exploration, electronics, politics and anything linked to sales and marketing. You are most compatible with the signs Aries, Gemini, Libra, Leo, Sagittarius and Aquarius but you do not favour the signs of Taurus, Cancer, Scorpio, Capricorn, Virgo and Pisces.

On first impression, you appear to be charming and courteous but you have a tendency to be offhand. You dislike pettiness, although this can be one of your own worst faults. You are the thinker of the zodiac and beneath your surface there is a lot going on that others would never guess at. You love excitement and what would appear to others as danger but the chances are that you will weighed things up before you act.

Your sign governs the calves and ankles, and exercise like hill-walking, climbing, aerobics or dancing will benefit you greatly and keep your constitution strong. In affairs of the heart you are easily hurt and hide your true feelings. Consequently, the object of your affections tends not to know how much you care.

As a friend you are loyal and supportive but can fall out of favour because of your hyper-critical attitude. Charming as you are, you always manage to find your way back into your companions' good books as though there was nothing wrong in the first place. Your earning capacity can be hampered by your vulnerability, which makes you easy prey for 'get-rich-quick-schemes'.

The Aquarius child is usually quite timid and will do whatever he or she is told. They do not handle any kind of stress well and need to feel safe at home and in their surrounding environment. They will be at their happiest with a good book full of adventure stories.

The Aquarius woman is independent, has a wide range of interests, and is capable of functioning on her own, having no need for masculine support. For this reason she is more likely to marry later in life and, although she will be loyal to her partner, if there is an important be reason to part, she will do so without hesitation.

The Aquarius man is a perfect gentleman most of the time. He treats everyone in the same way and is incapable of putting a lover or a partner on a pedestal, so don't hold your breath if this is what you want! Things to Avoid are criticism, thoughtlessness, aggression, selfishness and recklessness.

Famous people who share your sign are politicians Abraham Lincoln and Harold Macmillan and aviator Charles Lindbergh.

Pisces ♓
The Eleventh Sign of The Zodiac:
19 February–20 March

Born under the Water sign of Pisces, which is a mutable sign, your fortunate gemstones are moonstone, bloodstone, pearl and opal. Your ruling planet is Neptune, and the colour violet, in addition to the numbers five and eight will be fortunate to you. Your best day of the week is Friday and the most fortunate location for you to live or work is close to water.

Your best choice of occupation is in the fields of counselling, teaching, design, nursing, medicine, alternative therapies, aquatics and the arts. You are most compatible with the signs of Taurus, Cancer, Scorpio, Capricorn, Virgo and Pisces but you do not favour the signs of Aries, Gemini, Libra, Leo, Sagittarius and Aquarius.

You are kind, sympathetic and patient but are easily upset by others. You have a very soft nature and are easily led into bad company through trying your best to help and instead getting into tricky situations. Choose your friends wisely and do not believe every sob story that you hear.

Your sign governs the feet, the very foundation of your being. Keep them warm and dry to avoid colds, chills and throat infections.

As a friend, you would do without to help another and often regret it for seldom is this generosity returned. In affairs of the heart your feelings run deep but you are inclined to be in love with the idea of love rather than the person. This is when you are at your most vulnerable. Your financial security will depend on your ability to save wisely and make your money work for you rather than chancing your luck and speculating.

The Pisces child is easily impressed by the wrong company and should be taught discernment at an early age to help them avoid being manipulated later in life. They are studious by nature and have an amazing ability to retain anything they learn.

The Pisces woman is at her happiest when she is in restful, comfortable surroundings. Her home is her sacred space and, although she loves to be helpful and popular, too many demands weaken her spirit. She likes to socialise, be amongst acquaintances and generally have a good time but can only keep this pace up for a limited period and has to retreat back to her sacred space.

The Pisces man likes to have everything his own way. Where this becomes a problem is when he has a partner to consider because he can be very selfish. If his attributes are positive, he will be kind, considerate and caring, but if they are negative, he will be lazy and inconsiderate.

Things to avoid are mixing with the wrong type of people, and believing everything, you hear.

Famous People who share your sign are physicist Albert Einstein, inventor Alexander Graham Bell and actress Elizabeth Taylor.

Interpretations

WHETHER you are reading clouds in the sky, puddles in the ground or coffee in a saucer, the following interpretations will be helpful to you. Remember to trust your instincts, though, because things can have different meanings, associations or feelings for different people.

Abbey	A safe haven is being offered.
Acorns	Brings health, wealth, happiness and a joyful marriage.
Aeroplane	A journey is likely, for you or bringing someone to you. Changes will be experienced.
Alley	Indicates a loss of property or belongings.
Almond	A wedding.
Anchor	A symbol of safety and security.
Angel	This is a sign of safety and could be your guardian angel.
Anvil	Success and wealth, possibly through a new career.
Apples	Success in love, fertility, and growth in your life or business.
Archbishop	This can indicate a church service for a wedding or a funeral.

Interpretations

Arrow   This can be a warning of a threat to you, but if it is ornate it can be seen as an unknown admirer sending loving thoughts.

Axe   This can be threatening but is also the bringer of strength to handle difficult situations.

Baby   This is a sign of insecurity, a problem or responsibility, that you feel unable to deal with. A newborn baby can be a new beginning, as in a rebirth.

Bag   Although this is commonly a symbol for the womb, it can indicate hidden information.

Baggage   With too many problems to deal with, you are and feeling overburdened.

Bagpipes   A celebration of wealth and prosperity.

Balloon   Someone has grand schemes, which may not have the foundation required to make them successful.

Banner   A symbol of success in overcoming difficulty.

Battle   Indicates a difficult struggle ahead.

Beacon   Someone offers a solution or shows the way to solve a problem.

Beads   A sign of wealth to come.

Beard   This can represent someone who is trying to hide his or her true identity.

Bed   This can indicate that a rest is required to regain strength and vitality. It can also suggest the need to avoid hasty action; wait or rest before doing something important.

Bells A warning to you that you are not heading your instincts.

Bicycle A leisurely journey will be made or there will be delays in progress.

Birds In a flock, birds can indicate that circumstances will change very suddenly and that the whole family will be affected. One bird represents a message waiting; two bring merriment or marriage; three indicates a successful journey; four suggests good news and five signifies company.

Bird's Nest If it contains eggs, this indicates growth and success, but if it is empty, a plan will fail.

Boat A journey across water will be made, or a letter or call will come from afar.

Bones This can indicate a problem that someone keeps going over, which cannot be resolved. Bones can also indicate a death or an ending.

Book An open book shows that the answer to your problem is staring you in the face. A closed book indicates that the answers that you seek may be harder to find, or that someone is keeping a secret from you.

Boots New boots are a symbol of material success but old boots indicate a previous lover returning.

Interpretations

Bottle	If the bottle is full you will be invited to share a celebration, if empty you will experience a disappointment.
Box	If the box is open and empty you will lose something or someone. If it is contains something, look up the contents in this list to find out what it means.
Bracelet	Happiness and success can be expected and a gift may be received.
Bride	You will hear of a wedding.
Bridge	You will experience a change in your life. (Broken: the opportunity for a change lies ahead but you would be better to avoid it.)
Bugle	Good news will arrive.
Buoy	Problems lie ahead but you will find a solution.
Burglar	Your possessions are threatened so be careful whom you trust or have around you at home or in the workplace.
Burial	You will finally be rid of a problem and you will hear of a birth.
Butcher	Do not take any chances or speculate as good luck is not with you.
Cage	You or a partner may feel trapped.
Candle	If the candle is bright then hope lies ahead if dim information is being concealed from you.
Candlestick	Religious ceremonies are significant.
Cannon	An important announcement will be made.

Canoe   Something that you are waiting for will be slow in arriving.

Car   An unexpected visitor will arrive if the car is facing towards you. If the car is facing away, you will make a journey.

Castle   A symbol of wealth suggesting you can look forward to a prosperous future.

Cave   You may wish you could hide away from your problems or responsibilities.

Chains   You are in danger if being manipulated into something that you would rather not be involved in.

Chair   The more ornate the chair, the more fortunate the omen.

Chalice   Perfect truth and love will come to you.

Children   If they are playing, you have a desire to be free of responsibilities and return to a time when things in your life were easier.

Chimney   A wedding will be announced.

Christ   To see the face of Christ indicates that you are being given help and support in an unseen way.

Church   A religious ceremony is imminent.

City   This could indicate that you are or will feel overwhelmed by a situation or responsibility.

Clock   This is generally a sign that time is passing and that you will have to be disciplined in order to achieve your desires.

Interpretations

Clown	Someone may be trying to hide his or her true identity or character from you. This is not a good omen.
Club	You will be involved in a very sensual relationship and this will prove to be a very fertile period for you or someone very close to you.
Coals	A very lucky symbol denoting warmth and success in your future.
Colours	**Black** is for grounding and dispelling negative energies.
	Blue is for tranquillity and peace.
	Green is for healing, growth and fertility.
	Orange is for strength, power and courage.
	Pink is for love and romance.
	Purple is for protection, meditation and spirituality.
	Red is for passion, excitement and action.
	Turquoise is for communication, protection and travel.
	White is for purity, cleansing and knowledge.
	Yellow is for energy, vitality and motivation.
Corkscrew	Someone may try to glean information from you or about you.
Cornucopia	Good news is on the way.
Corridor	You will have to make a choice or a decision very soon.
Crescent	This is a very feminine symbol depicting

involvement, or very good news from someone of the female sex.

Cross Burdens may be heavy but look within to find solutions.

Crossroads A choice will have to be made and it must be made alone.

Crown You will be recognized for an achievement.

Crutches Help will be offered from an unexpected source.

Cupid Someone is thinking of you romantically.

Dagger You may or may have been betrayed in love.

Devil This depicts fear of making decisions or choices, or of making a commitment.

Dice The choice ahead will depend entirely on luck, good or bad.

Doormat A visitor will arrive unexpectedly.

Doors If the door is open a new opportunity will be offered. If the door is closed you will not get what you want.

Drum An important announcement will be made and you may not be happy with what you hear.

Eggs Birth or new beginnings that show great potential.

Enclosure This can be a sign that there is no way to avoid a problem and that you must face up to it and deal with it.

Execution There will be an unfortunate outcome to a plan or endeavour.

Interpretations

Explosion	Be prepared for an outburst of some kind.
Eyes	You are being watched or observed. This could be for promotion in your career or for other reasons.
Fairy	A fortunate symbol showing that the elements are on your side and will help where they can.
Fan	Although in some cultures this is the symbol for wealth and royalty, it can also show that a situation is in danger of becoming over-heated.
Feathers	Your ideas may not be as strong as you suppose and some additional information may be required.
Fields	An indication that you have many choices and can go anywhere or do anything.
Finger	You are being pointed in the right direction so listen to advice that is offered.
Fire	You will begin to regain your strength and vitality.
Flowers	Each flower has a specific meaning so look at the Flower List (pp 205) for an accurate description.
Gallows	You are heading in the wrong direction and may fall from a great height if you proceed.
Garden	The more abundant the garden, the more fortunate the meaning.

Garlands   A fortunate omen showing that you will succeed in your endeavours.

Gate   If the gate is open then the way ahead is clear and you can proceed with confidence. If the gate is blocked in any way then your progress will be blocked too.

Gems   An indication that you will be spoiled or pampered in some way.

Genitals   You are entering a very fertile period in your life and should make the most of it.

Ghosts   Something from your past will come back to haunt you.

Giants   Someone who is much older than you will have words of advice to offer, even if you do not want to hear them.

God   This is a very profound symbol regardless of your religion, and shows that your God is watching over you and communicating with your intellect.

Gondola   News from a foreign country will arrive.

Grapes   Recovery in health matters and good fortune in financial or material affairs.

Grotto   A place of worship and spirituality showing that you must develop your spiritual side and listen to your heart.

Guitar   You may be invited to a friendly gathering and participate in a celebration.

Gun   You will be protected from opposition.

Interpretations

Hair	A feminine symbol, 'a woman's crowning glory'. It shows the desire to be viewed as a feminine and graceful woman, or to have a beautiful woman as a partner.
Hair	**Black, short hair:** official business that may be difficult to handle.
	Dishevelled: problems can be expected unless you put your affairs in order.
	Long, flowing free: indicates, freedom from burdens.
	White: news or advice from an elder.
Hammer	This can be an indication that you will be provided with the tools to achieve your goals, but the going will be difficult.
Hands	Help will be offered.
Hanging	You may feel as though you are in a state of suspended animation and that nothing can change this, but sudden changes for the better will be experienced.
Heart	Romance is on your mind and you may be wishing that you had someone in your life.
Harvesters	Wealth will come to you.
Hatchet	Beware of treachery and deceit.
Hawk	Pay close attention to small details to avoid missing essential information.
Hay-cart	Prosperity in affairs to do with finances, land or property.
Hermit	Someone will show you a new way of life.

Honey	A fortunate omen indicating prosperity.
Horseshoe	If the open end of the horseshoe faces upwards then this is a very lucky omen, but if the open ends are facing down you are in danger of losing something precious, and good fortune is not with you.
House	If the house is standing strong then you are in a good position to deal with matters. If the house is dilapidated and falling down then you are at a weak point in your life and need the support of friends or loved ones.
Ice or Frost	A warning that you are about to make a mistake. Exercise caution in all areas of your life.
Iceberg	This could be an indication that you are only being made aware of some of the facts pertaining to a situation, person or issue. More is hidden below the surface.
Ice skates	With more experience you will be able to handle a difficult situation. Look to those who have experience for the answers.
Igloo	You are looking for a safe haven.
Indian	This may indicate that guidance is being offered and that you should look to your elders for this.
Initials	An important matter is connected to someone who has the initial in their name.
Ink Blot	The interpretation is dependent on the

	shape or form of the blot.
Island	You may feel as though you are having to stand alone and face all the difficulties that life and destiny is throwing your way.
Jester	Someone may give you false information.
Jolly Roger	This is a warning that danger lurks nearby.
Judge	You may be questioning something in your life and wonder what others may think of this.
Jug	A time to celebrate is close.
Kettle	You will have unexpected guests.
Key	A new home or opportunity will be offered to you
Kite	This is a desire to be free.
Knife	You will have the power, strength and ability to sever ties if necessary and forge ahead.
Knight	(in armour) Although problems may lie ahead, solutions will be found through the intervention of another.
Knots	This can be an indication that you feel as though you are tied in knots but others may experiences this as goals to be accomplished.
Ladder	New openings will occur but although the goal may be difficult to achieve, it is likely to be achieved providing you maintain a steady attitude and disciplined effort.

Interpretations

**Lamp or
Lantern**   You will be shown the answers that you require.

Leaves   This can be a sign that you feel as though your plans are falling apart.

Letter   Important news is on the way.

Lighthouse   A solution will be found or hope will be offered.

Logs   A sign of warmth and security.

Mask   Treachery or deception is around so be wary who you trust.

Maypole   You will be involved in a very physically exciting relationship.

Medal   This could be described as a desire for praise.

Mill   You will begin to reap rewards from the efforts that you have made.

Money   An indication that money may be coming to you from an unexpected source.

Monsters   You may have an underlying fear that must be faced before you realize that you had nothing to fear.

Moon   Beware of deception and depression.

Mother   This indicates that you are well protected and can proceed without fear

Mountain   Obstacles lie ahead but they can be overcome by looking for an alternative route or path to your goals.

Mouth   News will come and it may take the form of gossip or scandal.

Interpretations

Necklace	Guard your tongue as what you say may be misunderstood.
Needle	Beware of sharp objects or of annoying someone close to you.
Nest	You will be asked to care for a child or a pet.
Net	You could become caught up in an unsavory or difficult situation.
Nose	You may find something or find out about something.
Nuts	Rewards will be bestowed for efforts made.
Oasis	You will find a safe haven.
Obelisk	Fame and fortune will arrive for efforts and application already made.
Old woman	Guidance and inspiration will be given in answer to a prayer.
Orchestra	A time of great happiness lies ahead.
Organ	A wedding will be announced.
Oven	Someone close to you is planning something but keeping their plans to themselves.
Padlock	You will be unable to discover the answer to a mystery or puzzle.
Palace	You will find the answers that you seek and you will also find your destiny.
Paper	Someone or something is trying to give you information that you need.
Parcel	You will learn something new.
Path	You will find a new direction to follow. How easy or difficult it is depends entirely

	on the shape of the path, the smoother and wider, the easier your transition will be.
Pawnbroker	You may lose something of value or importance but will be able to substitute it with something else.
Pen	You will receive news.
Penis	A very powerful man will come into your life.
Phoenix	Good health will be restored to someone dear to you who is ill.
Pies	A party or gathering will be organized to celebrate an event.
Pillow	Someone may need to rest due to illness or injury.
Pincers	Be prepared for a betrayal.
Pipe	A disagreement will be resolved.
Pirate	An untrustworthy character will try to involve you in something shady although you may not realize this at the time.
Pistol	You will be protected from opposition..
Pitcher	You will have to work very hard to achieve your goals and no one will be willing to help you.
Pitchfork	You are in a very dangerous position
Plough	News of a pregnancy will arrive and you could be entering a very fertile period in your life.

Interpretations

Police   Uniforms and legal matters will be important.

Pool   Water is cleansing, healing and refreshing so if the pool is clear, good health can be expected, but if the pool is murky, sickness is close.

Portrait   You are being watched from afar.

Precipice   You may be afraid to take a chance.

Priest   Someone will show you a new way of life, and a prayer will be answered.

Prison   You may feel trapped in your present situation but release will come soon.

Prize   You may receive a reward or recognition for something that you have done.

Procession   A wedding or anniversary celebration will be announced.

Purse   You will be guarding your possessions and may feel threatened in a personal way.

Pyramid   You will achieve a cherished goal.

Quayside   A journey will be made and the parting will be sad.

Queen   You will be successful in your ambitions and reach the top of your chosen career.

Question mark   Someone will seek your advice.

Radio   You will hear news from afar.

Raft   Do not make any changes at this time, because luck is not with you.

Railway   A journey will be made.

Interpretations

Rainbow	This is a sign of hope for the future.
Reeds	You will have obstacles to overcome but if you are persistent, you will overcome them.
Rider	You will be swept off your feet in an exciting, romantic adventure.
Ring	A wedding or divorce will be announced, depending on the condition of the ring.
Road	You will find a new direction to follow. How easy or difficult depends entirely on the shape of the road. The smoother and wider, the easier your transition will be.
Rock	No one will move you from your chosen path.
Rocket	You will make progress faster than you anticipate.
Roof	You will reach the top in your chosen profession.
Rope	You may be reluctantly entwined or involved in something.
Rowing	Progress will be made but it may be slower than you would hope.
Ruins	You will rebuild from scratch and rebuild in strength.
Sailor	A journey across water will be made.
Scarecrow	There are people around you who cannot be trusted.
Scissors	If the scissors are open beware of quarrels and arguments, if they are closed,

arguments and disagreements will be resolved.

Scroll   You will receive a message from an unexpected source.

Scythe   A relationship will be severed.

Sentinel   You will be protected during both your sleeping and waking hours.

Seraphim   You will learn something to your advantage from someone much younger than you.

Shelter   Problems may lie ahead but you will be protected from them.

Shepherd   Someone will show you a new direction. Take it!

Ship   A journey will be made to a far-off place.

Shipwreck   Your plans will not go as you would wish.

Shirt   Official matters will go well if the shirt is whole and badly if the shirt is crushed or damaged.

Shoes   You have become discontent with your present situation are be longing for pastures new.

Sieve   You will lose your belongings or security if you do not exercise care and caution.

Skeleton   All pretence will be stripped away and plain speaking will win the day.

Skull   You are under threat of losing a hope, dream or possession.

Soldiers   Help will be offered but only if you ask.

Spade   You will have to work very hard to achieve your goal.

Spear　　Someone may stab you in the back, betray you or speak ill of you.

Spectacles　　You may be unaware of all the facts so ask more questions.

Steps　　You will rise to great heights.

Sugar　　You will be flattered and praised, and enjoy being the centre of attention.

Sun　　Your daily life will begin to improve.

Sundial　　Make better use of your time.

Swimmer　　You have almost reached your goal but not quite. More effort is required.

Sword　　You will be given more power to cut through your obstacles and overcome adversity.

Table　　Your material security will be strengthened.

Tambourine　　Good fortune will bless you and you will celebrate with others.

Tassels　　An official ceremony will be organized and you may be required to attend this.

Teapot　　Unexpected guests will arrive and a stranger will be brought to your home.

Tears　　Although you may shed some tears they will not be ones of sadness.

Teeth　　All is not well. Guard your health.

Telephone　　News will arrive that will excite you.

Temple　　You will experience some kind of mystical illumination.

Tent　　You may be worried about your stability and security. Exercise caution in financial matters.

Interpretations

Thermometer Unexpected changes will upset your plans.

Thighs The sign of Sagittarius may be significant.

Thimble A period of unemployment may be experienced.

Throne You will be praised and respected for your knowledge and experience.

Tinker Problems with neighbours can be expected.

Tomb You will find that you are stuck in a rut and unable to make any progress.

Torch You will be reminded of a past love.

Torpedo News will come that will shock or upset you.

Tower A crisis will unfold and nothing that you say or do can change this.

Train A decision will have to be made and the choice must be yours and yours alone.

Trapdoor Hidden information will be revealed.

Trench Beware of hidden obstacles.

Triangle You will hear of someone who is having an affair.

Tripod Your plans are not as secure as you would suppose.

Trumpet Someone will boast bout his or her possessions or achievements.

Trunk A house move is likely.

Tub Problems lie ahead.

Tunnel You will have a fresh start.

Umbrella You will be protected from a difficult situation or person.

Undertaker You will hear of a birth.

Unicorn You will achieve your dreams.

Urn You will hear of a death or a sudden misfortune concerning another.

Vagabond You will move home and it will be the first of several moves before you finally settle down.

Valley You will experience a delay in achieving your desires.

Vase You may feel as though no one cares and that you have to do everything yourself.

Veil You are uncomfortable about expressing your self or your desires.

Victory Salute You will be successful in your attempts to overcome obstacles.

Village You will wish that your life were more settled and content.

Violin You will be invited to a party.

Volcano There will be violent outbursts and quarrels.

Wading Good health will be restored.

Wall Barriers will be difficult to overcome in your personal, professional or romantic life.

Watch Good fortune will come but it may be slow in arriving.

Water Bearer The sign of Aquarius is important.

Water Mill Good health will be restored and good fortune will follow.

Waves Be patient, what you want will come to

you but if you force things now you will upset the outcome.

Wedding You may be wishing for romantic fulfilment.

Whale You will have the answer that solves another's problem.

Wharf While others around you may panic, you will be calm in the knowledge that all will be well.

Wheel You are about to experience a complete change in your life.

Whip Someone may threaten your peace of mind.

Whirlpool Unnecessary changes will bring disaster.

Whirlwind Unnecessary changes will lead to your downfall so allow things to remain as they are for the time being.

Wig Someone is showing you a false side to their nature and you are in danger of being taken in by this.

Windmill Changes for the better will surprise you.

Window You will hear of or be involved in a scandal.

Wings You will have the desire to escape from your everyday life.

Witch You will experience a stroke of unexpected good luck.

Wreath You will win an argument or a battle.

Wreck Good fortune may escape you so exercise caution in all your dealings.

Interpretations

Yacht   Progress will be quick or slow depending
          on the assistance that is offered or withheld.

**Zodiac
Symbols**   These generally depict someone who is
          born under that sign or something
          associated with it.

*

Creatures Great and Small

Alligator   A dangerous enemy.

Ants   A successful project which others will assist with.

Ape   This can be either good or bad depending on the image. It can indicate a strong ally or an enemy

Bear   An indication that you will find the answers that you seek within yourself. This inner wisdom will show you the way forward.

Bees   They can indicate a source of riches or sustenance, but if the bees are threatening or swarming you will be attacked from an unexpected source.

Beetles   Indicate someone who is hard on the outside but vulnerable inside, or someone who is trying to hide something.

Boar   A threat lies ahead, be careful who you trust.

Bull   An unexpected windfall or an amorous lover will arrive, and the sign of Taurus will be significant.

Butterfly   You will emerge from a difficult situation wiser and stronger.

Creatures Great and Small

Camel	You will have the ability to continue with a responsibility, task or aim even though the going may be difficult.
Cat	If the appearance of the cat is friendly then good fortune is around. If the cat appears aggressive then beware of jealousy. A new-found freedom could be the key to your future.
Cat	(Black) A sign of good luck if the cat appears to be resting or friendly. If the cat is threatening, problems that will be difficult to deal with lie ahead. (White) You are being given a warning.
Cattle	Indicate prosperity.
Chameleon	You are being deceived or are deceiving yourself.
Clam	This a good omen.
Cock	Someone will boast of his or her achievements to the annoyance of others.
Cow	A symbol of wealth, spiritual attainment and material abundance.
Crab	You may experience someone's anger.
Crocodile	Be careful of the company you keep as you may be associating with a dangerous enemy.
Dog	You will hear from a good friend, or a friend will help in time of need.
Dolphin	Someone close can be trusted to provide help or answers.

Creatures Great and Small

Donkey   You will be given assistance in moving home, or will offer to help someone changing address.

Dragon   A very lucky symbol in relationships, wealth and happiness.

Elephant   Known for its memory, the elephant will show you that what you seek lies within your own power to remember. Look deeper and you will find the answers.

Elk   This will bring you strength in times of need and is also the symbol of friendship.

Ermine   A symbol of wealth with royal connections.

Fawn   A symbol depicting innocence, and since the mother is usually nearby her fawn, protection is close at hand.

Ferret   Keep looking, with perseverance you will find what you seek.

Fish   The birth of a child will be announced.

Fox   You will have the ability to see and not be seen in order to find the answers that you are looking for.

Frogs   A spiritual, emotional or physical cleansing is required.

Goat   Keep trying to achieve your goals and, like the goat, climb to new and higher levels. The sign of Capricorn may be significant.

Goose   This is a symbol of male fertility and wealth.

Creatures Great and Small

Grasshopper You will be unable to focus on any specific task and will hop from one situation to another.

Hare Look for opportunities in strange or unusual surroundings.

Hedgehog You or your space may be threatened by outside influences.

Horse In Native American tradition, the horse is a symbol of power so seeing this animal is indicative of power or support coming to you.

Hyena You will hear of a robbery.

Insect An irritating problem may bother you.

Kangaroo This can be in indication that you feel responsible for someone younger than you who is unable to look after themself.

Kitten A desire to have someone or something to cherish and care for.

Lambs A hope for the future to be prosperous and secure.

Leopard You may have to be very cunning to achieve a desire, or information that is important to you.

Lion A very important person will be introduced to you and the sign of Leo is important.

Lizard You will have a prophetic experience that will safeguard you in some way.

Lobsters Generally bodes sorrow but fans of the TV programme 'Friends' may see this as the arrival of a soulmate.

Creatures Great and Small

Lynx	You or your actions are being observed.
Mice	Be wary of overindulging in food drink or self-gratification.
Monkey	Deceit and treachery are around and you may find something that you consider to be serious is laughed at.
Mushrooms	What appears to be a small unimportant idea may in fact be the solution to a problem.
Otter	Do not trust strangers.
Oysters	There may be some tears ahead for you or someone close to you
Ox	You will be tied to your responsibilities for a while yet.
Panther	This is a warning that danger lies ahead.
Pig	You may find that you have to search long and hard to find what you are looking for.
Porcupine	If you are careful you will be able to handle a difficult situation.
Porpoise	Joy and happiness will come to you.
Rabbit	You are afraid of something or someone and should rid yourself of this fear, because it is unnecessary.
Racoon	You will gather and reorganize your belongings.
Ram	The sign of Aries will be significant.
Rat	You will be cunning and clever, and find the solution to a problem.
Reindeer	A celebration is at hand and your friends will gather around you.

Creatures Great and Small

Reptile	Be wary, there is someone near you whom you should not trust.
Salmon	You will achieve your goals.
Scorpions	The sign of Scorpio will be important.
Serpent	You will experience a complete transformation.
Shark	There are hidden dangers around you be careful.
Sheep	Make your own decisions rather than following the decisions that others make.
Snail	Wealth and success will come to you if you take your time and be diligent in your attempts.
Spider	You will learn a new subject and from your learning you will change radically.
Stag	A successful businessman will assist you and may have more than business on his mind.
Tiger	An enemy is waiting to foil your plans. Keep them to yourself to avoid danger.
Toad	You will meet someone that you will instantly take a dislike to.
Tortoise	Success can be achieved by persistent effort.
Trout	Unexpected money will arrive.
Walrus	You are wasting your time and abilities. Do something radical and you will find fulfilment.
Wasp	You will experience a sudden quarrel from an unexpected source.

Creatures Great and Small

Weasel   Someone who pretends to be a friend is really an enemy in disguise.

Wildcat   An unexpected confrontation will be experienced among your circle of friends.

Wolf   You will teach others or study a new subject.

Zebra   Someone will be stronger and more reliable than you had at first thought.

Specific Types of Birds

Albatross   This is a warning of danger ahead.

Blackbird   Expect trouble and possibly a threat to your reputation.

Bluebird   You will meet a cheerful fellow.

Chicken   You will hear gossip.

Crane   Someone will try to take something from you.

Crossbill   An argument is imminent.

Crow   One crow for sorrow, two crows for mirth, three crows for a wedding and four crows for birth.

Cuckoo   A guest may wish to stay overnight or may overstay their welcome.

Dove   An argument will be settled or a broken mended.

Duck   One duck means a period of solitude can be expected, but two ducks indicate happiness in a relationship.

Eagle   This is a symbol of power and protection, and gives the ability to see problems from a different angle to help find a solution.

Falcon   A symbol of power over your enemies.

Geese   A fortunate omen indicating that good luck

	will come from an unexpected source. News will come from or for your mother.
Goldfinch	You will be entertained or admired by a wealthy suitor.
Hawk	You will receive a message that will bring enlightenment.
Humming bird	The symbol of joy and freedom of choice.
Jackdaw	You will have important mail or documents to attend to.
Kingfisher	Peace of mind and contentment will be yours.
Lapwing	News will come from afar.
Lark	You will celebrate within the week.
Magpie	

'One for sorrow,
Two is for joy.
Three for a girl,
Four is for a boy.
Five for silver,
Six is for gold.
Seven for a secret,
Never to be told.'

Another old rhyme says:
'One means anger,
Two brings mirth.
Three is a wedding,
Four is a birth.

Specific Types of Birds

> Five is christening,
> Six is a dearth.
> Seven is heaven,
> Eight is Hell,
> But nine is the very Devil's ain sel.'

Martin	Good luck around the home.
Ostrich	Do not hide from your problems but deal with them head on.
Owl	A mentor will provide the answers that you seek.
Parrot	Someone will betray you so do not divulge your secrets.
Partridge	You are likely to make a very silly mistake.
Peacock	A wealthy marriage or partnership.
Pheasant	Success and security will be yours.
Pigeon	You will be surprised by someone's unconventional behaviour.
Raven	Legal and business matters will be discussed and others will be responsible for the outcome.
Robin	Contentment around the home, news from an old friend, and you will make a new friend.
Rook	Pay attention to any rumours or stories and what you hear may surprise you.
Sparrow	Children, young pets or plants may need your attention.
Stork	News of a birth will arrive.
Swallow	News from afar is forecast.

Creatures Great and Small

Swan   (White) Contentment and love. Wealth and happiness to come. **(Black)** Sadness to follow.

Turkey   A celebration.

Vulture   Others may view you with envy.

Woodpecker You will spend time alone.

Wren   A small package will delight you.

Things That Grow

Acacia   You will overcome obstacles; this tree is associated with the sign of Aries.

Alder   You will begin to see things more clearly and the sign of Pisces is important.

Almond   Virgo will be significant and you will be required to be more organised in order to achieve success.

Angelica   Good health will be restored.

Apple   A problem on the home front will be solved. Taurus will be important.

Ash Tree   Legal matters will progress smoothly and the sign of Libra will be significant.

Bamboo   Quarrels and arguments can be expected.

Bananas   The fruit of the gods can indicate a blessing or a curse from above.

Basil   Courage will be with you when it is required and money will arrive.

Bay   Success will be achieved.

Bergamot   Success will be achieved

Birch   A fresh start will be offered and Sagittarius is significant.

Blackthorn   You are being warned to keep your secrets to yourself; Scorpio is associated witht his traditional hedging tree.

Things That Grow

Borage	Advice will be offered and should be taken.
Carnation	Peace, contentment and restful nights.
Cedar	Healing to someone who is sick, and news from an eastern country.
Cedarwood	You or someone you care for will be protected from harm.
Chamomile	Success will be yours.
Cherry	You are being advised to stand your ground; the sign of Aquarius is associated with this tree.
Chervil	You may study a new subject.
Chives	Courage will come to you when you need it.
Cinnamon	An unexpected windfall will arrive.
Clover	Lady luck will be with you in a speculative venture.
Comfrey	Good luck in overcoming obstacles.
Coriander	Good health will be yours.
Corn	This is a good omen indicating plenty to come.
Cypress	You may start again in a new place but will be sorry to leave your present one; the sign of Taurus may be important.
Daffodils	Health and happiness to follow.
Daisy	A time of brightness and celebration to follow.
Dill	Money will come soon.
Elder	You will have a prophetic or telepathic experience and the sign of Pisces will be important.

Things That Grow

Elm   You are being told that help will be offered when you need it most; Capricorn is associated with the Elm.

Fennel   You will make an unexpected journey.

Fern   You will have good luck in overcoming obstacles.

Feverfew   You will be blessed with joy and family happiness.

Fig   Pisces is associated with this tree and you are being told that someone will recover from a serious illness.

Frankincense   You will be blessed with joy and family happiness. You will be given protection from harm or harmful people.

Gardenia   Love and romance will be the focus of your attention.

Garlic   You will be given protection from harm or harmful people or energies.

Geranium   Courage will be with you.

Ginger   Money will arrive soon.

Grapefruit   The sign of Aquarius may be important and you are being told to think carefully before you make the choice that lies ahead.

Hawthorn   You are being given the protection of a guide on the astral plane; hawthorn is associated with the sign of Aries.

Hazel   You are being granted peace of mind and contentment; Gemini is associated with this tree.

Things That Grow

Heather   Good luck will be with you and you will overcome obstacles. You may feel frustrated in your attempts to change something but be persistent and you will win through in the end.

Hemlock   Danger is present so exercise caution in all that you do.

Hibiscus   You will have a psychic experience or prophetic dream.

Holly   This is the symbol of joy and brings news of good times to come.

Honeysuckle   This is the symbol for courage during difficult times.

Horse   Chestnut Expect quarrels and arguments.

Hyacinth   Good fortune can be expected. Good news will arrive concerning a member of your family.

Hyssop   Take care of your health and try to avoid chills, fevers and colds.

Ivy   The hand of friendship will be offered and can be accepted.

Jasmine   True love will be yours to embrace.

Juniper   Good health is forecast and good luck will be with you always.

Laurel   You will win a competition, raffle or a prize for your efforts.

Lavender   A new friend will be made.

Lemon   Peace of mind and contentment will be yours.

Lemongrass   You spirituality will be enhanced.

Things That Grow

Lilac	You will be protected from harmful influences or situations.
Lilies	Someone will be proved innocent of a crime. (Tiger) You may be tempted by envy or greed. (Water) Someone will recover from a troublesome illness.
Lily of the Valley	You will be shy about accepting praise that you do not think you deserve.
Lime	This will bring news from or a visitor from a far off place; lime is associated with the sign of Sagittarius.
Lotus	This is the symbol of new beginnings.
Marigold	This plant will bring success to new ventures and a happy marriage.
Marjoram	You will spend a few days away from home for business or social reasons.
Meadowsweet	Peace and contentment will be yours.
Mimosa	Love and romance will find you.
Mint	You will have a happy home.
Mistletoe	An admirer will compliment you.
Morning glory	You will find good reason to be hopeful.
Mulberry	An increase of wealth; this bush is associated with the sign of Sagittarius.
Myrrh	Brings happiness and contentment.
Nettle	Take advantage of opportunities that come your way but handle them with care.
Nutmeg	Good luck will come and help you overcome obstacles.

Things That Grow

Oak	The sign of Sagittarius is significant and you will be able to establish your independence one way or another.
Olive	An apology will be made and accepted.
Onion	Be wary of new people who may try to ingratiate themselves into your circle.
Orchard	If abundant the signs are good, if barren then your plans will fail.
Palm	You will have a successful outcome to a project or plan and a wedding will be announced; palms are associated with the sign of Leo and will bring victory.
Pansy	Your loved one will be true to you.
Peaches	You will be wined, dined and entertained.
Pepper	You will have the ability to dispel any negative influences.
Pine	Associated with the sign of Capricorn and will bring Good fortune and good health.
Pineapple	You will be invited to a celebration or a wedding.
Poplar	Associated with the sign of Libra and will bring an awareness and insight that will lead to justice.
Poppy	Good health will be yours.
Potatoes	You will reap the rewards of the efforts that you have made.
Primroses	Sad or upsetting news will come to you.
Pumpkin	You will have many admirers and be popular as a friend.

Things That Grow

Raspberries	You will receive news of a birth.
Rose	Love and romance will find you.
Rosemary	Success will be yours if you stay focused.
Rye	You will win an argument.
Sage	You will learn from someone who has wisdom, experience and knowledge.
Shamrock	You will cross water.
Sorrel	You will find the love that you are looking for.
Strawberries	You will have a good life and a happy marriage.
Sweet Pea	Success will be well earned and appreciated.
Sycamore	A wedding invitation will arrive.
Tansy	True love will find a way.
Thistle	A problem will have to be handled with care.
Thyme	You will embark on an education programme and you will probably be the teacher.
Toadstool	Speedy progress will be made concerning your plans for the future.
Tomato	Happiness may be slow to come and may not last long.
Turnip	You will have an unexpected advancement or windfall.
Vanilla	Romance will come to you.
Vetivert	Good luck will be with you and romance will follow.
Vines	Abundance will be yours

Things That Grow

Violet	You will learn something new and interesting
Walnut	Beware of treachery.
Watermelon	Guard your health
Wheat	You will receive an unexpected windfall.
Willow	You or someone close to you will shed tears. The sign of Cancer will be important.
Wisteria	A happy marriage is forecast.
Yew	Associated with the sign of Capricorn, this tree brings honour and great wealth.

The Crystal List

Agates
Agates come in a variety of colours and will help to eliminate negativity and cleanse the aura.

Agate Blue Lace
This pale blue stone has delicate markings in white, which usually have a lace effect, hence the name. It helps with communication and eases pain caused by breaks, sprains, fractures and arthritis.

Agate Moss
I have a piece that is completely clear with very well-defined pieces of fossilised moss within it, but moss agate is generally dark green with coloured markings. This is a stone that can be used to build your inner strength and stabilise your emotions.

Amber
This is one of my favourites and comes in shades ranging from the palest yellow, through green and red to the deepest brown. Amber is fossilised resin and in days gone by it would have been crushed and powdered to make a healing potion.

Amber brings good luck and protects the bearer from harm. I wore a gold amber necklace on my wedding day and only discovered afterwards that it is known as a symbol for renewing wedding vows and making promises.

It brightens the spirit, lifts depression and has been successfully used in the treatment of throat, kidney and bladder problems.

Amethyst

This is traditionally known as the elevator stone because it gives you a 'lift' and hence aids depression. A fabulous all-round healer, amethyst comes in many varieties and shades of lilac through to purple. It relieves tension and stress, and helps to give the bearer insight into situations that require a decision.

It can be used to improve posture and is commonly used for arthritis. For insomnia, place a piece of amethyst under your pillow or hold a piece in your hand as you go to sleep. Keep amethyst on you to enhance telepathy.

Ametrine

A mixture of amethyst and citrine, it combines qualities of both stones. Ametrine brings balance to the male and female qualities, stimulates the intellect in meditation and helps us to find peace and tranquillity.

Aquamarine

This is the stone you need to 'always be prepared'. Its gentle energy helps judgemental people to be more tolerant, and those who get swamped with responsibility to stand up for themselves, whilst also bringing order to chaos.

The Crystal List

Aventurine

A stone for the heart, it calms troubled emotions, attracts prosperity, and is a lucky stone. It helps enhance leadership qualities and strengthens the instinctive part of your nature.

Bloodstone

Use to revitalize love and friendship and to benefit the internal workings of the body. As its name suggests, it keeps the blood healthy and helps in blood-related diseases.

It lengthens the life span and eliminates anger. Helpful in court and legal matters, it is also a money stone. Carry it about with you or place it in the till to attract wealth. It is a good stone to use when your creative abilities or talents need directing.

Calcite

A major balancer of the body, this stone comes in every Chakra colour. It helps the body to remember what it was like when it was without illness, and go back there. Calcite is good for students of arts and sciences.

Use clear calcite for meditation and connection to the upper realms, pink for love rituals, green for money spells, blue for healing and orange for energy. This is a very useful stone.

Carnelian

This stone increases physical energy and stimulates the sexual regions. It eliminates apathy and stimulates inquisitiveness. It helps us to eliminate negative emotions and benefits the study of the arts.

The Crystal List

Celestite

This beautiful, blue crystal cluster brings about a feeling of inner peace. It creates calm and balance in times of despair, and love and light in times of pain.

Chrysoprase

This crystal helps banish greed and selfishness and can be used for protection and to attract money.

Citrine

Sometimes called the Merchant's Stone because in days gone by merchants would keep a piece of citrine in their moneybox to attract wealth.

Diamond

Known as a 'Girl's Best Friend' because it brings confidence to your emotions, and trust and fidelity to relationships. It fills the aura with healing light and attracts abundance into your life.

Emerald

This is a good stone to use when dealing with legal or business issues.

Fluorite

This is effective for all health problems and helps to bring order to chaos. Place a piece on your computer and help to eliminate negative energy.

Garnet

Helps to heal mental, physical, emotional and spiritual systems.

Hematite

I cannot wear this as I find that I become very depressed. However, do not be put off by my experience as it may help you achieve greater heights than you think possible.

Herkimer Diamonds

Another of my favourites – a pure, clear stone that can be programmed to dispel negativity and promote love and harmony.

Jade

The Warriors Stone so called because it was worn in the breastplates of warriors and high priests. It is best used for protection and challenging situations.

Jasper

A calming stone that promotes friendship and sharing.

Labradorite

Containing the energy of both the sun and the moon, this stone is a great healer as well as being beautiful to look at and comfortable to wear.

Lapis Lazuli

The success giver, this beautiful blue stone is a major healer and will help to eliminate depression and introduce joy.

Malachite

The stone of communication, music and courage also has the ability to enhance your immune system.

Moldavite

This is a very special stone that does not come from the planet earth. It will come to you when you need it and will suit any purpose.

Magical in its appearance and properties, it is a joy to own and wear even if only for a short time.

Moonstone

This will help to enhance femininity in women and will balance the menstrual cycle, and for men it will help them understand their feminine side and be more caring towards the female sex.

Obsidian, black

The most common grounding stone. It should be used with care as too much can bring depression.

Obsidian, snowflake

This unusual looking crystal can ward off and protect you from the negative attitudes and energy of others. It helps to bring repressed feelings gently to the surface.

Pearl

This beautiful stone symbolises all that is pure. It is calming and soothing and aids fertility.

The Crystal List

Pyrite

Known as Fool's Gold, this bright crystal will draw good positive energy to you and help to bring brightness into your life.

Rose Quartz

The Stone of Love helps you to draw love toward you, promotess self-love and eases heartache.

Ruby

This crystal aids concentration and brings protection.

Rutile

The fine lines in this crystal are sometimes known as Angel's Hair. This is another of my favourites and it is a very powerful crystal, which is beautiful as well as interesting to look at.

Smoky Quartz

This stone brings protection and harmony and is a good all round healer and balancer.

Numbers

Zero You are in between the end of your old cycle and the beginning of a new one. Be confident and make any necessary changes.

One The number of leadership, new beginnings, new ideas and inspiration. Exciting new changes lie ahead.

Two The number of tact and diplomacy, balance and harmony. Be prepared for some surprises.

Three The number of pregnancy, nursing or nurturing, socializing and having good times with friends. It indicates clubs, societies, organisations and also the countryside.

Four The number of security, assets and the home. Repairs, renovations and renewals may be expected around the home.

Five The number that shows the problem areas in your life, or any conflict that will be experienced. It is also linked with uniforms of any description and keys.

Six The number of tenderness, compassion, difficult choices, that have to be made, crossroads being reached and the eternal triangle. However, where five shows the problems, six is the number that provides the solutions.

Seven The number of control. This cannot be obtained

without full knowledge of all facts surrounding you. With inner questioning, you can then resume control in your life.

Eight The number of strength, determination and stubbornness.

Nine The number of completion and seeing the light at the end of the tunnel or finding your way after stumbling around in the dark. It shows difficult tasks being completed.